Human Behavior in a
Just World

Human Behavior in a Just World

Reaching for Common Ground

Rosemary J. Link and
Chathapuram S. Ramanathan

ROWMAN & LITTLEFIELD PUBLISHERS, INC.
Lanham • Boulder • New York • Toronto • Plymouth, UK

Acknowledgments: We extend our gratitude especially to Luz y Libertad; to Pravina Ramanathan, J. P. Nayak, Leila Narayanan, P. Ramalingam, and Sandeep Manchekar for their contributions to case studies; and to Vinni Thongthi, Anthony Bibus, Vinay Ramanathan, Amy Link, Sophie Link, and Boyd Koehler for their patient reading of drafts.

Published by Rowman & Littlefield Publishers, Inc.
A wholly owned subsidiary of The Rowman & Littlefield Publishing Group, Inc.
4501 Forbes Boulevard, Suite 200, Lanham, Maryland 20706
http://www.rowmanlittlefield.com

Estover Road, Plymouth PL6 7PY, United Kingdom

British Library Cataloguing in Publication Information Available

Library of Congress Cataloging-in-Publication Data

Link, Rosemary J.
  Human behavior in a just world : reaching for common ground / Rosemary J. Link and Chathapuram S. Ramanathan.
    p. cm.
  Includes bibliographical references and index.
  ISBN 978-1-4422-0290-0 (cloth : alk. paper) — ISBN 978-1-4422-0291-7 (pbk. : alk. paper) — ISBN 978-1-4422-0292-4 (electronic)
  1. Social service—International cooperation. 2. Social case work—International cooperation. 3. Human services. I. Ramanathan, Chathapuram S. II. Title.
HV41.L526 2011
361.3—dc22

2010013047

Printed in the United States of America

To our families

In loving memory of my father Reverend Donald C. Flatt and my sister
Josephine M. MacRae. Also, to my husband Andrew M. Link, my mother
Gwendoline D. Flatt, and my brother Donald G. Flatt, to let them know
that I cherish them as my constant companions and inspiration. Also to
my children, Sophie D. Link, Amy G. Link, and Alexander M. Link to
thank them for their encouragement and to wish them careers of joy and
usefulness to the world.

In honor of my mother Susheila Swaminathan, my father C. V.
Swaminathan, my wife Pravina Ramanathan, my son Vinay Ramanathan,
and my teachers, clients, and students, for having made me who and what I
am. Also, to my sister Sudha Krishnan, and brother C. S. Venkataraman to
let them know I cherish them as my companions and inspirations.

Contents

Figures, Tables, and Textboxes

FIGURES

TABLES

TEXTBOXES

Foreword

During the past decade there has been a dramatically growing interest in international social work. In the United States and in other countries increasing numbers of students have sought to prepare themselves for international social work practice. Schools of social work have expanded the opportunities they offer to prepare students for work in the international arena. The availability of jobs at the global level has also grown and more and more social workers are engaging in international practice. All of these changes have resulted in the need for professional literature to support the teaching and practice of international social work, and *Human Behavior in a Just World: Reaching for Common Ground* makes a significant contribution toward filling that need.

There are many reasons for the burgeoning development of international social work practice. First, global migration has created new population groups to be served by social workers. International social work means more than working in the profession in another country; it also includes working with clients at home who have come from other countries. In either case, however, effective practice with clients from other cultures requires special training beyond that which was offered in social work education programs in earlier years. Second, interaction among people from different nations and cultures has been facilitated and enhanced by developments in transportation and technology. The expansion of international travel has provided many folks opportunities to see and understand other cultures. Furthermore, the technology revolution has made it possible for everyone to know more about the lives of other people throughout the world with virtually no delay in the transmission time of this global news. Modern technology has done more than increase and improve the availability of world news; it has also enabled individuals to communicate in real time with persons from the other side of the globe. Increased information about the world, including the needs of citizens in diverse countries, has inspired many social workers to pursue careers in other parts of the world. Third, the "shrinking" of the world has not only increased the interactions among all peoples, but it has made us more aware of problems and needs in other nations. As we have become more knowledgeable of each other's cultures, living conditions, and needs, this increased awareness of the world has whetted the appetites of many social workers to engage in practice with clients from other cultures—either at home or abroad—and to develop the knowledge, skills, and values needed for international social work practice. Fourth, as Thomas Friedman has pointed out, the expansion of information sharing through the use of technology has also resulted in the "flattening" of the world. Work is now easily outsourced from one country to another, producing increased opportunities for people in some developing nations to earn better livelihoods. At the same time, however, everyone has not benefited from this job creation; wealth has not been shared equally, and many people have been exploited through outsourcing ventures. The resulting inequalities and injustices have motivated many social workers to work toward the amelioration of these conditions and the creation of more just and humane societies.

Higher education in general, and social work education in particular, have responded to the globalization movement. More and more courses dealing with international content are being offered in both undergraduate and graduate education. The use of online courses has expanded the number of such educational offerings. Most colleges and universities now offer study-abroad opportunities for their students, ranging from brief international tours, to cultural-immersion experiences, to entire semesters or years studying in foreign institutions. Social work education programs are integrating international content in their curriculums, adding more international social work courses, and developing increased numbers of international field placements. Social work schools are also creating a variety of means for their students to interact with persons from other nations, such as offering student exchange programs, arranging guest lectures by foreign scholars, establishing online connections between their students and students from other countries, and developing a variety of study-abroad opportunities. The international educational activities in schools of social work in the United States have been encouraged and supported by the Council on Social Work Education (CSWE), the accrediting body for schools of social work. Over the years CSWE has placed increased importance on the inclusion of international social work content in educational curriculums, to the point that such content is now mandated in all social work education programs. CSWE also offers a number of resources to enable schools to develop their international curriculums and programs. CSWE's resources are made available, for example, through its publications, its Global Commission, and its Katherine A. Kendall Institute for International Social Work Education.

The numerous international initiatives on the part of social work education programs in recent years have been enhanced by the growth in size and strength of many international social work organizations. These have included the International Association of Schools of Social Work (IASSW), the International Federation of Social Workers (IFSW), the International Consortium for Social Development (ICSD), and the International Council on Social Welfare (ICSW). These organizations provide forums for educators, researchers, students, and practitioners to come together to hear expert speakers, present papers on their own work, share ideas, and learn from each other in regard to international social work education and practice. These types of organizations also offer a variety of other resources to facilitate international collaboration and development such as publications, web-based information, and opportunities for online communication and data exchange among members.

Although the size and scope of international social work education and practice has expanded remarkably in recent years and has been supported by many organizations, the literature in this area has not increased correspondingly. Certainly there have been significant contributions to the literature by distinguished scholars such as Lynne Healy, Brij Mohan, James Midgley, Richard Estes, Michael Sherraden, Manohar Pawar, Rosemary Link, Chathapuram Ramanathan, and others. Furthermore, there are several important journals devoted to international social work such as *Social Development Issues, Journal of Comparative Social Welfare, International Social Work,* and *International Journal of Social Welfare.* But given the rapid growth of international social work, there is a significant need for more scholarly works that consolidate existing knowledge on this topic and develop new knowledge in this important area of practice. *Human Behavior in a Just World* helps meet this need in significant ways.

This book provides an excellent resource for faculty in social work education programs, the students in these programs, researchers, and practitioners in the field of international social work. One of the strengths of the book— and a quality that sets it apart from most of the other literature—is its focus on the impact of environment on human development from a global perspective. This global perspective enables readers to understand that they are truly citizens of the world. This view of person-in-environment recognizes that all of us are involved in a variety of complex relationships with many systems having fluid boundaries that we must negotiate successfully in order to survive and thrive. Understanding the human condition from such a broad, interactive point of view enables one to see that all of us are connected with persons from throughout the world in dynamic and ever-increasing ways.

Our lives are affected by what happens in other nations, and our behaviors in our own society impact the lives of others throughout the world. Although the complexity of life varies from culture to culture, we share what the authors call a "common human condition." That is, there are universal aspects of human existence such as the need for shelter, clean water, food, safety, identity, intimacy, and song, but access to resources for meeting these needs is not equal among people of the world. It is incumbent on social workers to recognize that all of us are vulnerable as individuals, but that we are stronger when we work together in community to help meet the needs of anyone who lacks access to basic resources.

The authors utilize a creative and helpful framework in order to analyze the global context for social work practice. In chapter 1 they describe six elements of social work practice in the global context—common human condition, knowledge, values, skills, cultural awareness, and sustainable life. Each of the following chapters of the book builds on these elements. Chapter 2 describes how we are citizens of the universe, focusing on the common human condition and the importance of sustainable development. Chapter 3 addresses the knowledge base of social work in a global context and does so through examination of issues of human rights and social and economic justice. Chapter 4 looks at values and ethics, making the case that there are universal values for practice (such as human dignity, worth of the individual, and sanctity of life) and that most ethical questions are global in nature. In chapter 5 the authors examine the issue of cultural competence in both local and global relationships. They describe cultural competence as a social worker's ability to work with people of many cultures within an attitude of inclusion and respect, and they emphasize that the rapidly changing demographics of the world require social workers to be culturally competent to practice in any setting. In chapter 6 the authors focus on assessment skills and inclusive practice with mobile populations. They discuss practice within the context of worldwide migration and its relationship to social and economic development. Chapter 7 examines the interconnectedness of life throughout the planet, the finiteness of the earth, the unequal distribution of resources on the planet, and the role of the social work profession in reducing the exploitation of people and working toward the well-being of all humans. Finally, chapter 8 reviews and consolidates the content in the preceding chapters and challenges the reader to embrace a truly global reality in supporting human rights and pursuing social and economic justice in all areas of social work practice.

Human Behavior in a Just World introduces the reader to many topics that are important for one to understand and appreciate in order to have a sound knowledge base for the practice of international social work. These include topics that are sometimes ignored or given only minimal attention in many other books dealing with international social work. The material on the

United Nations, presented in chapter 3, is an excellent example of such information. As the authors point out in this chapter, the deliberations, conventions, and accords of the United Nations since 1948 have resulted in a number of global policy instruments that have been critical elements of the foundation of international social work practice. It is essential for all social workers to understand this history and the influence of these policy instruments in order to practice international social work effectively and from a well-informed perspective. The authors describe this history in a straightforward manner. They then use one example, the Convention on the Rights of the Child, to demonstrate in detail how this Convention affects the lives of everyone, and how the basic elements of the Convention can be used as a framework for practice. Furthermore, the fact that this Convention, although passed in 1989, has not been ratified by the United States serves as an example of how social workers can strive to bring about changes at the macro level by addressing this issue.

Another example of a topic of significant import for an understanding of international work is that of global migration. In discussing this topic, the authors provide a succinct historical background before discussing the contemporary scene. They point out that migration within borders and across borders has occurred for centuries and has often involved some degree of tension and conflict, ranging from discriminatory practices to outright war. In modern times migration remains a contentious issue in many parts of the world and responses to it often threaten the ability of peoples and nations to live in peaceful coexistence. It is essential that social workers understand the reasons for migration, the positive and negative impact on the lives of those who migrate, the causes of the conflicts that often result, and types of policies and programs needed to facilitate more peaceful and effective settlement of people in new locations. It is also essential that social workers acquire cultural competence in order to engage successfully in professional practice with mobile populations, and that they develop the micro- and macro-level practice skills in order to do so. The authors use two case examples from the United States and India to illustrate how the requisite sets of knowledge, values, and skills can be developed and implemented by social workers.

The authors of this book have a unique ability to present to the reader in a simple, straightforward manner material that is complex, highly theoretical, and often difficult to comprehend. Their facility to make this material easily understood and directly relevant to social work practice is one of the key strengths of the book. An example of this is the discussion in chapter 4 of the concepts of cognition and relativism. The authors describe how all social work practice, at the local and global levels, must be informed by an appreciation of these two points of view. They then explain that in order for social workers to engage in ethical practice they must adopt a relativist perspective whereby their reasoning and decision making takes into account multiple points of view. They describe how various national and international social work organizations have adopted this viewpoint as reflected in their codes of ethics, constitutions, and statements of principles.

Another strength of this book is the use of numerous case examples to illustrate the concepts that are presented. Both of the writers have had extensive practice experience, which they call on to make their points. Regrettably, many publications dealing with global social work are written by authors who have had limited practice experience in international practice, and their writings, while conceptually sound and factually accurate, sometimes fail to connect the reader to the real world of practice. In this book, however, Link and Ramanathan make constant reference to their practice experiences in places such as the United States of America, the United Kingdom, India, Mexico, Norway, and Slovenia. They also draw on the practice experiences of others, including social work students, to illustrate the information they are presenting. This use of case examples truly makes the material "come alive" for the reader in ways that can be easily understood and applied to practice.

Human Behavior in a Just World is a valuable resource to anyone interested in the teaching or practice of international social work. And to repeat an earlier point, today *all* social workers must be knowledgeable in this area. This book can be used as text at all levels of social work education. Educators will find it to be an important resource that can easily be used in the classroom to equip students with a global perspective and to educate them in the practice of international social work. Used as a text, this book will not only inform students in a broad base of knowledge regarding international social work, but it will also challenge them to think critically about these issues. Students will be motivated to critique social policies, analyze their beliefs, question their stereotypes, reexamine their values, and develop cultural competence to gird their professional practice. The student assignments and questions at the end of each chapter are especially helpful in assisting students (and all readers) to review the content they have just read and to make sure they have mastered this information and can apply it. Everyone who has the opportunity to read this book—students, teachers, researchers, and practitioners—will not only develop a better understanding of social work practice from a global perspective, but they will also develop a renewed sense of excitement in applying this information to their own work in today's changing and shrinking world.

Frank B. Raymond
Past President, International Consortium for Social Development

Chapter One

Social Work Practice in a Global Society

I can never be what I ought to be until you are what you ought to be. This is the way our world is made. No individual or nation can stand out boasting of being independent. We are interdependent.

—Martin Luther King, Jr.

Is globalization leading us to a world of competition, injustice, and scarcity or to a just world where there is a place for all people to be valued? The implications for social work are that local and national borders are no longer sufficient limits for our information sources and ethical practice. The primary challenge for social work and social welfare is to ask, are we content to just live in the world or are we ready to seek social and economic justice for all members? Currently, students of social work can expect to work with a variety of cultures and economic circumstances in all aspects of their profession. This book holds that we place false boundaries on our potential if we stay in the place we know, with the people who are familiar, doing the same work we have always done. Technology has made the world more accessible than ever before and has helped to create the reality that effective assessment and practice require global awareness and understanding (Friedman, 2004).

When assessing situations in social work and human service, the focus is often on the individual's immediate problem of development or personal and family relationships, which may be referred to as the "microenvironment." There are valuable texts on human behavior that accept the influence of environment but focus on individual biological, psychological, and social development from conception to death. The focus of this text is broader, analyzing the impact of groups, communities, nations, and the world on human life and this broadest lens for assessment is sometimes referred to as the

1

"macroenvironment." In a just society consideration of both the immediate individual's situation and the larger structural issues of the macroenvironment are vital and constantly intertwined.

In the following pages we present a framework that illustrates the pitfalls of ignoring the world and, more importantly, presents the opportunities of gathering international knowledge (through case studies from country to country) and analyzing the effect of social and economic globalization (forces of change, including labor and migration across the globe that affect everyone). A combination of case studies and research data increases our understanding of human behavior as part of the common human condition and also provides expanded choices for practice. This framework reconceptualizes our approach to macro social work practice, which in the past has been dominated by domestic issues. In this context, macro practice both connects with individual needs of "micro" or clinical approaches and also takes these to a collective picture of communities, organizations, and global institutions constantly interacting with one another. The concept "community" is identified as dynamic and changing. Suddenly, we are familiar with the idea of "virtual" community; we all relate to "natural village" communities and simultaneously recognize imposed limits of "legal" community and the open possibilities of communities built on ideas of "shared experience."

WHY STUDY ISSUES OF HUMAN DEVELOPMENT FROM A GLOBAL PERSPECTIVE?

The dangers of focusing only on the local geographic community of traditional social work practice, ignoring global resources and limiting our cultural awareness, have been underestimated. Jane Addams challenged the profession to realize that it cannot be confined to country borders in her peace initiatives as long ago as the 1930s (Sullivan, 1993). Similarly our understanding of social work and human service is foreshortened if we only focus on the last 100 years of professional training for our history. Voluntary and traditional social services have existed for centuries. Prior to Indian independence, the approach to social welfare was more oriented toward social problems and social reform. "The Chinese traveler Hsuan-Tsang observed in the seventh century that the people of the Indus were always in the habit of planting trees to provide shade to travelers and voluntarily dug wells for drinking water for the community" (Gangrade, 1987).

It has taken a long time, however, for social workers to become aware of the importance of a global perspective in their practice, for example in their use of the International Classification of Diseases (ICD9) and the Convention on the Rights of the Child (Link and Healy, 2005). Given the increased attention to global issues—such as the constant movement of labor, migration of families and children, expansion in international adoptions, outsourced employment opportunities, and the World Health Organization's call for greater cooperation in the face of the spread of SARS, tuberculosis, and AIDS—we know that social work must respond to human needs on a worldwide scale. This global reach is energizing rather than intimidating when we identify case studies and realize the universal characteristics of human potential and response to crisis. We expect that, as a result of reading these case studies, faculty will encourage students to e-mail partners in other places and appreciate how much they can learn from colleagues in countries that they may have previously stereotyped or not fully understood. Many students underestimate the creativity of social workers in countries such as India and Mexico because they only see the images of overwhelming poverty and not the surge of innovation, resilience, and leadership there.

Social work is at the forefront of knowledge developers for a more integrated world, and this book offers case studies in each chapter to ground this claim. In chapter 2, the case study of Luz y Libertad brings these ideas alive. A group of women find food and family provisions too expensive to purchase in Morelos, Mexico. In their work to build a cooperative, they illustrate a widespread dilemma in the United States and many countries of the world: the children must eat. Luz y Libertad (Light and Freedom) came together to organize around common concerns to establish dependable access to affordable nutrition and moved beyond food to education, health, and rights.

We also study global issues because social work uses an ecological perspective. Germain has made a helpful distinction between systems theory (where the sum is always greater than the parts) and an ecological framework. The former is an interdisciplinary theory of how units are organized and can be related to technology or formal organizations as well as to human relationships in the organization of social life (Germain, 1991). Ecological theory, however, always reflects cycles of human interdependence and healthy and dynamic biological and psychosocial growth. There is no boundary in terms of human needs: polluted groundwater from maquiladoras (U.S.-owned plants operated in Mexico and Central America) has seeped back into Brownsville, Texas, and recent birth deformities are being attributed to water that knows no political boundaries (American University Case Study, no. 374, *Maquiladoras and the Environment*, www.american.edu/TED/maquila.htm). As stated by Sachs, "Sustainable development can be achieved only through an approach that considers everything from geography to infrastructure, to family structure" (Sachs, 2005).

In this text, we use the ecological perspective under the umbrella of systems theory; the whole is our universe, completely interrelated and without boundaries. Despite Friedman's discussion of the new "flat earth," where everyone potentially has access to the Internet and the playing field has become more even for the economic development of countries such as India and China, the reality of our rotating, interdependent universe is unchanging (Friedman, 2004). Although we know it, we persist in the optical delusion that we are all separate parts, acting unilaterally, rather than part of each other's sustainable being.

Another practical reason for studying human behavior and social work through a global lens is the recent encouragement from the International Federation of Social Workers (IFSW), the International Association of Schools of Social Work (IASSW), the International Consortium for Social Development (ICSD), and the new requirements of the U.S. Council on Social Work Education (CSWE). In recognition of these global paradigm shifts the IFSW and the IASSW collaborated in a revised definition of social work presented in chapter 3 of this book. Also, the CSWE adopted new standards in 2001 that identified the need for social workers to understand their neighbors and their role in the world in order to practice effectively. Although the latest standards have altered the wording, the emphasis is the same, recognizing that the profession is caught up in "social and economic justice worldwide" and offers leadership in a global context (Council on Social Work Education, 2008).

Increasing global awareness expands our vision for practice and is empowering, as stated by an Augsburg College student after her semester in Mexico: "I suddenly realized what it means to complete a critical analysis, to think about the causes of poverty from a structural as well as personal point of view" (Augsburg College, 2003). Following many experiences of learning from colleagues worldwide, the authors believe "that social workers across the globe can always learn from each other in an atmosphere of reciprocity where social and economic justice are twin goals" (Ramanathan and Link, 2004).

The goals of the book, therefore, are to

- Expand awareness of global interdependence and implications for social work and human service;
- Define the common human condition and ethical assessment of human behavior;
- Promote cultural awareness and ability to examine and explain one's own culture;
- Provide opportunity to expand skills in culturally competent assessment;
- Alert students to the array of United Nations global policy instruments that are frameworks for human service;
- Increase knowledge of diverse communities;
- Introduce innovative approaches to city life and problem solving in social work; and

• Learn what it means intuitively, conceptually, ethically, socially, and legally to be global citizens.

Broad goals include engaging students in realizing that their having excesses may be creating hardships for others; and the Oxfam statement on global citizenship includes awareness of interdependence as a key learning element, as set out in textbox 1.1 (Watkins, 1995). An illustration is the reality of children dying from hunger and poverty in Honduras, despite the country's being a major producer of bananas. In Western countries students eat this fruit regularly without a thought to whose labor they benefit from and at what cost. Encouraging students to look beyond their usual domain as they seek to understand the common human condition opens the way to increased insight and effectiveness for their future practice with people from diverse cultures.

Certainly the goals of Oxfam, especially in developing more global commitment to a "new sense of responsibility" for others outside our own nation-state, has been slow to evolve in recent years. For example, Oxfam has more recently been successful in encouraging policymakers toward a human-rights-based approach to global trade policies (Aaronson and Zimmerman, 2006). The ideal of international cooperation espoused in the Declaration of Human Rights has been challenged by discussion of a New World Order where economic and military might dominates social life (Singer,

---

Textbox 1.1. Oxfam: An Agenda for Change

People are not developed, they develop themselves. Julius Nyerere

Working for an alternative approach to development has to be seen as a process. . . . It implies continuous changes, as well as uniting people from across the entire social spectrum in a common purpose. Eduardo Klein, Oxfam Deputy Regional Representative, Central America.

A new sense of responsibility for the rights of others is needed, together with an emphasis on building new alliances to achieve change. The five critical elements of that enabling environment are

• democratic participation
• enhanced opportunity
• increased equity
• peace and security
• a sustainable future

Source: Watkins, K. (1995). *The Oxfam Poverty Report.* www.oxfam.org

2004). It is not the first time that social workers are practicing at the cross-roads of economic and social development, where peaceful relationships are jeopardized by human aggression (Adams, 1930; Barash, 2000). Social workers are key actors in contributing to this sense of increased responsibility and sustainable growth in the context of human well-being. Such ideas are at the core of social work practice and social development and will be explained in the following pages.

It is our ethical obligation to the oppressed—wherever they are on their journey—to unite in effective strategies and bring global issues, such as the causes of family disruption and migration, to the forefront of socioeconomic change. Politicians are saying that we should put a human face on the global economy, but this is yet to be actualized, and we are concerned that the goal not stagnate or be seen as too idealistic. Certainly, UNICEF brought a powerful image to the fore in its picture of a small child falling asleep over the pile of baseballs he is sewing for a wealthier domain (UNICEF, 1997). In his discussion of the "truth about globalization," Craig Kielburger, who began his human rights work as a teenager in Canada, points out the consequences of exploiting children, just as we find child workers demonstrating in New Delhi against harsh conditions and low pay. Simultaneously, children are overflowing from homeless shelters in the United States and struggling to survive natural disasters (Kielburger and Kielburger, 2004; www.freethe children.com).

In the last decade, students have increased their understanding of their purchasing power and have made an impact on clothing manufacturers such as Walmart and GAP and vendors such as Starbucks (www.business-human rights.org). Through their travel exchanges, volunteer work, and electronic mail campaigns, students are recognizing that as social workers, we have an important contribution to make to human relationships, including fair trade, across the globe (www.newint.org/issues/past/). Since the millennium, the painful images of war, natural disasters, and consequently the increasing numbers of refugees, have spurred renewed impetus for global cooperation in social work.

Perhaps in response to these images the curriculum of social work is changing, for example, with the infusion of references to formal documents such as the International Federation of Social Workers' Statement of Principles, the Indian Declaration of Social Work Ethics, and the Convention on the Rights of the Child. In the midst of apparent chaos we are optimistic that this is a time of opportunity, where we can see afresh the multitude of ways to work together as neighbors in creating a planet concerned more with human well-being than accumulation of wealth, trading weapons, and winning wars.

As we build insight and critical awareness of the potential for cooperation we also recognize the tension between personal (it's your fault) and collective responsibility (the fault of the current social and economic system). In the United States for example, income statistics present startling data to indicate that the poor are getting poorer and the rich are getting richer:

> In 2004, according to the Congressional Budget Office's latest official analysis, households in the lowest quintile of the country were making only 2 percent more (adjusted for inflation) than they were in 1979. Those in the next quintile managed only an 11 percent rise. And the middle group was up 15 percent. The income of families in the fourth quintile—upper middle class folks with an average yearly income of $82,000—rose by 23 percent. Only when you get to the top quintile were the gains truly big—63 percent. (Roger Lowenstein, *New York Times Magazine*, June 10, 2007, pp. 11–36)

Social agencies benefit from the donations of wealthy families and they often generate wealth for society as a whole. The difficulty with these jarring statistics is that people experiencing poverty are walking up a very steep sand hill, never able to keep their grip, while the wealthy are taking flight with ease. The structure of such a society is wasting the potential of those trapped in surviving from day to day on minimum wage or temporary assistance, unable to feed their children or pay for health care. Another illustration of structural policy rather than individual behavior influencing social circumstances lies in access to handguns. We are all responsible for acts of violence; however, some countries of the world have dramatically lower rates of death by handguns than others. The discrepancy is not because Canadians or Japanese people are so much more peaceful than U.S. citizens; it is the policy that makes the gun available or not (see textbox 1.2).

Thus some of the personal/professional questions addressed in this book are

1. How can I become more aware of my role as a global citizen and what is happening in other parts of the world?
2. What are some of the universal elements in the common human condition, which I can anticipate as I work to understand diversity and human interaction that is new to me?
3. What are some international policy instruments that can enhance my understanding of human behavior and my assessment skills?
4. How can I increase my cultural competence and thus facilitate the cultural efficacy of the institutions I interact with?
5. What would truly globally aware practice mean for our service recipients and partners?
6. What is the role of the social work profession in promoting social justice worldwide?
7. How can I learn from other countries?

Textbox 1.2.   Private Troubles—Public Policy and Common Ground

DEATH BY HANDGUN (1986)

Canada	6
West Germany	17
Great Britain	4
USA	9,800
USA (1993)*	38,077
Legal Intervention	259
USA (2006)**	30,242
Legal Intervention	300

*National Safety Council, *1994 Accident Facts*, Itasca, IL, Library of Congress Catalogue, Card #91-60648.

**National Vital Statistics Reports, 54*(10), January 31, 2006. www.cdc.gov

"Homicide is the second leading cause of death for teenagers. The leading cause of death for African American men and women 15–34 years."
D. Prothrow-Stith 1991

To assist the reader in reaching the goals of this book, which include responding to the questions above, we introduce "six elements for social work in a global context" to help in reflection, analysis, and action as global citizens: common human condition, knowledge, values, cultural awareness, skills, and sustainable life. These elements are inspired by the ancient sites of the pyramids in Mexico City and the museum and exquisitely maintained site at Xochicalco, south of Cuernavaca. The six elements refer to the four compass points as well as the two axes of earth and sky that form the universe for all humanity. At Xoxicotl, the ancient teachers used reflecting pools to study the heavens. Similarly, ancient peoples in what is now New Mexico (for example, at the Jimenez Pueblo) shared a seamless frame of reference with their Mexican relations, as can be seen in their use of father sky, mother earth, and the four winds in their artwork and sculptures. The political border is meaningless to the age-old traditions of tribal lands and human migration.

Each chapter builds on these six elements, and in conclusion, vital steps for social work practice in a global context are identified. This framework is based on ancient ideas from the First Peoples of Mexico, but also the First Peoples of Asia, Africa, and Central and South America. In ancient pyramids, sculptures, and carvings, people like the Aztecs and Maya honored the uni-

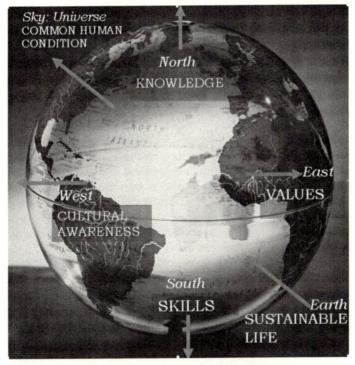

Sky: Universe
COMMON HUMAN
CONDITION

North
KNOWLEDGE

East
VALUES

West
CULTURAL
AWARENESS

South
SKILLS

Earth
SUSTAINABLE
LIFE

Figure 1.1. Social Work's Response to Globalization

verse and the whole-systems approach; this approach includes the individual, group, community, and global levels of interaction, which we erroneously and naively attribute to twenty-first-century thinking.

As the book unfolds, the connections between these elements become clear. The framework is offered as a constant reminder of our interaction with the natural resources of the earth and our common humanity. Thus, chapter 2 focuses on the *universe* of all the compass points as the lens of the concept of a common human condition (CHC) and sustainable development. In response to our earlier book, *All Our Futures*, students commented that the concept of CHC was not defined but rather assumed. In chapter 2 the concept of CHC is defined with their help. It includes a personal/professional review of global awareness and the implications for assessment in social work when we avoid blaming the victim and understand the vulnerabilities and opportunities that belong to everyone. Sometimes, those who "have" become associated with being different or superior because of their pile of material goods, while those who "have not" are judged more harshly. Examining the common human condition, rather than individual development on its own, assists in laying aside the false impressions of resilience or capacity that the acquisition of wealth brings. The existence of core human values is discussed together with the theory that culture represents difference in behaviors but not in our common human needs.

There is a tension between establishing universal principles of social work through international collaboration in research and practice, while respecting indigenous uniqueness, distinct local traditions, and cultural strength. We seek common bonds across uniqueness:

> I was admiring the intricacy and beauty of lace made in Idrija, Slovenia and commented to a Slovenian colleague that it reminded me of the lace in Cuernavaca, Mexico. My colleague was offended and said the lace is unique and could not be the same. I had intended to refer to the sharp juxtaposition of acute poverty and maintained loveliness, demonstrated in the ability of women in impoverished circumstances to transcend their deprivations, to maintain and cherish their artistic skills. The comment was received however, as undervaluing the uniqueness of the lace itself. (Link and Čačinovič, 2004)

The resilience displayed in the dignity of work and art is a characteristic of the *common human condition*, while the details of the art are spectacularly unique. When social workers recognize the tension between what is locally established tradition and what is open to change, there can be flexibility in the way we partner with people receiving services. In the place of a hierarchy of client and professional transactions, which is the "norm" in some countries, a wider global view identifies models of practice based on empowerment and more equal status of service user and those who serve (Link, 1995; Saleeby, 2002).

In New Delhi, a social worker, Rachel, has organized self-employed women into a cooperative for sewing garments and accessories where they have more influence in arranging child care and fair trading practices. Although a very different environment than India, Slovenia facilitates similarly creative practice opportunities. For example, their practice is to place students in multiservice "social work centers." This approach allows students to work flexibly with different age groups and community initiatives, such as the family and senior cooperative program, in order to reduce drug addiction in the coastal area of Koper. In this instance, isolated seniors are not "clients" but "mentors" to families recovering from drug addiction. Although hampered by long traditions in social work education in the Global North of putting individual and micro practice in the forefront, students are now being encouraged to think more globally and to engage in macro approaches to practice. The micro approaches may speak to "local uniqueness" and the "macro" to globalization; each is in dynamic tension with the other, and we need both perspectives to practice effectively.

Chapter 3 looks to the north in the framework, which represents the knowledge base for social work in global context through the prism of human rights and social and economic justice. The chapter presents global policy instruments as yardsticks for social work, where a policy instrument is defined as policy approved at the highest levels of global cooperation, usually through the United Nations. This includes knowledge of mutual learning, such as Luz y Libertad (Light and Freedom) and their model for women's community organizing; it also means coming to an understanding of what causes people to leave extended family and beautiful places. As villages surrounding Oaxaca in southern Mexico become deserted or inhabited only by elders, women, and children, what is happening at the structural and institutional levels of their communities? Examining these changes leads to deeper insight when social workers are offering services to migrant workers. Similarly in Mexico, in the community organizing of Salud Integral, social workers expand their skills in developing neighbor-to-neighbor networks of communication and health resources.

In southern India in the state of Kerala, the expansion of women's and children's education has resulted in one of the highest rates of literacy and immunization in the world (UNICEF, 2003). Also in India, in the states of Karnataka and Tamil Nadu, the engineers of Atkins Corporation, based in Cambridgeshire, England, have realized the importance of identifying local leaders and social networks. As they identify the community leaders they can build commitment to long-term maintenance of dams and irrigation channels. The most astute engineers in the world cannot impose a sustainable irrigation plan on a state without the cooperation and rapport of the farmers and local community. California is now finding this out with their renewed dam projects. They would do well to visit Karnataka but may not, due to a dangerous, outdated North American view of the world that there is not much to learn beyond their shores. Be it engineers or social workers, we serve our customers better when we open ourselves to a world of learning from the experience of others. The experience of others includes moving beyond the profit motive as the governing force toward social responsibility. In the Larsen and Toubro case study (textbox 1.3) Ramanathan documents an alternative path that corporations may choose for community well-being.

Another act of corporate social responsibility similar to Larsen and Toubro was demonstrated by a Mumbai, India–based pharmaceutical company (USV) that is providing free insulin to poor and needy diabetic children in the city of Bangalore. About 1,200 children suffer from diabetes in Tamil Nadu, and the pharmaceutical company is providing the insulin for one year, in order to reduce the family's monthly financial burden (Oneindia, 2007).

Following figure 1.1, chapter 4 looks east to focus on values, international ethics, and case examples for social workers. The chapter discusses values and ethics in general and then the specifics of international and large system (macro) approaches to human dilemmas. Examples cited in this chapter include

---

Textbox 1.3.   Actualizing Social Justice

Chathapuram Ramanathan

An integral part of actualizing social justice is the concept of social responsibil-ity and socially responsible and responsive behavior. Although the noted econo-mist Milton Friedman highlights profit and profitability as the sole or exclusive criteria for evaluating organizations, Schumacher (1973) takes issue with that notion. During the twentieth century, to some, corporations gained social le-gitimacy, and emerged as perhaps the most influential institution (Ghoshal and Bartlett, 1997). Ghoshal and Bartlett, however, also write that toward the end of the last century, both in the United States through President Clinton's White House conference on corporate social responsibility with regard to downsizing, and Prime Minister Blair's review of the role of the corporation in the United Kingdom, the standing of corporations reflects social ambivalence. Globally, there is public tumult over executive pay, in stark contrast to community well-being or, more accurately, lack thereof. Paradoxically, in such circumstances, according to Schumacher (1999, 1973), economics is to be revised, and there is a need for a fresh start, if the meaning of ideas such as democracy, freedom, and human dignity is to go beyond national income, rate of growth, capital output ratio, capital accumulation, and so on, and if it is to be processed in the context of human realities of poverty, alienation, and health status. Therefore, social responsibility and profits must not be viewed as mutually exclusive. A subset of social responsibility is corporate social responsibility.

In the Indian scene, corporate organizations have been associated with phi-lanthropy. Philanthropy is a desirable ingredient, but not adequate, and not a substitute for socially responsive behavior of corporations. This is all the more true when, globally, industrialization is viewed as an integral part of develop-ment. Corporations need to recognize their broader mission and be actively involved in change that increases quality of life for people.

CORPORATE SOCIAL RESPONSIBILITY: CASE STUDY OF LARSEN AND TOUBRO GROUP OF COMPANIES

Larsen and Toubro Limited is one of India's leading engineering companies. It is a widely diversified, multilocational company with several manufacturing complexes. It has offices both across India, as well as in Asia, Russia, Europe, and North America. It was founded by two Danish engineers in 1938. Larsen and Toubro employs over 25,000 people, and according to President Nayak of Larsen and Toubro, the corporate philosophy is to extend itself to the commu-nity and help in the preservation of the environment. President Nayak includes the human condition and people as part of the corporate environment in which the company does business (Ramanathan, 2005). This is clearly articulated in the Larsen and Toubro Vision Statement: "We shall be committed to community services and environmental protection." For example, the Larsen and Toubro Welfare Centre in Mumbai offers medical and diagnostic services to both Larsen and Toubro employees and their families, as well as to the neighboring community. The center offers services free of cost to the community in the areas of family planning, mother and child health care, and tuberculosis and leprosy control. The center is staffed by physicians, nurses, social work professionals, and so on (Nayak, 2005).

In a rural location, Larsen and Toubro offers the "VIKAS Programme" (Village Improvement Know-how and Skills). This project focuses on improving the quality of life in a cluster of villages that surround the Larsen and Toubro factory. The project initiatives include provision of medical care, building schools for children, employment opportunities, and imparting skills for self-employment. Larsen and Toubro is also actively involved in AIDS education of its employees and the surrounding community. In areas where Larsen and Toubro has factories, it is engaged in tree plantation efforts, and other afforestation efforts, to sustain the environment. It has planted upward of 500,000 trees (Nayak, 2005).

In recognition of Larsen and Toubro's contribution to the larger community, it was selected unanimously by the panel of judges, and was awarded the 1999–2000 Bombay Chamber Civic Award for the category of Community Development (Bombay Chamber of Commerce and Industry, 2000). Five years before that, in 1994–1995, Larsen and Toubro was awarded the Good Corporate Citizen Award by the Bombay Chamber of Commerce and Industry. The criteria used for this category include evaluation of company policy and activities in the areas of environment issues, health and sanitation, rural welfare, education, urban development, help to the disabled, and social welfare (Nayak, 2005).

REFERENCES

Ghoshal, S., & Bartlett, C. (1997). *Individualized Corporation: A Fundamentally New Approach to Management*. New York: Harper Collins Publishers.

Nayak, J. P. (2005). President, Operations, Larsen and Toubro, Ltd. Personal interview by C. S. Ramanathan, at Bangalore, India, and at Mumbai, India.

Schumacher, E. F. (1973). *Small Is Beautiful*. Abacus.

Schumacher, E. F. (1999). *Small Is Beautiful: Economics As If People Mattered*. Hartley and Marks.

gender selection, stolen identities, treatment of children in adult courts, and the decision to separate conjoined twins. Students learn and practice from the international code developed by the International Federation of Social Workers (IFSW). It becomes apparent that most ethical questions are global in nature. Social workers are revisiting their universal values, in areas such as human dignity, worth of the individual, and the sanctity of life, in the context of their international code of ethics (www.ifsw.org).

Some of these values have been under assault as we debate the ethics of cloning, selling parts of the genome project to the highest bidder, or suicide bombing. Social workers involved in hospice, refugee resettlement, torture victim services, and health settings are often at the forefront in helping their profession provide leadership in ethical decision making (Skarnulis, 2004). The IFSW Statement of Principles is under constant revision and represents a dynamic document to support practice decisions. Many ethical debates refer to individual and family well-being, including the implications of reproductive health policy. In this regard, the innovative work of the Green Star Services in Pakistan is reviewed and offers insights for pregnant, unsupported teenagers worldwide.

Chapter 5 turns to the west in our framework to study *cultural awareness*, or cultural competence in local and global relationships. Cultural competence refers to our ability to work with people of many cultures in an attitude of inclusion and respect. Gould has said, "Do not look at culture as white people versus people of color, established immigrant versus new immigrant, American minorities versus Global South cultures; rather, reach for thinking at a trans-cultural level" (Gould, 1995). From this transcultural vantage point we hold cultures in genuine regard, realizing that communities are becoming much more complex and fluid.

In many parts of the world, nations are experiencing an inward flow of migrants in the pursuit of safety, economic opportunities, and family reunification. In addition, continued conflicts and full-scale wars result in displacement of populations and an increase in refugees and internally displaced persons (IDPs). The United Nations High Commissioner for Refugees reports that in 2007 the number of refugees under UN care topped 11.4 million, and the number of internally displaced under UN care topped 25.1 million. These numbers do not include asylum seekers or stateless people; all together the UNCHR believes there are over 31.7 million displaced populations worldwide (UNHCR, 2007).The social work literature in several countries reflects an increased attention to the needs of immigrants, refugees, and minority groups; this is a critical issue for this text. The concept of *cultural competence* has proven valuable in heightening awareness of our cross-cultural communication at the micro, mezzo, and macro levels. This attention to cultural competence for social work practitioners is essential for several reasons:

- The unprecedented movement of people across the globe, including to the United States and Europe and between Asian nations and African countries;
- The globalization of labor, as transnational corporations relocate manufacturing and agricultural production plants from country to country, seeking the least restrictive economic, safety, and health conditions;

- Outsourcing of labor from a company headquarters in one country via electronic and web networks to another country, often in the form of "call centers" (e.g., British Telecom, U.S. Dell Computers in Bangalore); and
- Increased attention to educational exchange of students in preparation for their work in an interdependent world.

One example of the use of multiple locations within one corporation is British Telecom. Service calls made in the UK are now routed to a company in Bangalore, India, which dispatches local service technicians for performing repair work in England, Scotland, and Wales. It is an indicator of the fast-changing demographics in the world that students come naturally with a wider view of their domain. There is recognition that domestic issues are now global concerns. No social worker in any country can expect to work only with the people of a culture they are familiar with, in their hometown, in the place and way they know well.

In chapter 6, we turn to the south in our framework and consider assessment skills and inclusive practice with mobile populations: understanding migration and its relationship to social and economic development. Assessment is particularly assisted by the framework offered by documents such as the ICD and the work of designing international policy instruments. International human rights instruments such as the Convention on the Rights of the Child, the Geneva Convention on the Rights of Refugees, the International Covenant on Civil and Political Rights, and the Universal Declaration of Human Rights will be reviewed in every chapter. Becoming familiar with these policies is a prerequisite for social work practice (www.un.org). As students step into the rich materials offered by the United Nations and global organizations such as the World Health Organization, they find frameworks and case examples to enhance their own practice experience.

For example, the number of refugees worldwide continues to expand dramatically, with more than 50 percent being children. Although refugee numbers decreased from 2002 to 2006, in 2007 they increased globally (UNHCR, 2007). The 1951 Geneva Convention on the status of refugees establishes the basic rights to sanctuary, documentation, and safety, commitments that are now being questioned. The Convention has helped "millions of civilians to rebuild their lives and it has become the wall behind which refugees can shelter . . . the best we have, at the international level, to temper the behavior of states" (Erika Feller, director of the Department of International Protection of the UN High Commissioner for Refugees [Feller, 2001]). In this context a refugee is someone "with a well-founded fear of being persecuted for reasons of race, religion, nationality, membership of a particular social group or political opinion" (Geneva Convention, 1951, Article 1A(2)).

Chapter 7 explores the fifth element: mother earth and ecological aspects of human well-being and sustainable development. Planet Earth is a precious resource that is only just being realized as being finite in its gifts. Differential access to water, clean air, farmland, and the implications for human flourishing are discussed. The film *Earth on Edge*, with Bill Moyers (2000), explores the tight circle of life, which often can only be perceived through a leap of the imagination. Farmers in the Midwest tell Moyers that they now realize that their farming practices often led to pollution of the Mississippi and ultimately to the dead zone that is developing in the Gulf of Mexico, where nothing survives. When fishing people lose their livelihood, they move north and become migrant workers, and this is happening the world over, off the coast of Nigeria as well as in parts of the Americas. Farmers in the Midwest are now following natural patterns of allowing some weeds and sewing hardy grasses among their crops. The rivers of the Mississippi are responding quite quickly to the efforts of farmers and environmentalists, not to mention the work of the Environmental Protection Agency in holding corporations accountable for polluting groundwaters.

Chapter 8 looks to our place in the universe and draws together key ideas and research for the social work profession to truly embrace global reality, where every student is familiar with international policy instruments, international values, global definitions, and goals for the profession. Challenging topics, including terrorism and its impact on families plus the spread of tropical viruses, are also being addressed with designated social work roles. Concepts of spirituality and the reality of common humanity are connected to social work assessment. The data presented in this book also demonstrates that a broader view of ourselves can promote peaceful coexistence.

GLOBAL INTERDEPENDENCE AS A VALUE IN SOCIAL WORK ASSESSMENT

Terrible events elicit immediate attention, crisis management initiatives, and a briefly heightened awareness of the frailty of peaceful coexistence worldwide. Since the millennium, we have experienced the United States and allies' ongoing war in Iraq and Afghanistan; the violence of November 2002 in Palestine and Israel; the explosion in Bali in October 2002; the attack on the Indian Parliament in January 2002; the attacks of September 11, 2001, in New York, Pennsylvania, and Washington, DC; the tsunami in December 2004; and the attacks on July 7, 2005, in London and November 26, 2008, in Mumbai. It seems that students in Western nations truly learn their knowledge of geography through war and disaster rather than a peaceful curiosity about fellow human beings. A *National Geographic* survey conducted in

2002 across nine nations found that only 13 percent of U.S. people between 18 and 24 years of age could identify Iran on a map, and only 12 percent could identify Afghanistan. Overall, the United States came in eighth in the survey, and Sweden was top, with the highest international knowledge (Garcia, 2002). We consider curiosity and knowledge of the world and the causes of social and economic injustice to be foundations of social work—and geography is the first step.

The philosophy here is to accept the reality of *global interdependence* and grasp our role as world citizens for the advancement of humanity, for all time. Desmond Tutu spoke powerfully to this theme: "One day we are going to wake up as though hit between the eyes; we will realize that we are all family, not in a sentimental sense, in our realization that we have need of one another" (interview on the *Charlie Rose* program, September 16, 2005). Therefore, in this text we learn about the world through examples of human service and social work that focus on justice, conflict resolution, and pursuit of human rights in a spirit of *social inclusion and interdependence.* The definition of social work from the IASSW and IFSW, agreed on in 2001, reflects this philosophy:

> The social work profession promotes social change, problem solving in human relationships and the empowerment and liberation of people to enhance well-being. Utilizing theories of human behavior and social systems, social work intervenes at the points where people interact with their environments. Principles of human rights and social justice are fundamental to social work. (www.ifsw.org)

The IFSW definition strengthens the focus on systems and social action as well as cooperative responses to man-made disasters: "Providing all people with access to basic social services and transfers to boost their incomes would cost $80 billion, less than the net worth of the planet's seven richest men" (Aslam, 2002; Singer, 2004). Liberation is an elusive concept—it can be used in relation to economic freedom and social and gender equality, but also in more sinister and less positive ways as a camouflaged form of influencing weaker countries. This book draws on the *Oxford English Dictionary,* which defines liberation in positive terms, as expressed by the International Food Policy Research Institute:

> In order to eradicate poverty and liberate people from it there is growing recognition that we need more women in leadership. Securing land rights for women can lead to greater agricultural productivity and improved environmental stewardship. (Aslam, 2002)

The issues lie not in the leadership or intelligence of men and women, but rather in who has access to and ownership of resources, and this will be discussed further in chapter 5. War is driven by the arms trade and the need for resources such as oil and water—when the majority of wealth is held by one gender (at the moment, men), it seems likely that war will continue. Margaret Mead asserts that war is not a biological necessity; we have yet to live that belief (cited in Barash, 2000, pp. 19–22).

As part of our practice elements, social work has a tradition of faculty and students partnering with communities for peaceful change during social upheaval. Examples of such upheaval include the world wars and U.S. civil rights movement of the 1960s, social justice initiatives in the Global South, and the emerging economies of Eastern Europe (Link and Čačinovič, 2004). We utilize the learning of these partnerships to identify, analyze, and expand frameworks to encourage and invite international cooperation and learning at a variety of levels.

In clinical work we have some accepted norms of practice, such as self-awareness, confidentiality, use of self, assessment, goal setting, contracting, engaging, and evaluating. Often, however, this work lacks the global lens. Ironically, in macro practice we have identified global issues of social development and poverty without adequate attention to the skills that will ameliorate harmful social conditions for people existing, or barely existing. Therefore, we tend to focus our change efforts more on individuals, families, and local communities (at best looking at the national level) and neglect work in the global sphere that requires skills such as cultural competence, negotiation, techniques to achieve distributive justice (such as micro lending), and linguistic facility. For example, the influenza strain H5N1(bird flu) is an international phenomena that requires cooperative efforts toward management—politicians can't simply say, "Stay where you are and don't infect others." We already know that airline travel takes people swiftly from points of infection to uninfected regions. The recent SARS epidemic was addressed effectively in Singapore but less effectively—even with panic—in Toronto and China (Tan, 2004). The profession of medicine cannot say we will only address the quarantine structure; they must find a cure. In terms of social work, similarly, we can no longer say we focus only on the poverty on our doorstep and ignore the wider structural reasons for it and its cure. These are the kinds of discussions, ensuing skill sets, and collaborative actions that are part of the macroenvironment of human behavior.

Contemporary social work knowledge, skills generation, and practice cannot operate in isolation. Globalization is providing us opportunities to operate on at least these four levels:

- The individual student-to-student, personal Internet connections;
- Faculty, student and practitioner, client, community exchange across borders in physical and video settings;

- The larger institutional, agency, United Nations agreements, and NGO (nongovernmental organization) programs;
- A holistic universal approach to the worldwide practice of social work encouraged by the IFSW and partner institutions, including the IASSW and, in the future, the fledgling Social Workers without Borders.

Instead of seeing international concerns as additional material in an already packed curriculum, students are often the driving force in integrating global materials in all they do. In many schools, social work students find that a literature search is incomplete without international references. For example, the *Diagnostic and Statistical Manual of Mental Disorders* for the United States, referred to as the *DSM IV*, is too ethnocentric to be helpful when working with immigrant groups; thus the International Classification of Diseases (ICD) is essential resource material for mental health assessment. The ICD9 is now the standard for all U.S. medicare claims (Mayadas, Ramanathan, and Suarez, 1999). Furthermore, utilizing the learning of cross-national exchanges expands our thinking and often gives us a wider array of solutions and approaches (Link and Čačinovič, 2004).

Some countries, including the United States and Europe, have been challenged by their colleagues in the Global South, for focusing too narrowly on individual "client" problems, rather than social and economic justice and human rights, and the implications of human migration (Potocky, 1996). In this context, social justice relates to the distribution of resources so that all people have access to basic means of well-being (clean water, safe shelter, food, health services, and education). The connection between economic and social conditions necessary for development to occur is vividly portrayed in the *Progress of Nations* report (UNICEF, 2000).

Writers from the Global South (Arundhati Roy, Merlai Desai, Amartya Sen, and Vandana Shiva) call attention to the ways some countries of the Global North neglect social justice in preference to blaming individuals for their poverty. This dynamic of "blaming the victim" was widely recognized by activists in the 1960s (Ryan, 1976) but lost momentum in the European/ American/Austral-Asian economic boom of the 1980s and 1990s. Blaming those in poverty for their plight is currently most evident in punitive social policies, such as sanctioning people who need "welfare" support (Link and Bibus, 2000) or restricting access to affordable housing.

In 1968, Richard Titmus proposed the notion that we are all recipients of welfare (defined as the government disbursement of tax dollars to maintain income). This notion is based on a framework of occupational welfare (workplace benefits, flexible accounts), fiscal welfare (corporate tax exemptions and individual tax allowances), and public welfare (public income maintenance) (Titmus, 1968). Dominelli recently included the middle class in this framework as the insecure wealthy. She explores the impact of structural unemployment, corporate bankruptcy, and the shaky foundations of pensions and U.S. social security touching the lives of over 98 percent of the world's population (Dominelli, 2009). The framework prompts insight into our web of financial supports and vulnerability. None of us stands alone and the sign of humanity in a peaceful world is not independence, but interdependence.

SUMMARY

As the framework of six elements for assessment (figure 1.1) is applied in this book, there are basic principles for a macro approach to human behavior which underlie the work of becoming social workers in a global context. When students come to realize the multicultural character of their service communities they may naturally be interested in other countries and world regions. However, many have not received the grounding in geography and the history of nations and peoples necessary to give context to their practice. For social workers, we begin by expanding our global knowledge in every arena of our professional and personal life. Where do our coffee beans or bananas come from, who picked them, what are they paid, and why are we seeing the migration of farmworkers from the south to the north in the Americas? Often, small nations may not make the global CNN news, but they are crucial to our well-being; for example, in Suriname deforestation threatens flora used in developing chemotherapy drugs. Recently, students tracked the "fair trade" policies of companies such as Caribou and Starbucks. Following electronic mail pressure, Starbucks has finally agreed to offer a fair trade bean, one that is guaranteed to be picked by people who are paid a fair wage. One of the authors (Link) found that students wrote vividly of their increased understanding of global issues when they came to know a farmer who spends part of his year in a Minneapolis coffee shop and part at his Mexican brother's farm.

The basic premise of this book is that we learn from international dialogue and that it is oppressive and demeaning for countries of the Global North to assume superior knowledge. There are always opportunities for mutual learning in social work and in economic development. The first decades of "international development" supported by the United Nations and the various national aid organizations saw a focus on economic assistance as the key to progress. Recently we have recognized the failures of development and the need for a combination of social and economic progress, with attention to human rights and sustainable social development. The ideas behind this term "social development" are familiar to the social work profession in the form of community organization, empowerment, and social action. The UN refers to social development as the only way we can achieve "sustainable" improvements in the challenges of infant mortality, unsafe water, illiteracy, poverty, and famine (UN, 2000).

Essentially, the case studies and analysis presented bring currently sporadic international collaboration between social work educators, students, and practitioners into focus to assist our understanding of human behavior. We anticipate that students will be able to mobilize and inspire each other and their faculty and supervisors as they take up some of these ideas. For example, the report of the Detroit Project is just one example of student and practitioner action in taking a group of inner-city youth to Africa for a transnational experience focusing on self-esteem and identity. The Detroit Project 1993 initiative of the School of Social Work worked with a sample of public schools in the inner city of Detroit and created lasting change for participants (Ramanathan and Link, 2004; Ramanathan and Beverly, 1999).

Building partnerships between colleagues in the northern and southern nations that are most intensely impacted by globalization generates opportunities for students to enhance and sharpen their skills in critical analysis. Social workers have a central role to ensure that the politicians' rhetoric about recent immigration is translated into dignified, realistic programmatic and service initiatives. Such services can only be built on an understanding of the social and economic conditions that fuel migration in the first place.

Educational institutions are playing "catch-up" to the global realities of international trade, work outsourced from one continent to another, electronic communication across borders, and new economic alignments. In class in Minneapolis, students discussed the origin of the bananas they buy. No one had thought about this simple food and its connection to social work. They completed an assignment to see how many they could buy for one dollar and to identify the marketing companies. Students compiled their data and discovered that the "Big Three" (Chiquita, Dole, and Del Monte) control the banana trade in the Midwest of the United States. The banana trade is run by a few large corporations in Central America, while there is a trend toward smaller ownership in the Windward Islands of the Caribbean. The effects on local families and communities in Central America can be devastating when transnational corporations control their lives (Martin, 1999). In Honduras there is now a "dead zone" of land overtreated with chemicals. Local people struggle with poverty and the impact of pesticides on their health, or they migrate. Despite the earlier fertility of their land and the abundance of basic crops, they leave the land of their ancestors. Now, when students stop to buy, they can pause to ponder the source of their food and the human cost. They may also choose to recognize and exercise their purchasing power by seeking fair trade bananas from the Caribbean.

Although humans have achieved startling technological advances in the last century, including worldwide communications systems, we are also still caught up in the paradox of narrow national interests competing with one another and dangerous escalations in aggression that threaten whole regions, if not the planet. Vaclav Havel (former president of the Czech Republic and playwright) writes in his essay "The Politics of Responsibility" about awakening a new sense of recognition and responsibility for the world as a precious, shared place (Havel, 2000). Havel asks how countries, such as the United States, can learn to lead without dominating, and learn to develop large productive corporations without exploiting labor and the natural environment. Vaclav sees the key in recognizing our interdependence and avoiding controlling while role-modeling compassionate leadership:

> Whether our world is to be saved from everything that threatens it today depends above all on whether human beings come to their senses, whether they understand the degree of their responsibility and discover a new relationship to the very miracle of Being. The world is in the hands of us all. (Havel, 2000)

This book also asks how the social work profession can endeavor to make the world more hospitable, to hold precious our own stories yet also transcend our local experience and learn what can bring us together. Havel reminds us that we have to make the psychological, social, and emotional leap beyond defining ourselves by our clan.

There is a new narrative forming in parts of the world, including in the United States, where President Barack Obama speaks to our need to listen to one another. In his address to the G20 summit in London in 2009, President Obama said the time for one nation to lecture another is over; we are ready for new relationships of respect and negotiation. The film series *In Her Own Image* contains a segment describing the work of a Colombian cooperative (*Hell to Pay*, 1991). The focus is rural poverty and the struggle for communities who receive dwindling public funds due to the national debt repayment plan. The film is called *Hell to Pay*, and it reminds us of the costs of neglecting schools, health, and housing in favor of the interest payments demanded by banking systems of the Global North, where the thread of common humanity has rarely been part of the dialogue. In the economic turmoil of the failed banking systems in 2010–2011 and the changing political climate, there is renewed attention to human rights and global interdependence, which raises awareness of struggling communities and oppressive monetary practices. In his State of the Union Address in January 2010, President Barack Obama reminded his country, "The best antipoverty program is a first-class education. A high school diploma no longer guarantees a good job, which is why we will pass a bill to revitalize community colleges, increase tax breaks for families and increase the Pell Grant and tell students that no one should go broke because they chose to go to college" (Obama, 2010). In this book we suggest that education as a right for children worldwide is a goal we must work to achieve and that the profession is on the cutting edge of living out a recognition of global interdependence and responsibility.

In this text, we offer social work students ways to appreciate the diversity in the world, to understand the complex reasons for poverty (especially that structural conditions such as lack of employment are not the fault of individuals), and most importantly to learn from one another internationally, and to reach for common humanity in their practice and their narrative. The final chapter considers this question of the role of social work practice in the context of globalization. What are some common concepts and where must unique indigenous patterns be respected and maintained? Methods of establishing international standards and components of practice are identified, and a comparative framework of social work in six countries is presented. It is timely that we strike a note of optimism, that the social work profession can embody more trusting and respectful relationships at all levels of community—from personal to global. If not, there is, indeed, hell to pay.

STUDENT ASSIGNMENTS

1. Test your knowledge of countries by identifying blank maps or country borders: for example, what are the six countries bordering Iraq?
2. Write your definition of "globalization" as it relates to social work. What are some opportunities and some challenges of this concept? Revisit your definition at the end of your course or reading.
3. Write in your journal about your current knowledge and encounters with international social work or interventions with a global reach (such as work with refugees or recent immigrants).
4. Use the Internet to visit the United Nations site and identify one social development document; discuss its connection to social work practice.

Chapter Two

Common Human Condition

A human being is a part of the whole, called by us "universe," a part limited in time and space. He [she] experiences himself, his thoughts and feelings as something separated from the rest—a kind of optical delusion of consciousness. This delusion is a kind of prison for us.

—Albert Einstein (1899)

What are the factors that lead us to become more aware and appreciative of one another, and what are those which separate, isolate, and even tempt us to judge others hastily? UNICEF'S *Progress of Nations* report states: "The day will come when nations will be judged not by their military or economic strength, nor by the splendour of their capital cities and public buildings, but by the well-being of their peoples" (UNICEF, 2000, preface). This expectation seems a long way from 2010, when countries continue to wage war, corporations continue to destroy the natural environment as though this precious earth is limitless, and people struggle on low wages in underresourced communities.

For social workers, it is essential to recognize common human needs that have to be addressed for people to achieve a sense of well-being. Effective assessment is based on the ability to focus on the wide array of causes of behavior and to balance the internal and personal motivations with *human conditions* in the surrounding environment. Although it may be hard to truly understand the experience of refugees and their separated families, everyone can relate to degrees of hunger, cold, loneliness, and devastating loss. Sometimes this understanding requires fully conscious effort.

One might assume that the concept of a "human condition" is universal; however, more often than not, human condition is described within a particular context. When people have access to resources, they forget what it

25

means to be without them and often judge those less fortunate adversely. In this chapter, we address the notion that all of us are subject to a "common human condition" and cannot live with dignity without our basic needs' being met. It is a distinctive characteristic of the social work profession that we always consider the situation of the person and his or her behavior in the surrounding social environment in tandem. When a child is restless in the classroom, what space is there at home for free play? How safe are the streets, stairwells, and playgrounds? The study *The Rainforests Are a Long Way from Here* vividly portrays the challenges of living in housing projects (estates) in Scotland (Burningham and Thrush, 2001). Thus, we draw on our understanding of people's behavior in relation to their conditions to guide social work assessment and practice decisions. This does not mean that we absolve people of their responsibilities, but it does require social workers to take a broad ecological view (see the example of gun control in chapter 1). Sometimes, human service professionals have emphasized the individual's behavior and undervalued the impact of the environment (Specht and Courtney, 1994).

Linked to the common human condition are the concepts of social exclusion and sustainable social and economic development, which are also described here and analyzed for their contribution to assessment and practice. The International Labour Organization (ILO) uses the term "social exclusion" to identify ways in which whole groups of people are placed outside the means of survival. If we accept the notion of a common human condition, the realization of social exclusion follows. Using this analysis leads to assessment that starts from a structural position, analyzing the way our local, national, and global society works, before "blaming the victim" (Ryan, 1976). There are many excellent texts describing theories of individual development because the practice of social work has tended to focus more on individuals and their family than on structural concerns (Ashford, LeCroy, and Lortie, 2006). Here the focus is the impact of the environment on human development. It is a deliberate professional lens for social workers to focus with full attention on the environment and human condition before assessing the individual and his or her family as deficient or behaviorally disordered. There are times when the focus on the individual is entirely appropriate and urgent; however, this book argues that the first step is to absorb and assess the surrounding conditions.

Often we discount the effects of poverty because of our own easy access to resources. This means that many educated professionals and students are separated from the reality of existing in conditions with the barest minimum of utilities, which is frequently the experience of clients or people using social services. An unintended consequence of automatic access to electricity, clean water, faucets, paved roads, and dentists is a numbing of human survival skills. Thus, some researchers in human development have underestimated both the flexibility and skills of people living in underresourced human conditions because their own abilities in staying warm, gathering fuel, lighting fires, or sanitizing water are rarely put to the test.

Affluent people have been caught up in the results of pampering and they may fail to see the capacities of people labeled as indigent, underdeveloped, or illegal migrants. Maslow's hierarchy of needs, for example, implies that people without basic means are unlikely to self-actualize (Maslow, 1968) While the challenges of impoverished conditions are recognized (for example, children need food in order to learn), the capacity of people and their coping mechanisms are evident in even the toughest circumstances and should never be underestimated (UNICEF, 2006).

Following the definition of three concepts—common human condition, social exclusion, and sustainable development—an assessment and practice model with case examples will provide a synthesis of these ideas. Thus, the chapter will address four elements that constantly interact. An understanding of these elements is the foundation for assessment of any situation:

1. The common human condition;
2. The nature of social exclusion and its impact on human well-being;
3. The connection between exclusion and sustainable social and economic development; and
4. A new model for assessment and practice as a holistic understanding of our inner and outer worlds.

COMMON HUMAN CONDITION

In a BSW program at Augsburg College, Minnesota, students were invited to seek and comment on definitions of "common human condition." Several spoke of the complexity of the term and drew on scientists and philosophers such as Albert Einstein and the Dalai Lama. The class highlighted the idea of embracing a holistic approach to the world and spoke of these new ideas as both daunting and inspiring (see textbox 2.1). The term "common human condition" invites complexity as the variation from culture to culture, place to place, individual to individual is considered, but it is also a means to identify the building blocks of human life that are part of everyone's development. It is the ancient tradition of Buddhism to meditate on the flavor of the food we eat, our means of transport, shelter, and the refreshing miracle of clean cold water. Social workers can practice such reflection in order that they never forget what it means to lose these things and to become more conscious of what is common to us all. As one student suggests, the common human condition is "what people must endure, struggle, and live for" (see textbox 2.1).

**Textbox 2.1. A Student Writes about the Concept:
Common Human Condition**

A human being is a part of the whole, called by us "universe," a part limited in time and space. He [she] experiences himself, his thoughts and feelings as something separated from the rest—a kind of optical delusion of his consciousness. This delusion is a kind of prison for us, restricting us to our personal desires and to affection for a few persons nearest us. Our task must be to free ourselves from this prison by widening our circle of compassion to embrace all living creatures and the whole of nature in its beauty. (Einstein, 1899)

Einstein has captured the essence of what we believe the human condition to be. This quote has large implications on micro, mezzo, and macro levels that create a global village. He explains that humans have a tendency to interact and survive within a small circle of people because it is easiest to do this. We concentrate on those things that affect us personally and in the process limit our responsibility to a larger world.

The Dalai Lama has explained the human condition as "the need for all sentient beings to pursue happiness." The global implications of this definition depend on the social and cultural environment in which we each live. These are different and the definition of happiness is culturally defined. We must understand this reality and accept it, if we intend to bridge the human condition into one specific definition. I believe the human condition is a difficult term to define because it encompasses the essence of what makes us human.

The human condition could have a different definition every place in the world. The variations can be as large as from one country to another or as small as the difference between two towns only a mile apart. The human condition will be defined by an individual's life. Where one lives, works, spends free time, and what one's family and friends are like, anything that affects the person will have an effect on the definition of his or her human condition.

Source: Essay by Kendra Roberg, 2002. Quoted here by permission.

To grapple with and come to an understanding of common human condition is a central part of the assessment process. For the purposes of this book, we define "**common human condition**" to include *the universal aspects of human existence such as the need for shelter, clean water, food, safety, identity, civil rights, intimacy, and song, and the idea that we step back from judging people without access to resources and recognize that all of us are vulnerable as individuals and stronger when we work in community.*

This is a giant leap, but it begins with accepting ourselves as citizens of the world and is followed by a vision of the complex relationships and systems of resources and fluid boundaries that we constantly negotiate in order to sur-

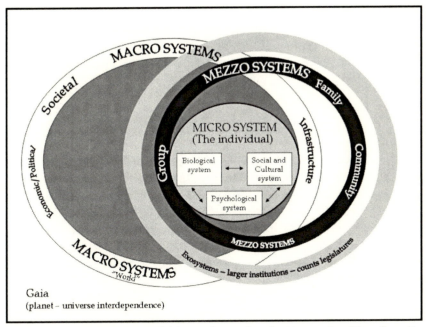

Figure 2.1. An Interactive Model for Understanding the Human Condition (from Ramanathan and Link 1999, 2004)

vive. This approach to the environment surrounding human existence is best understood in the context of **systems theory**, which identifies at least four spheres of constant interaction (see figure 2.1): the micro level of interaction and immediate nurturing relationships; the mezzo level of community connections and **sustaining environment**; the exosystems of larger institutions such as courts and legislatures; and the macro level of national and interdependent international relationships. We also add the fifth known system, also referred to as the Gaia system of our world, seen as a fragile planet in an ever-changing universe subject to global warming and solar energy surges (Wheatley, 2000).

In schools of social work over the last sixty years, the primary focus has been on the micro aspects of social work intervention with less research and focus on broader issues. By this, we do not imply that focus on the individual is inappropriate, but disproportionate attention has created an imbalance in our vision and use of resources. If we utilize Cooley's "looking-glass self," the other is the immediate other, even in the macro content, such as policy confined to national boundaries or human condition in one's domestic environment. At a personal level, this translates to challenging the idea: if it does not affect me immediately, I do not need to worry. An example is the extent of HIV in many African countries and the increased attention to public health policies. In "My Voice Counts Too," Hortense Bla Me, an AIDS campaigner in the Cote d'Ivoire, is concerned at the lack of recognition that education is the key to AIDS prevention (UNICEF, 2000). When the universal vulnerability and creativity of the human condition is accepted, the door opens to a wider variety of solutions and cooperation.

THE NATURE OF SOCIAL EXCLUSION

Historically, social exclusion has been used as a tool to deny people civil rights and freedoms. Civil rights movements worldwide demonstrate that the need for civil rights is part of the common human condition. These movements use nonviolent social inclusion as a means to gain access to civil rights. For example, Mohandas Gandhi (respectfully referred to as Gandhiji) first used a nonviolent civil disobedience technique, called satyagraha (resisting tyranny through massive civil disobedience), in South Africa, where he worked as a lawyer in the Indian community struggling for basic civil rights. After witnessing some success using satyagraha in advancing civil rights in South Africa, Gandhiji returned to India and organized protests and campaigns by farmers, urban laborers, and the educated elite to advance women's rights, promote interreligious harmony, ease the hardships of poverty, and above all gain independence from British domination (India gained independence on August 15, 1947). Gandhiji spent years in jails both in South Africa and in India, as the authorities were intimidated by people demanding civil rights and freedom. Dr. Martin Luther King Jr. replicated the nonviolent movement in the United States during the civil rights struggles. In fact Dr. King had traveled to India and spent a month immersing himself in the nonviolent movement there.

In 2009, Secretary of State Hillary Clinton, while commemorating the 50-year anniversary of Dr. King's visit to India remarked, "Dr King's trip to India stands as a landmark of the Civil Rights Movement and a real testament, ambassador, to the bonds of affection and shared history between our two nations" (Clinton, 2009). The scenario depicted here is a clear testimony to the universality of the common human condition. The authors of this book view civil rights as a required condition for social and economic development. In the Western world, and democratic societies, civil rights are often taken for granted, while they continue to be denied in other parts of the world, be it for the Tibetan people, or the Iranians, or in Mayanmar. The authors of this book believe that the denial of civil rights anywhere is a threat to civil rights everywhere, and therefore, ought to be a concern of social workers and others working in the human service professions.

Connected to a narrower micro focus is the unnoticed effect mentioned earlier of easy access to resources. This means that many people in economically thriving communities are separated from the reality of existing in conditions with the barest minimum of utilities. It takes a deliberate, conscious effort to notice when our values push us to overhasty assessment.

Although social work has struggled with the societal tension of blaming individuals for their circumstances, a focus on human condition prompts us to think first of the impact that social conditions make on people's lives. Part of our common human condition is to be sharing a fragile planet at a time of serious destruction of natural resources and increasing tension over access to precious reserves of our most critical natural elements, most especially water. Although much of the focus in the U.S. war on Iraq has been the protection of oil resources, it is now argued that water is the next worldwide crisis (Shiva, 2002).

Social workers are often witness to the suffering of adults and children excluded from shelter and adequate means of survival. Sometimes whole groups of people suffer together, for example, as refugees, or through natural disasters, mass layoffs, and plant closings. Their suffering is often compounded by lack of resources and exclusion from normal social behaviors, such as shopping, recreational activities, taking a holiday, or eating in a café. Despite this lack of access, there are alternative means of survival, which can be supported when newer forms of assessment are used. The concept of social exclusion came into being with the influence of the French writer Jean-Paul Sartre and his book *Roads to Freedom* (Sartre, 1960). His writing identified group alienation and has inspired French social policy analysts and, more recently, international organizations.

The term "social exclusion" has been adopted by the International Labour Organization to refer to "the sinister reality of a world of have-not: the homeless, jobless, powerless, penniless" (Gaudier, 1993, cited in Ramanathan and Link, 2004). The concept of exclusion addresses the structural changes in whole communities following mass layoffs, migration, war, global warming, fires, and urban corporate development. Social exclusion has many layers of meaning, from the exclusion of a class of children who live in projects, on estates, or in refugee camps without access to basic technology, to the wider exclusion of some adults and people with disabilities or those who seem to be outsiders. Excluded adults and children are described by some as in poverty, but it goes beyond income to the exclusion from access to health care, viable employment, official language, political participation, and access to light and clean water (Shiva, 2002). More recently the language and response of the United Nations has been to examine the policies that would ensure inclusion.

Thus, when we focus on human condition as opposed to human behavior, it gives us increased opportunities to make assessments (or in Mexico, **reality**

Textbox 2.2. Example of Reality Analysis

LEAVING FOOTSTEPS

Rosemary Link

(With thanks to Luz y Libertad for their permission to quote their work and for their suggestion that we include the Spanish translation)

Settling back into the chilly fall of Minnesota, I caught myself thinking back to Cuernavaca, looking for bougainvillea and the hanging vines in the Jardin Borda. I was also looking for ways to apply the wisdom of community workers we met in Mexico who look for human dignity and liberation from exploitation rather than "development" or "case management." In June 2002, we visited a number of community centers, and met with families and social workers to hear about their work. Mexico is currently a country of spectacular opulence that you can see in the whitewashed weekend houses of Tepotzlan and fancy districts of the capital, but also a country of acute poverty in the colonias and barancas of the cities and countryside. As social workers in the United States, we are used to contrasting wealth and poverty, but our approach is often to assess the individuals and their families in terms of *their* problems, as though they are somehow separate from the majority. In Mexico, we frequently hear the term "reality analysis," and it has stayed with me.

We were sitting in a warm, sparsely furnished meeting room with a central table replete with good food. We were 14 people at Luz y Libertad (Light and Freedom). We heard from Alma Chaires, Eustorgia Estrada, and Teresa Andrade about the origins of this women's organization. Conscious of the increasing costs of food and essentials for families with children, a group of women came together to "learn how to be in solidarity and to organize." We heard that the group carried out a "reality analysis" and "found we had creative skills, self-esteem, and respect for each other in working for justice." Now they help each other with nutritional education, run workshops on self-esteem and health, cook with soy and amaranth, and maintain vegetarian menus. They buy in bulk and share the food on a cooperative basis. Also, they sell their crafts at meetings such as ours (I have my exquisitely crocheted purse by me as I write), and they hold weekly sessions to train themselves and others in making the footsteps to "solidaridad." Another workshop is about self-esteem, in which they help other women to elevate their self-esteem. They also told us, "We have weekly Bible study meetings, and this is the motor that drives us to these and other activities."

Later we listened in another part of town to community organizer Carmen Granados tell us about the brutal struggle for land reform in Chiappas and the risks people take on behalf of their community. She told us, "As I work to understand, I am filled with the richness of the people . . . [and] we avoid the summary: no this, no that, no other. It is much better to ask ourselves, what should be done? We start to create a program, the propositions and initiatives and we start." We heard that, similar to Luz y Libertad, the steps of this work included (1) a reality analysis, (2) a celebration and recognition of work that is being done (leaders from Chiappas have recently been honored in a Cuernavaca ceremony), (3) cooperation to escape exploitation in wages and costs of basic goods, (4) awakening of strengths, (5) seeking and evaluating results of solutions, and (6) developing advocacy (Carmen Granados, 2002).

As I walk to a meeting of people in the Phillips neighborhood of Minneapolis, Minnesota, I am thinking deeply about the solidaridad of Luz y Libertad and Carmen's words. She suggested that one of the best aspects of being a social worker is that "you never walk alone . . . you are always leaving footsteps with others." I shall be joining a regular meeting of capable Minnesota women who are struggling with acute poverty and the isolation of being "cut off" welfare due to the time limits. The images of Mexico and our conversations will linger as we discuss our own reality analysis and ways we take footsteps to "solidaridad" to avoid the oppressions of one of the richest countries in the world unable to feed its children.

Ejemplo de Análisis de la Realidad

DEJANDO HUELLA

Rosemary Link

Tratando de volver a acostumbrarme al frío otoño de Minnesota, me di cuenta que estaba recordando Cuernavaca, buscando sus bugambilias y enredaderas colgantes y abundantes del Jardín Borda. Pero también estaba buscando maneras de aplicar la sabiduría de los que hacen trabajo comunitario, los que conocimos en México, los que buscan la dignidad humana y la liberación de la explotación en lugar del "desarrollo" o "manejo de casos." En Junio de 2002, visitamos varios centros comunitarios y nos reunimos con familias y trabajadores sociales para escuchar de su trabajo. México actualmente es un país con una riqueza espectacular y opulento que se ve en las enormes bardas blancas de las casas de fin de semana en Tepoztián y en las lujosas colonias de la capital, pero a la vez es un país de pobreza extrema que se ve en las colonias y barrancas de las ciudades y el campo. Los trabajadores sociales en los Estado Unidos, somos acostumbrados a los contrastes de riqueza y pobreza, pero nuestro metodo frecuentemente es para evaluar al individuo y su familia en términos de sus problemas, como si fueran, separados de alguna manera de la mayoría. En México frecuentemente escuchamos el término "análisis de la realidad" y éste se ha quedado conmigo.

Estamos sentados en una espaciosa y cálida sala de juntas que tiene una mesa central repleta de apetitosa comida. . . . Había nosotros 14 y nuestras 6 anfitrionas del grupo "Luz y Libertad." De Alma Chaires, Eustorgia Estrada, y de Teresa Andrade aprendimos de los orígenes de esta organización de mujeres. Conscientes de los continuos incrementos de los costos de comida y necesidades básicas de las familias de bajos recursos y con niños, este grupo de mujeres se juntaron para "aprender a ser solidarias y organizarse." Aprendimos que el grupo hace un "análisis de la realidad" y "descubrieron que tienen habilidades creativas, autoestima y respeto por ellas mismas y luchan por la justicia."

Ahora ellas ayudan a otras mujeres, con los diferentes Talleres como el de educación nutricional a bajo costo y que ayudan a las personas a mejorar su salud, al cocinande con soya, trigo y amaranto, creando menús vegetarianos. Otra actividad es hacer las compras por mayoreo, organizándose con otros grupos de mujeres, en donde todas se ven beneficiadas por adquirir los productos a costos más bajos, realizado en base de una cooperativa. También ofrecen talleres de manualidades (tejido de bolsas y blusas y diseños navideños en material de fieltro y en listón) cuyos productos son vendidas en reuniones como la nuestra. (Yo tengo mi preciosa bolsa tejida junto a mi mientras escribo.) Otro taller ofrecido es el de autoestima en donde ayudan a otras mujeres a elevar su autoestima. Tienen reuniones semanales de Reflexión Bíblica, que "es el motor que les impulsa a estas y a otras actividades," para mejorara ellas mismas e ir marcando el camino hacia la solidaridad con otras mujeres.

Entonces fuimos a otra parte de la ciudad a otra persona que hace trabajo comunitario, Carmen Granados. Ella nos habló de la brutal lucha contra las reformas agrarias en Chiapas y sobre los riesgos que la gente tomados en nombre de su comunidad. Ella nos dijo: "Tratando de entender, me lleno de la riqueza de la gente . . . evitamos un resumen con reglas: no a esto, no a aquello, no a esto otro . . . más bien preguntamos . . . ¿qué hay que hacer? Empezamos a crear un programa con sus proposiciones e iniciativas y empezamos." Escuchamos algo similar en Luz y Libertad, los pasos de su trabajo, que incluyen: (1) Un análisis de la realidad, (2) una celebración y un reconocimiento del trabajo que se está haciendo (a líderes de Chiapas se les hizo recientemente un reconocimiento en una ceremonia en Cuernavaca), (3) la cooperación para escapar de la explotación en cuanto a salarios y costos de productos básicos, (4) conciencia de fortalezas, (5) buscar y evaluar los resultados de las soluciones, y (6) apoyo a una causa (Carmen Granados, 2002).

Mientras camino a reunirme con la gente del barrio Phillíps de Mínneapolis, pienso profundamente en la solidaridad de las palabras de Luz y Libertad y de Carmen Granados. Ella nos sugirió que uno de los mejores aspectos de ser un trabajador social es que nunca se camina solo . . . siempre está "dejando huellas con otros." Pronto me uniré a reuniones regulares de mujeres capaces de Minnesota que están luchando contra la pobreza extrema y el aislamiento causado por ser quitadas del sistema de bienestar social debido a sus vencimientos. Las imágenes de México y nuestras conversaciones estarán conmigo mientras discutamos nuestro propio análisis de la realidad y maneras en que tomaremos pasos hacia la "solidaridad" para evitar la opresión en uno de los países más ricos del mundo que es incapaz de alimentar a sus propios hijos.

El ejemplo de Luz y Libertad ilustra el trabajo que promueve la inclusión social en vez de la exclusión causada por la pobreza. También nos modela la conciencia del medio ambiente, la comida sana y nutritiva, y el desarrollo sustentable. El grupo se alimenta y enriquece entre si, desarrolla habilidades, se conecta con la red local de productores de alimentos, organiza compras al mayoreo e influye la economía local. Un acercamiento de valorar al individual podría identificar si cualquiera de ellas tuviera un crisis personal o con sus niños, quien quizás no fueran a la escuela, si algún miembro de la familia puero desempleado, si hubiera violencia, faltara acceso a empleos bien remunerados. El análisis de la realidad sostenido por una valuación de la condición humana común, suspende.

Se sugiere este orden de ideas para "Luz y Libertad."

analysis) based on dignity, awareness of social exclusion, concern to promote social inclusion, and well-being (see textbox 2.2). This approach to assessment will then reflect capacities and coping repertoires at the community and individual levels and the interaction between people and resources with the view that all of us are included in the human race. For example, when we assess the resilience of people in poverty according to their capacities, we need to simultaneously assess our own abilities to cope with crises and the uneven distribution of basic necessities (in this context, identified by the United Nations as access to health care, shelter, food, employment, education, and human services). Otherwise, we risk projecting our biases on both the perception of the problem and the generation of solutions.

The Labour government in the UK established a Social Exclusion Unit in 2000 and announced a commitment to end child poverty by 2020 through a variety of policies including one called "Sure Start." Although the timelines have been criticized as too long, there is widespread support for the idea of targeting areas of the country that struggle with economic and thereby social depression. The term "social exclusion" is used to denote a cluster of characteristics that hamper individual and community progress. One area targeted by the Sure Start program is south Bristol, particularly the Hartcliffe, Highridge, and Withywood areas. In those areas family and early childhood learning centers have been set up with the following aim:

To build a confident community, of confident parents, giving children a Sure Start in life. Parents, carers and local agencies will work together to ensure that there are opportunities for ALL children under four and their families to have: high quality play and learning experiences; access to high quality health care and information; good support networks; opportunities to learn new and develop existing skills; services that are designed with them and for them. (Fulford Family Centre, 2002)

At the Fulford Family Centre in Hartcliffe, the program emphasizes partnership with parents, and their brochures and artwork speak to "happy parents, happy children, programs designed to give children back their future" (Fulford Family Centre, 2002). The focus is to combat social exclusion by identifying a geographical area and including everyone in that area who is interested in taking part. There are no means tests or categorical requirements: if you live there you are included in the services. Some of the parent comments in the annual reports include

"They showed me that my role as a mother is valued."
"We have a say in what we want . . . [so] we make the difference."
"There are lots of things for the children and myself to do."
"Actually getting out and doing something has made me feel better about myself and much more positive about the future." (Fulford Family Centre, 2002)

The Sure Start program is completely new in some areas and builds on existing initiatives in others. Link's research in 1995 identified the role of parents as partners in service provision and presented data from both service providers and users concerning the challenges of working together to address larger community issues of social exclusion. Since that time, the funding of the Sure Start program has strengthened the agencies and given them the staffing and resources to realize the inclusion of hard-to-reach parents. Their methods include the affirmation of strengths of all families, deliberate power sharing across layers of the community, and most significantly a larger step into reality analysis of the social and economic development needs of the surrounding areas. For example in Hartcliffe and Withywood, there is an industrial park and superstore development which broke ground 2004 and was completed in 2006. This development supplies jobs, training, and work experience for local schools and families.

The process of weaving an appreciation for the common human condition together with our own biases and access to, or social exclusion from, resources is complex wherever it is—in the UK as described in the Sure Start initiative or other parts of the world. In Mexico it is illustrated in the involvement of the workers in joint community action with women cooperative organizers described in the journal excerpt "Leaving Footsteps" (see textbox 2.2).

The example of Luz y Libertad illustrates work that promotes social inclusion rather than exclusion as a result of poverty. This work also role-models an awareness of the natural environment, healthy foods, and sustainable development. The group nurtures one another, develops skills, connects with the local food-producing network, sets up bulk buying, and influences the local economy. An individual assessment approach might identify any one of many personal crises with children out of school, unemployed family members, violence, and lack of access to adequately paying employment. The **reality analysis**, underpinned by a valuing of common human condition, suspends judgments and moves into what can be accomplished.

The project Luz y Libertad is, however, fragile, surrounded by a macroeconomic environment that is in flux. U.S.-owned maquiladoras arrive in Mexican communities and offer employment, but exploit labor in the hours, conditions, wages, and lack of attention to family needs such as day care and sick pay. It is ironic that in the time between visiting "Nustart" in Morelos in June 2002 and writing this chapter, a seemingly family-friendly maquiladora, producing apparel such as Jantzen swimsuits and offering day care to employees, has been closed and moved to Asia.

Although neither part of a Sure Start program nor a conscious reality analysis, a family center in the United States is working to include families in a nurturing experience that promotes healthy child development and better futures in a context of sustainable development. In a recent study, Bibus and Link identified census tracts of the poorest families in a neighborhood known as Phillips in Minneapolis, Minnesota. The researchers set up focus groups to listen to the voices of families living there and using the services at a selected agency: Southside Family Nurturing Center (see textbox 2.3).

Textbox 2.3. Southside Family Nurturing Center

CASE STUDY

Rosemary Link

Entering its thirtieth year, Southside Family Nurturing Center (SFNC) is based in the area known as the Phillips Neighborhood of Minneapolis, Minnesota. The agency was established to work with whole families, rather than identified "problem" members, and has been recognized as innovative in its holistic systems approach. Aware of the costs of poverty and social isolation, the agency aims to avoid judgment and be patient while families find their way to work in unison for better futures. Most of the 130 families receiving services in 2003 have experienced neglect, poverty, drug abuse, child protection inquiries, and housing and transport concerns. Southside believes in the strength of families and in cooperative strategies to prevent child abuse and neglect. In order to present the agency more effectively, Fayol's framework (1949) for understanding organizations will be used, addressing *planning, organizing, staffing,* and *controlling.*

(continued)

1. Planning

Set in a Victorian four-story house, the agency is a welcoming place to be and is inviting to both adults and children. At a 2003 accreditation event, one of the Early Childhood Association site visitors commented: "If I were a child I would want to be here." To many observers, it is also a nurturing place to work. Approximately 35 workers and over 100 volunteers offer a range of services with one mission: "Together with families and community, we nurture children, build on family strengths, and find alternatives to violence" (SFNC brochure, 2003).

The goals of the agency for parents include "to work with you to provide a respectful, caring place in which you will be encouraged to learn some new and positive ways of relating to your children and to recognize your strengths and the things you are already doing well" (SFNC brochure, 2003). For children, goals include to provide a nurturing, safe, and stimulating educational environment with opportunities for social, emotional, intellectual, and physical development. For fathers, goals include "to offer advocacy, support and resources, and help with parent skills in order to emphasize the vital importance of the father's role in the family" (SFNC brochure, 2003). There are three main programs that help to meet these goals: the Center Base Program, the Home Base Program, and the Father's Program. Smaller additional and complementary programs working across the three core units are a community resource program, a holiday store, and an interns program. A variety of resources is needed to reach these program goals, and they include public funding through county contracted services, private foundations, United Way, and individual donations. In-kind contributions come from area businesses, such as the Target stores, and educational institutions, such as Augsburg College. Also, the local community contributes to the holiday store, local churches provide help with the nutrition program, and a variety of neighborhood businesses support fund-raisers and reciprocal events. An example of reciprocity would be the contribution of time by interns and faculty in service to the agency and the opportunity for students to be supervised by excellent practitioners and faculty to conduct research.

2. Organizing

The agency began in a church basement with volunteers in 1974 and then established itself as a nonprofit agency with three directors. The organizational structure from the start has been "flat," nonhierarchical, and more of a wheel of relationships. The three directors have very specific roles: administrator and fund-raiser, director of home-based services, director of center-based services (since this research, the founding directors have retired and the agency has adopted since 2006 a single executive director position with supervision of program director roles). Role relationships are clear within the staff and sometimes more complex with the board and community. Interns experience the agency as a welcoming place with ease of access to supervisors and open communication. At a recent retreat for strategic planning and realignment, staff praised the agency for its levels of supervision and support. The agency has a higher than average child to teacher ratio in the early childhood program (3:1 for 16–36 months; 4:1 for 36 months to kindergarten) due to high needs and the combination of education and family service; staff are identified by the county for example as master teachers. The staff work in their program teams and have regular (weekly) meetings plus meetings across the teams for community planning and events, such as the holiday store or Thanksgiving meals. The Victorian building is aging gracefully and has remained a deliberate choice of space for the programs, despite maintenance costs that are higher than a more modern building. The building has the feel of a large, warm home, with stained glass windows, newly painted classrooms, and a fresh yellow meeting room with sofas and plants for parent and staff meetings.

3. Staffing

There are approximately 33 workers at the agency and over 100 volunteers. There is a board of 12 directors that includes a parent-liaison quarterly meeting; a separate Capital Campaign Committee comprising representatives from staff, board, and community; and a Building Committee that coordinates contractors and maintenance companies. The staff serve approximately 150 clients (parents and children), and this includes program services, community outreach, food program (daily meals for all the children attending and at least one family meal per week), and transport (the agency owns three buses for transporting children).

4. Controlling

Elements of control in an agency include directing and maintaining work standards, evaluation, and accreditation, motivating staff, and monitoring the impact of the agency on the community as well as the impact of policy and community on the agency and families served. Regular supervision and monthly data gathering for reporting to funders such as the county all contribute to a high level of direction and work standards. All programs have goals and outcome measures, and these are reported both for accountability to funding streams and for fund-raising purposes. At a recent accreditation meeting, the agency received positive reports on the nature of relationships between families and staff. One of the agency's directors wrote a thank-you note to staff, which represents the atmosphere at Southside Family Nurturing Center well:

> "It's so clear that you have to cherish everyone . . . every soul is to be cherished . . . every flower is to bloom" (Alice Walker). The truth is it is not clear to everyone, but I am beyond grateful to work in a place where cherishing is attempted every single day. "If I were a child, I would want to be here." Those

(*continued*)

are the words of the woman who came to validate our preschool and toddler class-rooms. She recognized in each of you the undeniable radiance that comes from your tenacious effort to cherish. Thank you for your support, effort and dedication during this process. (Olson, 2003)

The impact of the outside environment, particularly in terms of the reduced public funding of families in poverty, is probably the hardest aspect of the work of Southside. While staff work tenaciously to cherish children and their parents, the larger community is often ambivalent about people labeled as "poor" or neglectful. The larger system is often unaware of the resilience and capacities that all families have. The Bibus, Link, and O'Neil (2005) research gives parents an opportunity to voice their experience of the current policies relating to the alleviation of poverty, known in the United States as "welfare reform."

REFERENCES

Fayol, H. (1949). *General and Industrial Management*. Trans. C. Stours. London: Pitman.

Olson, Barbara (2003, September). Executive Director address to staff at Southside Family Nurturing Center, Minneapolis.

The research utilizes the concepts of common human condition and social exclusion. For example, the neighborhood was mapped for a wider view of the conditions in which the families were trying to survive. It is an area well known to police, service providers, and activists, and these groups have very different approaches and interpretations of the reality of problems here. Within policing units, the individuals are blamed for their drug use, gang behaviors, and violence. In the social agencies, some workers describe families as hard to reach, even uncooperative. For others, particularly the social workers and activists concerned with social exclusion, there is a recognition of the complex picture of economic and social depression. The research reveals that families are working to survive and do the best for their children in very challenging circumstances. The application of the concepts of common human condition and social exclusion helps social workers to step back from hasty assessments to absorb the day-to-day perils of existence on low wages, limited welfare or income maintenance, high housing costs, intermittent transport, and complicated relationships between health and education services.

SUSTAINABLE SOCIAL AND ECONOMIC DEVELOPMENT

In the past, social development has been a separate area of study and only recently has it been recognized as part of social work. Sustainable social and

Textbox 2.4.   Capacity and Skill Retention

Chathapuram Ramanathan and Sandeep Manchekar

In recent times, as a result of contributions to the field of computer technology, the economic expansion of India has been taken note of by the Western world. Expansion of the urban economy in and of itself is not likely to improve the standard of living of India's rural population. This requires systematic development of policy initiatives at both the central government and the state levels. Therefore, Indian policymakers, political leaders, and corporate leaders have embarked on a tripartite partnership between the governmental, nongovernmental, and the private sectors for effective and sustainable growth and development among India's poor. The number of active NGOs in India is a testimony to this. Similarly, CEOs of major industries, including the computer software industries, systematically collaborate to increase the standard of living for all citizens. For example, the world-renowned IT guru and chief mentor Narayan Murthy (Infosys Corporation) asserts that "the hardest challenge we face is how to make available all good opportunity to poorer section of people for development on all fronts." As he reiterates his mantra of "performance brings recognition, recognition brings respect, and respect brings power," with equal fervor, on development, Mr. Murthy insists that government has done all for the corporate sectors and now it is time for corporate leaders to deliver what people expect from the corporations: namely, "advancing their quality of life through development projects that improve their employability" (Murthy, 2006).

This kind of effort takes place both in urban and rural India. For example, farmers in a remote village in Honavar, 600 kilometers away from India's Silicon Valley of Bangalore, are using ATM machines to open a bank account. This village is in the southern nation of India, and the ATM machines provide banking access to 22,000 odd villagers, covering over 3,500 villages. This project, as described in "Bridging the Digital Divide" (Carless, 2009), is a culmination of pilot projects that showcased the marvel of information technology in rural India, through tripartite collaboration of government, NGOs, and corporations. In addition the same group is involved in developing e-governance projects for village-level governments (Gupta, 2006).

The following case scenario is an example of potters from the village Pudukottai, in the state of Tamil Nadu, in India. Their only occupation is pottery. They make clay lamps (which use oil and wick) and Ganesha idols (Hindu deity). Men can make large figures, usually 10 feet tall and taller, of horses and bulls that are usually found at the entrance of village shrines. Their pottery is fired in kilns for which the women carry "head-loads" of wood over long distances. The men work on the wheel, and women make hand-built articles alongside.

The significant fact is that this traditional craft is no longer seen as economically viable. The "next-generation" families are keen on a formal school

(*continued*)

education and mainstream work opportunities in cities. Although there is nothing wrong with people aspiring for formal education, and exploring opportunities in cities, people who migrate to urban settings are not very happy being
in urban settings, but feel that they have no alternative, as their skills do not
produce sustainable levels of income. *DakshinaChitra* (Art of the South), is
the brainchild of Deborah Thiagarajan, an American woman living in India for
many years (http://www.dakshinachitra.net/). DakshinaChitra, which is a not-
for-profit organization, has a center for living traditions of art, folk performing
arts, and crafts. The center aims to preserve and promote the rich heritage and
culture of the people of South India. Their concern is to upgrade existing skills
and help extend craft markets. This involves sustained training programs such
as the workshop discussed below. During the workshop, potters who had successfully upgraded their skills were certified by the regional Office of the Development Commissioner (Handicrafts). This is a significant step and opened
up opportunities to access urban markets through cooperative societies.

During March 2006, DakshinaChitra conducted a terra-cotta glazing workshop for village potters. It was the first of its kind for the Heritage Centre
in Chennai. Ten traditional potters, both men and women, chosen from a
well-researched database attended this residential training program. Sandeep
Manchekar, a ceramist from Mumbai, trained them in the basics of glazing on
terra-cotta. He had even fabricated a gas kiln (1,300 degrees, downdraft) for
the organization. Keeping in mind the urban consumer of pottery, products
like snack trays, agarbatti (incense) stands, candle and lamp holders, wind
chimes, and so on, were produced. This involved rolling the clay out flat with
rolling pins into the precise length and thickness using simple tools and creating a variety of natural textures, using leaves, seedpods, gunnysacks, and so
forth.

At the workshop, one of the acknowledged master potters in the group, artist Rengasami, was inspired by Sandeep to try flat mural forms, much like the Orissa "patta chitra," with each small clay tabloid telling a story from the *Mahabharata* (Hindu epic). This required not only a leap of skill but of imagination as well. Rengasami Ayya brought the workshop to an end by eliciting the ancient text "Kula Puranam" or the story of creation, from the standpoint of a potter. It states that a potter is the quintessential creator, like Lord Brahma. It is this belief that gives potters their strong sense of identity and their sense of sacred purpose. Finally, the bright and magical results from the glazes along with slips on terra-cotta culminated the process. Each of them was exhilarated with the "high" from the creation. The glazed terra-cotta pieces were available for sale at the DakshinaChitra shop on the premises.

With this effort, yet another set of village potters were encouraged to inculcate imaginative techniques in clay and aid in the marketing of their skills through cooperative societies.

REFERENCES

Carless, J. (2009). "Bridging the Digital Divide in Rural India with Unified Communications." News at CISCO feature story, March 9. http://newsroom.cisco.com/dlls/2009/ts_030909.html.

Gupta, S. (2006, April 7). "How IT Is Changing Rural India." Rediff India Abroad. www.rediff.com/money/2006/apr/07spec.htm

Murthy, N. (2006, May 5). "Murthy Stresses on Opportunities for the Poor." *Deccan Herald*, Guwahati, India.

Pictures reproduced with permission from Chathapuram Ramanathan and Sandeep Manchekar economic development is revisited in most chapters and is introduced here because it is impossible to separate economic progress toward well-being from healthy human development (as illustrated in the case of the potters in textbox 2.4). In Luz y Libertad there is the social interaction of the families in conjunction with practical solutions to daily economic needs. At Southside, families consistently identify income and housing as their top priorities. Simarly for the case of the potters in textbox 2.4, control over their own lives becomes empowering and a source of healthy and sustained development as a community.

Midgely describes social development as a "process of planned change" designed to promote the well-being of the population as a whole in conjunction with economic development (Midgley, 2003). In the daily lives of people trying to make a basic wage or sell their produce for a fair price, the social and economic issues are intertwined. However, it is not always clear whether people who control the economics of new advances in technology or production understand the connection with sustainable development and human conditions where families can thrive. For example, with the rapid expansion of coal mining in the UK in the Victorian period, conditions for the miners led to lung disease and short life span; only the owners could safely benefit (Cronin, 1937).

In Nigeria, a local protest vividly highlighted that economic development of a locality without attention to the social context is a distorted form of development. In Ugborodo a group of women became frustrated at the obvious progress of a large Chevron plant just across the river from their village. They heard stories of clean water and modern air-conditioning at a time they were struggling with polluted streams, infant mortality, dehydration, and poverty. In a peaceful demonstration, they quietly crossed the river and infiltrated the plant. Their shock at what they found is eloquent: "We found heaven just across the river."

The Chevron plant has a deal with the government that takes the profits out of the country and leaves a small percentage to the government. Nothing comes directly to the village of Ugborodo. The women have simple demands: clean up our river, share clean water, and offer us jobs. Although Chevron Nigeria Ltd. has acknowledged some contribution to human rights abuses in the Niger Delta, a report by Amnesty International describes continued activities by Chevron Nigeria Ltd. and Shell Nigeria, which continue to lead to violence, human rights abuses, and isolation of the local communities (Amnesty International, 2005).

As social development and community macro-level projects are studied across the globe, common elements can be identified that generate a model for social work. In a number of countries, for example, micro credit banking is being established as a way for people without savings and collateral to access funds for self-help and community business projects. While the Grameen Bank in Bangladesh is becoming famous, the variety of micro-lending institutions are expanding in India and Africa and more recently in the United States (see discussion of the Grameen Bank in chapter 4).

When students compare and contrast micro-lending initiatives with traditional banking, they identify very different conditions: micro lending is based on trust and the right of all people to credit; traditional lending is based on privilege, collateral, and suspicion. As these lending projects encourage community initiatives such as Luz y Libertad and rice mills in northern India owned and run by women a new model of social work based on the recognition of common human conditions and needs is emerging. The work of Sherraden and his colleagues has connected U.S. researchers and interns with projects in Africa and they have focused on the mechanics of setting up effective micro-lending schemes (Sherraden, 2003).

Midgley has suggested that we have the instrumental aspects of social development (such as credit) without enough collective theory of social development. In the 1990s most social workers were introduced to institutional and selective approaches to welfare and human well-being. Many had been familiar with the state-sponsored "welfare state" and more recently "welfare reform." With stringent cutbacks in state social programs, the work of the Blair government in the UK to introduce a "third way" in politics and social welfare gained attention. It has been identified as a "pluralist" approach, where the old notions of entitlement to basic well-being are abandoned in favor of a mix of public and private responsibility in the Western "more developed countries" (MDCs). However, the economies of many "less developed countries" (LDCs) mean that the majority of people are in poverty due to stringent structural adjustment programs that are the conditions of international and World Bank loans. As people struggle to feed their children, more radical approaches to social welfare—including the organizing of groups such as Luz y Libertad in Mexico, the BRAC or Bangladesh Rural Association bank community projects in Bangladesh, the Nigerian women's group challenge to Chevron in Ugborodo, and the Nu asset-building project in China—have called for a different approach that is less reliant on government "welfare"; this new approach is known as developmentalism. Midgley has identified at least three theoretical levels of developmentalism:

> Creation of organizational arrangements at national levels to harmonize economic and social policies;
> Recognition of the importance of macroeconomic approaches to promote employment; and
> Encouraging social programs that are "productivist" in that they incorporate economic needs with human programs; the conditions have to be eased before human well-being is feasible. (Midgley, 2003)

As this theory base is applied to social work, we can identify steps for assessment and practice that truly focus on common human condition, celebrate capacities, and avoid judging people for economic circumstances that surround

---

Textbox 2.5.   SOWSEEDS

Steps to achieve social work for social and economic equity development that
is sustainable:

1. A social *network* is built that finds common ground (for example the women
   farmworkers of Tolmin in Slovenia gather monthly from far hills to talk
   about their work and provide solidarity to one another);
2. Through *narrative* sharing of experience, history, and concerns the "reality
   analysis" begins (Cacinovic Vogrincic, 1997). Luz y Libertad has demonstrated that reality analysis avoids identifying what is not present "no this or
   that" and focuses on what is present, what the skills and experience of the
   group are in the actual social and economic situation;
3. To build community and recognize capacities; *celebrate* early and often.
   Southside Family Nurturing Center celebrated their thirtieth anniversary
   with a quilt that many families helped to sew and now hangs in the agency
   hall for all to take pride in;
4. *Cooperate* to escape oppression or exploitation. The Domestic Workers'
   Center in Cuernavaca for example, was closed due to threats to the women
   workers (Ramanathan and Link, 1999);
5. Awaken insights and strengths by claiming and naming them through the
   processes of "conscientization," whereby what we are "told" by government
   administrations is matched to what we "know" through our experience. The
   women of Ugborodo were told that the plant was benefiting the country, but
   their experience showed them pollution and exploitation.
6. *Evaluate* the results and solutions.
7. Develop and claim advocacy skills in concert with international women's and
   human rights movements and credit organizing groups such as FINCA (Foundation for International Community Assistance; www.villagebanking.org).

Source: Čačinovič Vogrinčič, G. (2000). *Family Social Work.* Ljubljana, Slovenia: The
University Press.

---

their families and hamper their development. The assessment and practice model
that students in Link's classes in social development identified as SOWSEEDS
(Social Work for Social and Economic Equity Development that is Sustainable)
takes the "developmentalist" approach as its theoretical base and includes the
following **strengths-based assessment** and action steps (see textbox 2.5).

As students use the concepts of common human condition, social exclusion, and development, they add dimensions of macro assessment to their
understanding of the world that are both complex and enlightening. This new
model, SOWSEEDS, gives us the tools to act, to invite the narrative and to
ask questions about why poor, why here and not there, why so much knowledge and so much vulnerability. As we explore the common human condition

we realize the essential combination of social and economic development and the effects of globalization. In social work that is concerned with development we ask: where is the human dimension in economic globalization and how can we learn from Luz y Libertad, the farmworkers of Tolmin (a rural cooperative of farmworking women in northern Slovenia who invited the author Link to spend time with them in 2002), the community capacity builders in China, and the micro lenders in Bangladesh or Nigeria. Human development depends on this shift in gears to incorporate the economic with the social and sustainable, where the environment and community come first in our assessment and "reality analysis."

STUDENT ASSIGNMENTS

1. Use the learning outline "What Do We Mean by Development?" to help you create your own definition of development as it relates to social work.

What Do We Mean by "Development"
a learning outline

- The process whereby a country improves the well-being of its people.
- The year 1961 was the first UN Development Decade.
- Well-being through social and economic means: "Development is a process of improving the capability of a nation's institutions and value system to meet increasing and different demands, whether they are social, political, or economic."
- Economic development on its own is not enough . . . why?
- Which countries are developed . . . developing . . . underdeveloped (in UN documents and many publications less developed countries are referred to as LDCs and more developed as MDCs).
- The term "developing country" is used to contrast the lower income, less industrialized countries of the world, with the more industrialized, higher income countries, labeled by some as MDCs.
- How is the definition of "development" or the label "developed" changing?
- Countries are recognizing that economic development is not viable without a simultaneous focus on sustainable human development and human rights.
- Human development indicators (HDIs) of "developing" countries, such as high infant mortality, low rates of immunization, low rates of education, and poverty, coexist with characteristics of "developed" countries in the same nations. What might be some examples?
- Why is this definition controversial?
- Developing "may suggest that there is a particular path or end state to be pursued . . . [but] it also suggests progress, which is not a reality in all countries" (Healy, 2001).
- Who is developing—are men and women included equally in statistics?
- From what and to what are we developing?

Development in the future must include dwelling on the work of women (Patel, 1998).

Development "must be redefined as an attack on the chief evils in the world today: malnutrition, disease, illiteracy, slums and unemployment" (World Bank, 1982).

DEVELOPMENT RELIES ON HUMAN RIGHTS

The 1948 UN Declaration of Human Rights includes a statement that "the recognition of the inherent dignity and the equal and inalienable rights of all members of the human family is the foundation of freedom, justice and peace in the world."

Human rights = political, legal, economic, and social rights.

Justice = a question of development—the development of a population raised to its full creative potential.

Human Rights + Justice = Peace and Development

FAILURES OF GLOBAL DEVELOPMENT

"There are two major reasons why the global development movement of the last half of the twentieth century has been a disastrously destructive misadventure:

1. It has emphasized aggregate increases in economic output and consumption without regard to either equity or human needs . . . resulting in expanding demands on earth's ecosystem beyond what the earth can sustain . . . even while leaving some 1.3 billion people living in destitution . . .
2. The favored development models have called for the deregulation of markets and the elimination of national economic borders to facilitate the unrestricted free flow of goods and money." Korten, 1995

Recognized as economic globalization, the process Korten describes has led to the perception that economic organizations of global scale have resulted in too much power over resources concentrated in too few hands. Many analysts consider that hidden decision making by a few large corporations and banks has in turn led to the depression of the first decade of the twenty-first century.

2. Explain what is meant by the "gap in imagination" when we see a photo of a young child asleep with thread in hand over a pile of baseballs he is sewing (UNICEF, 1997).

3. Why has it taken so long for social work to focus on economic development in relation to human development?

4. What is your definition of the concept "common human condition"? How might you apply it to your assessment processes?

5. Draw two circles and label one the **nurturing environment** and the other the **sustaining environment**; cut out the nurturing circle and place it according to your level of acceptance and feelings of congruence, on top of or to the side of or separate from the sustaining environment. As an example, although the authors are not Lutheran, one of their employers is a Lutheran organization where the concept of vocation is held dear. For a Lutheran student, coming from a Lutheran family, attending and later even being employed by a Lutheran college is a very close fit in terms of traditions, language, expectations, commitment to vocation, calendar of events such as Vespers and Holy Week, and ways of life. For a student from Somalia, however, the fit of the circles is very different; they may hardly be touching. To understand this dissonance is a powerful opening to a social work relationship. (See chapter 5 for discussion of these ideas.)

6. Complete a reality analysis of a community you know—but *only* if you carefully *prepare* through a discussion with your adviser or supervisor and identify the time and skills you could offer this community if invited or appropriate. At the first meeting, begin with the work to understand by inviting the story and deeply listening, avoiding the temptation to judge "no this or no that," and asking what is to be done, what is the plan, how is it going, what are some current initiatives, and what are some ways I could participate.

KEY TERMS

common human condition. The universal aspects of human existence such as the need for shelter, clean water, food, safety, identity, intimacy, and song and the idea that we step back from judging people without access to resources and recognize that all of us are vulnerable as individuals and stronger when we work in community.

nurturing system. The place called home; where family is, where one is most comfortable and accepted unconditionally, where the door is open.

reality analysis. Carmen Granados tells us, "As I work to understand, I am filled with the richness of the people . . . [and] we avoid the summary: no this, no this, no that and ask what should be done? We begin to form a program, their propositions and initiatives and they start."

strengths-based assessment. An approach to assessing communities or individuals that begins by identifying their abilities, their skills, their examples of getting through previous crises, their hopes and dreams, before a focus on problems that are getting in the way of their current journey. Instead of seeing sickness to be treated, this form of assessment engages in mutual, respectful endeavor to find solutions.

sustaining environment. The network of services, supports, employers, officials, government organizations, and health environments that surround individuals, who must negotiate with them on an impersonal level and cannot live without them.

systems theory. A constant awareness that the whole is more than the sum of the parts and that individuals are constantly part of a dynamic exchange, interacting and making an impact on one another in their face-to-face relationships, in their collective family and local community participation, and in their national and worldly experience.

Chapter Three

Human Rights and Social and Economic Justice

There is enough wealth in the world to meet everybody's need, but, not enough to meet everybody's greed.

—Mahatma Gandhi

This chapter focuses on the knowledge base for macro social work through the lens of human rights and social and economic justice. As mentioned in chapter 2, the existence and respect for human rights are founded on our understanding of a *common human condition*—that no one, by virtue of birth, wealth, inheritance, gender, or glory is set above others in his or her right to certain basic needs for existence, including safety and protection from discrimination and torture. The United Nations Declaration of Human Rights states:

Whereas recognition of the inherent dignity and of the equal and inalienable rights of all members of the human family is the foundation of freedom, justice and peace in the world,

Whereas disregard and contempt for human rights have resulted in barbarous acts which have outraged the conscience of mankind, and the advent of a world in which human beings shall enjoy freedom of speech and belief and freedom from fear and want has been proclaimed as the highest aspiration of the common people,

Whereas it is essential, if man (or woman) is not to be compelled to have recourse as a last resort, to rebellion against tyranny and oppression, that human rights should be protected by the rule of law.

(UN, Universal Declaration of Human Rights, 1948, General Assembly resolution 217A)

Gradually, the rule of international law is gaining ground, but it has been a long road since this statement of intent in 1948 and even earlier commitments by groups of former combatants. Some countries of the world began uniting during the nineteenth century to set up conventions for treatment of prisoners of wars. The Geneva Conventions came into being in 1864 with the First Geneva Convention; they were then revised and greatly expanded in 1949. It has taken 146 years to generate commitment to the idea of human rights through the work of the United Nations. Ball and Gready's *Guide to Human Rights* suggests that the 1990s were a time of ratification of human rights conventions and that the first decade of this millennium has been a period of serious acceptance and application in many areas of abuse and exploitation. Attention has turned, in particular, to people being held accountable for war crimes, children's rights (for example international identity theft, particularly in relation to adoption), exploitation, and human trafficking (Ball and Gready, 2006). These rights are part of the values of social work, as defined by the United Nations: "Human rights are those rights, inherent in our nature and without which we cannot live as human beings" (UN, 1987). Furthermore, although the UN Declaration of Human Rights has helped advance individual rights, it is a continuing challenge to adequately address cultures with more collective orientation, for example the ancient cultures of China, India, Pakistan, and many Asian countries, where the majority of the world's population now resides. The interplay of individual and collective rights is the current reality and one in which social work leads the way in its attention to ecological systems, healthy communities, and cultural awareness.

The deliberations, conventions, and accords of the United Nations since 1948 have generated a series of global policy instruments that are crucial frameworks and yardsticks for social work practice (Reichert, 2007). These conventions and declarations assist us in a wide focus on the roots and consequences of poverty. The policies address the basic needs of men and women to be treated humanely in civil life and during times of war; they address the needs of children in order to survive and the widespread violations of childhood (for example, through exploitative labor and sex trade), the lack of access for women to property ownership or credit, and extensive, often camouflaged gender disparities in employment and wealth. The UN policies and conventions are broadly addressed in categories of political, civil, social, and economic rights. Reichert categorizes these into three sets of rights: (1) political and civil rights such as a fair trial, free speech, and protection from discrimination; (2) social and economic rights to "a standard of living adequate for the health and well-being of himself and of his family, including food, clothing, housing and medical care and necessary social services" (UN, 1948, Articles 16–27), and (3) collective rights that foster cooperation amongst nations, for example in relation to sustainable development (Reichert, 2007, pp. 3–5). All of these rights are considered basic needs of families to survive and thrive and are central to the endeavor of social workers to enhance human functioning. It is difficult to understand why it has taken so long for the social work profession in the United States to benefit from the work of the United Nations, but certainly it is now accepted as a key part of our work to research and use these resources. Other countries of the world have woven UN policies into their political and social fabric; for example, the child welfare services of Jamaica and Slovenia are based on the Convention on the Rights of the Child. The role of the Ombudsman for Children in Slovenia and Norway functions as a direct result of the expectations of the Convention (*Human Rights Ombudsman of the Republic of Slovenia*; Wenstøb, 2006: see textbox 3.2).

Following a brief history of the United Nations and reference to a number of conventions, this chapter takes as an example that relates especially to social work the Convention on the Rights of the Child. In a combination of policy and case example, the chapter analyzes the Convention and lays out the ways in which it is implemented and how it overlaps and reinforces other instruments. Simultaneously, the dangers of ignoring global policy become apparent—for example, in relation to international adoptions and the rights of refugees and migrants. Case studies include the shutting down of Seattle International Adoptions in 2003, the success of the Milk Marketing Board in India, the KLJUC organization to prevent child trafficking, and health programs currently offered by the giant cement manufacturers Larsen and Toubro (Shukovsky, cited in Link and Healy, 2005).

The spur to deliberate about human rights has often been the atrocity and aftermath of human aggression. There are records of ancient debates about treatment of prisoners in both Chinese and Hindu archives, and the Red Cross/Red Crescent have researched these regional but unsustained initiatives (Ball and Gready, 2006). The nineteenth- and twentieth-century efforts to provide rights to people in times of war ushered in more broad interpretation of human rights and human family as a direct result of the worldwide involvement in hostilities. "In 1859 Henri Dunant, a Swiss merchant . . . was horrified to witness an appalling battle near Solferino. His efforts to aid some of the 40,000 wounded soldiers were to change his life" (Ball and Gready, 2006). Together with colleagues, the work of the International Committee of the Red Cross drew up the document that has become known as the Geneva Conventions, signed by 16 countries and enduring to this day. The following timeline helps to track progress in collaboration toward human rights:

1864: International Peace Conference at The Hague adopts "A Convention for Peaceful Settlement of International Disputes."
1918: World War I Treaty of Versailles.
1920: League of Nations; United States did not join.
1921: League brokered disputes successfully.
1942: 26 nations ("allies") met in New York to draft first declaration of the UN.

1945: In San Francisco 50 nations signed the UN Charter; ratified by five permanent members of the Security Council (United States, United Kingdom,
China, France, Russia).

1950s–1990: Cold War undermined UN, but view of success depends on
individual country perspective.

2006: United Nations peacekeepers become the hope for peace in Lebanon
and Darfur. Several conventions, including the conventions on the rights
of children and on social and economic rights, became lifelines in the aftermath of disasters and conflict.

The United Nations remains a controversial but crucial body, that has developed into a complex organization at several sites internationally, including
New York, The Hague, Geneva, and Nairobi. In 2009 the General Assembly
represented 191 countries. The most powerful body of the UN is the Security Council, which has five permanent members and 10 rotating members
and is based at the headquarters in New York. The secretary-general is appointed by the General Assembly for a term of five years, and he or she is
based in New York. He has an extensive staff of nearly 7,000 people in the
major offices and in supporting programs in Geneva and New York. Some
of these programs and funds include the United Nation's Children's Fund, or
UNICEF, which focuses on children and poverty and publishes the *State of
the World's Children* reports; the United Nations Development Programme,
or UNDP, whose focus initially (1980s) was on economic development and
is now on sustainable social and economic development; and the United Nations High Commissioner for Refugees, or UNHCR, which focuses on human
rights and recently established the new High Commission for Human Rights
in Afghanistan.

The International Court of Justice in The Hague has 15 judges on nine-year
terms and settles disputes between countries, for example fishing rights disputes between Iceland and Canada. The International Criminal Court tries individuals for crimes against humanity and has become better known for holding people from Serbia and Iraq accountable for such crimes. Recently, there
has been concern that the judges appointed to the criminal court are not suf-
ficiently aware of cultural bias in legal systems dominated by Western thought
and process. In response to this, antidiscrimination training is being sponsored
by the European Community Action Programme and a recent report identifies
the goals: "Finding justice at courts in cases of discrimination is the ultimate
protection a democratic state can provide; judges and prosecutors represent
the constitutional state and their response to a multidimensional society needs
to be comprehensive" (*Anti-Discrimination for the Judiciary*, 2006). Many
organizations work closely with the United Nations and provide research data,
policy initiatives, and alerts on human rights violations; these groups include

United Nations Educational, Scientific and Cultural Organization (UNESCO)
International Labour Organization (ILO)
World Health Organization
World Bank
International Monetary Fund

These organizations are gathering information globally and acting in concert with one another in ways that underscore the positive results of increased globalization. For example, the medical community responding to the the SARS outbreak in Singapore benefited in their crisis response from the coordination offered by the World Health Organization (WHO), which is currently assisting countries in tracking the spread of the H5N1 virus, also known as bird flu, and enabling people to cooperate across borders in ways that lead to more effective communication at a number of levels.

Currently, the public view of the UN's work depends on the country or region being surveyed. Some countries see the UN as the hope for the future. For example, the UN was responsible in helping make elections possible in Iraq, even though the outcomes have been so mixed. The UN has also served as peacekeepers effectively in some parts of the world, though it has experienced terrible failures in other areas, such as Rwanda. Unfortunately, a powerful country like the United States resents some of the potential of the UN, as portrayed by the disrespect from the U.S. ambassador to the UN, John Bolton, in 2006, and the comments made by President Bush, who said he needs no "permission slip" to make decisions in the U.S. national interest. However, other groups see global issues beyond national borders, including human trafficking, peacekeeping, and the spread of disease as key opportunities for the UN to make a difference. Simi Samar, current chairperson of the Afghan Independent Human Rights Commission and UN special rapporteur to the human rights situation in Sudan, gave a presentation to the Augsburg College Nobel Peace Prize Forum in 1993. She spoke of her work as the first human rights commissioner in Afghanistan. Her clear belief is that "the UN is indispensable" in bringing about worldwide respect for individual and collective human rights. In the video *Peace One Day*, students can see the research of those seeking cease-fires and an end to the military machine and arms trade that perpetuate conflict as something they can imagine and help come into being in their lifetimes (www.peaceoneday.org). One of the most encouraging global policy instruments for social workers is the Convention on the Rights of the Child, which provides us with a variety of learning points for assessment and practice.

In his introduction to the 2003 *State of the World's Children* report, Kofi Annan invites the voices of children into the United Nations General Assembly and anticipates that adults will make room for children's views and experiences. The UN record shows exuberant pictures of young people under 18 and some of them under 10, finding their feet and sharing the microphone to discuss the Convention on the Rights of the Child:

> We are not asking too much! You said this Summit is about taking action! We need more than your applause and comments of "well done." We need AC-TION. Think about the children, what kind of world do you want for them. Please hear us, we need time to learn. (UNICEF, 2003, p. 1)

The children address all components covered in the 54 articles of the Convention on the Rights of the Child, ranging from education, protection, preservation of identity, and health services, to protection from armed conflict and dangerous labor (UNICEF, 2003). In the last 25 years, countries have slowly ratified the Convention. In addition, in May of 2000 two additional protocols were added to the Convention, addressing the issues of children in the military and the sale of children, child prostitution, and child pornography. As of December 2008 these additional protocols had been ratified by 120 states. States have come to realize the multiple ways this richly layered document may be used, particularly in the field of social development and social work.

In the following pages, a vignette plus a brief history will introduce and alert readers to the ways we are utilizing the articles of this policy in social work; these are followed by a more detailed presentation and analysis of the Convention in the context of human service and future work. As an international policy instrument, the Convention is relatively new. It was passed in 1989 and has now been ratified by most countries of the world, with only two exceptions, the United States and Somalia. What is even more recent is the way the articles have been implemented and are gathering momentum. For many countries, the Convention has become a template for human services concerned with families and their children. The articles of implementation (Articles 42–54) and the reporting mechanisms to the United Nations ensure consistency in both planning and implementation. It is an unfolding story to see the various ways the Convention has provided frameworks and support for intervention to maintain the human rights of children—a story often overlooked in human service literature. While adults have claimed the rights of parents to know what is best in disciplining children, the Convention commands attention to the safety of children from abusive punishment and recognizes that

> In all countries of the world, there are children living in exceptionally difficult conditions, and (we recognize) that such children need special consideration . . . and have agreed as follows . . . Article 19: State Parties shall take all appropriate legislative, administrative, social and educational measures to protect the

child from all forms of physical or mental violence, injury or abuse, neglect or negligent treatment, maltreatment or exploitation including sexual abuse, while in the care of parent(s), legal guardian(s) or any other person who has the care of the child.

INTRODUCTORY VIGNETTE AND HISTORY

A student on summer-school field placement in Koper, Slovenia, spoke of the indelible impression made by an evening picnic organized for her group (Link and Čačinovič Vogrinčič, 2000). A child played an accordion and others danced, while their parents shared good food and stories with visiting students and senior citizens. All the families present were recovering from drug addiction, and all the children had experienced the consequent stresses on their lives at home, at school, and in the community. The families were assigned mentors from the community: older, retired, previously isolated citizens who were their listeners, their encouragers, and their history. That evening, the U.S. visitors became aware of the mutual respect between children, parents, and seniors. Circumstances of *service* in relation to addiction vary considerably in different country contexts. Where the "medical model" dominates, service often becomes "treatment" with professionals in control of clients, where intervention is separated from the needs of the children. The primary distinction at this picnic was the respect and seemingly equal power of all present. Here in Slovenia, the families and children are participants in recovery with their mentors and the agency; everyone is equal in status and value. The families are matched with seniors who receive family help with transport, friendship, and meals; in turn, the elders become "grandparents" to the families and encourage their progress. A number of the group members had organized to run in a marathon and the whole community focused on supporting them in this goal (Link and Čačinovič Vogrinčič, 2000). Although Slovenia is a young country (it gained independence from the former Yugoslavia in 1991), its commitment to social services that use the Convention on the Rights of the Child as a template is exemplary (Slovenian Committee for UNICEF, 1995).

Social workers need to be familiar with the circumstances of World War II that gave rise to the United Nations and the concern for greater cooperation between peoples of the earth. Unlike preceding wars, during World War II children became the victims as bombing took the lives of more civilians than military personnel; for example, firestorms in Dresden and Coventry; the "London Blitz"; and the nuclear bombings of Hiroshima and Nagasaki (Strong, 1998, pp. 498–499). The appalling loss of life led directly to the deliberations and agreements of the Declaration of Human Rights in 1948 and later, the articles devoted to the rights of children (which stipulated that they not be pressed into serving as soldiers).

The specific focus on children manifested in the UN Convention for the Rights of the Child was a long time in coming, however. It moved through many iterations during its 10-year passage through the UN in the 1970s, before approval in 1989.

Arguably, the Convention on the Rights of the Child affects all our lives, but it is rarely cited in U.S. agency documents. This is not just a negligent oversight; it may be another reflection of the more deep-seated antipathy to international "interference" in U.S. affairs. But such an oversight is also a threat to ethical professional practice, as demonstrated by the example of Seattle International Adoptions' recent plight, when it was closed down by federal agents (Shukovsky, 2003). The following passage presents the basic elements of the Convention; then a case illustration demonstrates ways it can be used as a framework for practice.

THE CONVENTION ON THE RIGHTS OF THE CHILD: ARTICLES, GOALS, AND A FRAMEWORK FOR SERVICE AND RESEARCH

The UN Convention on the Rights of the Child is a natural, albeit complex, framework for social service and research. The document has 54 articles that can be grouped into eight categories with standards and guidelines within each category, and they are outlined as a framework for social work practice in textbox 3.1. To ignore the Convention leaves the United States in danger of being at a disadvantage in a narrow vision for child development. Also,

---

Textbox 3.1.   Clusters of the 54 Articles

1. Definitions of the child;
2. Guiding principles (these include nondiscrimination, the best interests of the child, survival, development, and participation);
3. Civil rights and freedoms;
4. Family environment and alternative care;
5. Basic health and welfare;
6. Education, leisure, and culture;
7. Special protection; and
8. General measures of implementation.

Source: Adapted from IFSW, 2002.

---

the Convention draws attention to the reality that these rights are more than child protection—they involve respect and inclusion in decision making. For others, however, there is growing recognition of how useful it can be, and the following summary identifies the articles, some goals, and elements that particularly inform social work practice.

In these eight clusters of the 54 Articles, the Convention covers a wide array of issues that are vital for children's healthy development. For example, the plight of children pressed into fighting and killing as soldiers, the exploitation of young mothers who give their children up for adoption under the pressure of poverty, and the exploitation of child labor are highlighted issues. Also spotlighted are issues ignored by contemporary communities, such as the need for control and obliteration of sexual exploitation (which includes trafficking of children across borders), and consent to marriage rights critical for children. To cover all these eight categories at every level of practice would require separate discussion; for this chapter, the focus is on an overview of the implications for social work practice of the clusters of articles of the Convention, with at least one level of social work practice identified for each cluster. Table 3.1 lays out the systems theory levels of practice, whereby social work recognizes that every individual is part of a family and community system that interacts with surrounding systems, nations, and the world.

A key goal of the Convention is to speak a universal form of language. In reaching for this it highlights how misleading many terms are—whether they refer to local term for marketplace negotiations, or more abstract ideas. For example, the concept of "childhood" varies in age and cultural expectations from country to country, especially in relation to betrothal and marriage. The Convention makes it clear: "child" applies to an individual under the age of 18 years. Similarly, issues of child labor are interpreted differently: in Jamaica, "haggling" is an exchange of fruit and vegetables from family gardens and often takes place in schools among students during the school day and is accepted as a way for families to survive.

Similarly, the term "welfare" has different meanings from country to country; in many European, Asian, African, and Pacific countries, it refers to well-being in a wider context. For example, in countries with national

Table 3.1. Systems Theory Levels of Practice

Level	Description	Practice Illustration
Micro practice	person-to-person	Punishment or discipline (positive reinforcers)
Mezzo practice	person-to-group	Immunization
Mezzo practice	community-to-community	International adoptions
Macro practice	institution-nation-world	Trafficking, child labor

health services, access to affordable day care, emphasis on public transport, and availability of housing, the reform of "welfare" is less harsh than in the United States (Scott and Ward, 2005).

THE CONVENTION ON THE RIGHTS OF THE CHILD AND IMPLICATIONS FOR SOCIAL WORK PRACTICE: APPLYING THE FRAMEWORK OF EIGHT CLUSTERS OF ARTICLES FROM A U.S. LENS

For some policymakers, the fact that the United States has failed to ratify the Convention may have led to the false assumption that it is irrelevant or that the United States has its own satisfactory systems in place. This is a serious barrier to sharing knowledge and gaining the benefit of the experience of countries that have established their processes of participation, self-study, and reporting mechanisms. Furthermore, it means a lack of attention in human service to children's issues—such as clean water—that cross all borders and know no boundaries.

Thus while the essential elements of the articles relate to the social and economic well-being of children who are born into and endure acute poverty, there are aspects of children's rights that cross all socioeconomic groups and all cultures, including the questions of identity, health, adoption, and sexual exploitation. Perhaps most important is the theme of worldwide cooperation invoked by the Convention, which Nelson Mandela discussed at the Conference for Children in Johannesburg in May 2000:

> This global partnership will be guided in its work by the Convention on the Rights of the Child, that luminous living document that enshrines the rights of every child without exception to a life of dignity and self-fulfillment. (Mandela, 2000)

The following paragraphs present the articles in ways that illustrate the response of the social work profession to this "luminous living document" and the connection to fields of practice.

1. Definition of the Child

The eight clusters of articles represent the framework for connecting these policy ideas to social work. For example, the opening statement relates to the definition of "child" as under 18 years old. This is crucial to discussion of culpability, military service, marriage, and employment protections. It is taken for granted in many Western countries that children have the luxury of childhood and adolescence without the adult pressure of economic survival.

In the Oxfam testimonies, children express their concerns about access to clean water and their responsibilities as siblings rather than adults. For example, Surma Begum moved from Bangladesh to Britain and she speaks of people not having money for water wells and not understanding public health: "Some people, when no one is looking, they just pee in the water . . . [and] that is how people get ill" (Oxfam, 1996). The definition of the child is part of the expectation that "State Parties shall respect and ensure the rights set forth in the present Convention to each child . . . irrespective of the child's parent's race, colour, sex, language, origin, disability, birth or other status" (UN, 1989, Art. 2).

For social workers, the right of every child to have his or her status defined and to have a name is crucial for practice. In the author's experience as a school social worker in London during the 1980s, it was normal practice for a child born with a disability and placed for adoption to be called by a capital letter, such as Baby M or Baby P. Being without a name implies that children do not exist in their own right until named by an adoptive parent, and this reduces their independent status and influences attitudes toward practice. Recently in Minnesota and Wisconsin, laws have been passed to shelter newborns. A desperate mother can now take her child to a hospital (rather than abandon it) and know that she will not be prosecuted by the state. The child has immediate status at birth. The law affects social work practice in that it demands that we support and ensure these protections and the right to a name as the first step in our encounter. No child should be just a number or a category.

2. Guiding Principles

The second cluster relates to "guiding principles and the best interests of the child, including the right to survival and healthy development" (IFSW, 2002). Pistoia is a town in northern Italy that has been deemed a "child-friendly city." The town abides by the Convention on the Rights of the Child, and the mayor and administration of the city define "child friendly" as placing children's needs as top priorities for the adult community. The Department of Education has developed preschool "nests," and interdisciplinary teams discuss the most effective ways to serve children, so that those in less resourced circumstances are put "at the front of the line" (GNP Media, 2002).

In reviewing and becoming more conscious of the terms we apply to children's services, we begin to realize how long it has taken to place them center stage and to truly understand that they represent our future. This town of Pistoia in Italy and the country of Norway demonstrate the multiple ways adults can work to create the ideals of the Convention on the Rights of the Child by promoting safe and nurturing urban environments.

The idea of converting Boston or Minneapolis or Madison to a "child-friendly" set of policies and practices (which includes banning physical punishment) seems outlandish and impossible until you see and hear the mayor, teachers, social workers, police officers, parents, and children working together in this sanctuary of commitment. The case study of the Norwegian ombudsman (textbox 3.2) tells us of the innovative work in preserving children's rights that is developing, and the report of the European Network of Ombudsmen for Children (ENOC) is clear in its commitment to end physical violence in the guise of discipline, stating that

> The Assembly considers that any corporal punishment of children is in breach of their fundamental right to human dignity and physical integrity. The fact that such corporal punishment is still lawful in certain member states violates their equally fundamental right to the same legal protection as adults. Striking a human being is prohibited in European society and children are human beings . . . [so] the Assembly therefore invites the Council of Europe's Committee of Ministers to launch a coordinated campaign in all the member states for the total abolition of corporal punishment of children . . . to make Europe, as soon as possible, a corporal punishment–free zone for children. (ENOC, 2005)

Social work practice is involved in myriad ways to enhance child development, and reviewing the explanations of these articles reminds practitioners of their obligations to see that children are free to learn and develop separate from their parent's impeding actions or crises. The meal program put in place by social workers at a number of agencies in Minnesota, including Southside Family Nurturing Center, addresses just this concern; if children are hungry it is harder for them to play and to learn. Issues of safety and hunger are central to child development and a priority for social work everywhere (Scott and Ward, 2005).

3. Civil Rights and Freedoms

The third cluster refers to civil rights and freedoms to protect children from adults inclined to exploitation. The setting up of ombudsman authorities in several countries, first in Norway as mentioned above, then in Sweden, and in some states (including Michigan) in the United States, has led to a delineating of the rights and protections that children can seek of their own volition. This includes the rights of children not to be incarcerated with adults and not to be held on death row.

The 1999 case of the boys who bludgeoned a toddler to death in the UK shocked citizens into greater dialogue concerning the rights of children to due process, rehabilitative treatment, and anonymity. Following dissension in the UK courts, the case appeared before the European Union and the boys, who

Textbox 3.2. Norway's Ombudsman for Children

Bengt Morten Wenstøb

THE EARLY YEARS

In 1981, when Målfrid Grude Flekkøy became the first Ombudsman for the children of the world, a historical milestone concerning children had been reached. Since then we have had three more people in the position, including the Ombudsman today, Reidar Hjermann. They have all focused on different areas. In the beginning the focus was children who experience divorce and children who were physically and emotionally abused by their parents. Then it was a strong focus on mass media and especially video/DVD, and the impact of the Internet, and this focus continues.

THE INSTITUTION TODAY

In 2004 Reidar Hjermann was elected as the fourth Ombudsman for children. During his term several European countries established Ombudsmen following the Norwegian example; also countries outside Europe followed suit. A European network (ENOC, European Network of Ombudsmen for Children) has been established to work especially with children's rights in Europe, based on the principles of the UN Convention on Children Rights.

Organizational Structure

1. **Staff:** The staff includes 12 people, and the budget for 2005 was around 8 million NoK (1.4 million U.S. dollars).
2. **Legislation**
   Article 3, Duties of the Ombudsman, stands as follows:
   In particular the Ombudsman shall:
   a. On his or her own initiative or at a hearing, protect the interests of children in connection with planning and reports of well-being in all fields,
   b. Ensure that legislation relating to the protection of children's interests is observed, including checking whether Norwegian law and administrative routines are in accordance with Norway's obligations according to the UN Convention on the Rights of the Child,
   c. Propose measures that can strengthen children's safety under the law,
   d. Put forward proposals for measures that can solve or prevent conflicts between children and society,
   e. Ensure that sufficient information is given to the public and private sectors concerning children's rights and the measures required for children.

(continued)

Based on these duties, the Ombudsman for children can play at least three important roles. First, he or she can be a politician on behalf of the children. Second, he or she can be an activist and propose different issues that are important for children, for example, the Internet. Third, he or she can be an adviser for parents, children, organizations, schools, and kindergartens.

He or she has also developed a direct line so children can get in contact by phone with one of the professional staff members, who helps them solve their problems.

3. Election

The Ombudsman is elected for four years. If he likes to he can stay for another four years. After the second period it is time to choose a new person.

4. Report

Every year the Ombudsman for children makes a report on the situation for children in Norway. The report is also sent to the UN.

Focus Areas

The Ombudsman for children always has some focus areas he wants to stress more than others, while "the best interests of the child" are always most important.

1. UN Convention on the Rights of the Child

The UN convention is now a part of the national laws thanks to the Ombudsman for children. He has been aware of the importance and symbolic effect of integrating the UN convention into Norwegian society. Through this work more and more institutions and people are concerned about the child perspective in their work. Still there is much to be done for children who live in asylum or residential care, and also in schools in general.

2. New communication technologies

The Ombudsman for children works on at least two levels related to the impact on children of mass media. The first level is to promote good relations between the new media world and the child. It is important to start early, so that children, teenagers, and family have a mutual understanding of the games and images that are age appropriate.

The second level is to go actively into the media arena and protect young people and give them advice so they can avoid potential dangers, for example, pedophiles who get in contact via the Internet and later sexually abuse them.

3. Children and their right to be protected

Some children in Norway are living in families with violent parents, or other family members who abuse them. The Ombudsman for children wants to help these children by promoting more focus on protection, access to services, and safety.

4. Children traveling on their own

Norway has many families who divorce after some years of marriage; often these families include young children. When a family splits, it sometimes ends up with one of the parents moving to another part of the country, but sometimes also to another country. Normally the children move into one of the parent's homes, and travels to visit the other. In some situations, the result is that children have to travel far away on their own. The Ombudsman for children wants to motivate parents to think about what is in the best interests of the child in these situations, both related to traveling but also the daily contact between the parents.

5. **The Sami population and their rights**
   The Sami children need a special protection concerning language and culture. The Sami language is not understood by most of the people who live in Norway. To take care of their historical roots the Sami need to be given opportunities to bring their culture to schools and public institutions.

6. **Manifesto against bullying**
   In Norwegian schools many children have experienced bullying. Every day a child is oppressed by the bullying of another child. Therefore programs have been developed that target the fight against bullying in schools. Children who are bullied can develop problems later on in their lives with drugs or depression. The Ombudsman for children evaluates the programs and gives comments if they do not reach the identified targets.

7. **School meals**
   In Norway there is no tradition of serving food in schools. In primary and elementary schools it is possible to buy milk or fruit. Politicians have discussed several times whether it is time to start school meals. So far no one has succeeded. As always it is about money, even though we know many children could have achieved better school results with better nutrition.

CASE STUDY (1) TO ILLUSTRATE
THE ROLE OF THE OMBUDSMAN

In January 2007 an old man is driving his daily tour in the local district with his car. This morning he discovers a teenager, 15 years old, who is lying close to the street. He very quickly finds out that the teenager is drunk and probably cold. He calls the local emergency services and asks for help, and then he gets out of the car to try to help the teenager. The teenager responds negatively when the old man wants to help him. The teenager starts to argue with the old man and thereafter beats him. The old man tumbles down and can't get up again. The teenager steals the car and drives away. After some hundred meters he crashes the car and walks away by foot. In the meantime, the police have reached the place where the old man has called from. They try to help him, but he is already dead. The police start looking for the teenager. They use dogs and after some hours they find him and arrest him.

(continued)

A debate starts in the newspapers about whether it is acceptable to put teenagers in jail or place them in special institutions. The Ombudsman for children
participates in the discussion as a representative for the children's voice. He
says that no teenager should be placed in jail. He also stresses that this has
nothing to do with the teenager's innocence in the crime against the old man.

SUGGESTED READINGS

Ariès, P. (1960). *Centuries of Childhood.* Harmondsworth, UK.
Cunningham, H. (1996). *Barn og barndom.* Oslo: Ad Notam forlag.
Hagen, G. (2001). *Barnevernets historie.* Oslo: Akribe forlag.
Hauglund, E. (2001). *Barnets århundre og Ellen Key.* Oslo: Akribe forlag.
Kvello, Ö., & Skaalvik, E. M. (1998). *Barn og Miljø.* Oslo: Tano-Aschehoug.
Slagstad, R. (1998). *De nasjonale strateger.* Oslo: Pax forlag.

have now been released for their crime, are sequestered under new identities with the full protections of the Convention (*Financial Times*, May 10,
2005). Similarly, the U.S. Supreme Court has been criticized for its recent
action whereby Justice Anthony Kennedy authored the ruling that found the
death penalty unconstitutional for juveniles. In writing his decision, Justice
Kennedy referred to international approaches to the death penalty and the
Convention on the Rights of the Child (*Financial Times*, March 2, 2005).
Waldmeir, in reporting on this decision, writes:

> Bowing in part to world opinion, the U.S. Supreme Court abolished the juvenile
> death penalty in a ruling that immediately sparked controversy over whether
> the justices should listen to the views of foreign countries when interpreting the
> U.S. constitution. . . . Amnesty International welcomed the ruling saying that
> the U.S. court has ruled to protect child offenders in the United States from the
> premeditated cruelty of the death penalty. (Waldmeir, 2005)

Justice Anthony Kennedy argued that "neither retribution nor deterrence
provides adequate justification for imposing the death penalty on juvenile offenders" (cited in *Financial Times*, March 2, 2005). However, the dissenting
judges rejected the idea that the United States should look to world opinion or
practice in interpreting the Constitution, and during the summer of 2005 there
was continuing anxiety about the longevity of this decision given the nature
of the political response and recent vacancies on the court.

In the view of social work researcher James Garbarino, however, public attention to these civil rights came not a moment too soon. In the United States
attention and questions were already being raised despite the opposition of the

Bush administration, which is committed to an independent United States that should never be in a position "to ask for a permission slip from the United Nations" ("State of the Union Address," 2003). The idea of abolishing the death penalty for juveniles had reached its own national momentum, including the series of interviews in correctional settings recently documented by *Oprah Magazine*. For all their media glare, the interviews speak to the suffering of the 70 plus young inmates incarcerated with the ultimate penalty hanging over them (Goodwin, 2005). On a more formal scholarly level, Garbarino has documented his interviews with boys in adult prisons, including on death row, and speaks powerfully of the destruction of their spirits and of "the light going out in their eyes" (Garbarino, 1999). In every case Garbarino describes, the boys had role models of violence and in some instances had watched unspeakable crimes against family members, including coercion and manipulation. In the view of many countries, children are born innocent and thrive through the attachment to and nurturance of adults and community surrounding them. The PBS documentary *Childhood* vividly portrays the positive results for children when they are in the circumstances of Japanese culture, which expects that "children live with the Gods until seven years of age," meaning that they are treated as honored and central to family well-being (PBS, 1998).

4. Family Environment and Alternative Care

The fourth cluster relates to family environment and alternative care. This includes international adoptions. Article 18 relates to recognition of parental responsibility, Article 20 relates to children "without family," and Article 21 to adoption.

There are very few social work agencies worldwide that are not involved in global issues relating to families. However, agencies offering international adoptions are particularly at risk if their staff is not globally aware and educated to use international policy instruments, which include the Convention on the Rights of the Child. As with "child," the term "family" is recognized by the Convention to include extended family. Social work agencies such as the Southside Family Nurturing Center in Minneapolis (www.ssfnc.org) or the KLJUC center for youth who become victims of human trafficking build their missions on the Convention. The diversity of family life, represented by the extended family networks of African American or American Indian families, is not yet adequately addressed by the Convention.

In 2003 Seattle International Adoptions was closed due to concerns about protocols with their partners and questions of money laundering and exploitive exchange. The agency would have benefited from knowledge of the articles, for example relating to the drive to give refugee and migrant children their full rights to identity and natural family participation in finding a home.

As reported by Shukovsky (2003), some of the infants offered for adoption as "orphans" had inadequate identification and in some cases lived in extreme poverty with parents desperate to find ways for their children to survive during economic migration.

Some people in the United States are criticizing adoption agencies for their lack of knowledge of the social and economic development of the countries they are working with (Trenka, 2003, p. 138; Traylor, 2002). Also, there is concern that the agency decision making on choice of partner countries is based on political and market availability criteria rather than on social need—moving for reasons of expedience rather than human concern, from Korea to Colombia and, most recently, China. This search for infants at any price for infertile American couples has taken on a troubling image of exploitation. In a touching and assertive presentation to students at Augsburg College, Minneapolis, Jane Jeongh Trenka explains her journey as a Korean adoptee in a European American family and community: "The way I think about myself these days is with the word that best describes me: exile. I hadn't thought of myself as an exile or immigrant before—just a lucky adoptee. But now, I see that 'exile' is the word that fits me best" (Trenka, 2003, pp. 188, 199). Trenka also developed a list of questions for social workers involved in adoptions, which includes the following:

1. Was there advertising for Korean adoption in rural Minnesota in the 1970s?
2. What was the nature of the advertising?
3. What kind of training was provided for the adoption social workers who placed children?
4. What kind of information did the agency provide adoptive parents about international/interracial adoption?
5. Were there mandatory classes for prospective parents?
6. What kind of follow-up took place in the adoptive families?
7. How are the agency records used?
8. What is the logic of having a law that records must be kept if they're not accessible to those who need them? (Trenka, 2003)

Traditional pressures to place babies for adoption quickly (and part of the reasoning relates to crucial periods of attachment in the early years) undermine a complex reality. For years adoption and correctional agencies have focused on facilitating early placement of infants with the presumption of thorough search and due rights for parents. Recently a student intern was alarmed by the rapid placement of children born to women incarcerated at the Shakopee Correctional Facility for Women. She found that it is legal policy for women with over a year to serve to be encouraged in this way if they have no immediate family to care for the child (Augsburg College social work field seminar, spring 2005). Professionals have avoided the tough, long-term questions of the repercussions for children placed without the fullest possible resolution of obstacles for the birth parent(s) to raise the child. In her vivid memoir as a Korean American, Trenka speaks to the isolation, self-doubt, and loneliness for children who are uncertain of their natural parentage. There is a persistent undercurrent of questioning: "why" was I given up, "mothers are supposed to love their children aren't they?" (Trenka, 2003). Now children are finding their voice as young adults and have high expectations of support in searching for and resolving their full identity.

In addition to the common human need to be with a family and culture of origin and to have an identity and medical history, the Declaration of Human Rights is a reminder of the way we agree to treat each other respectfully, and the Convention on the Rights of the Child affirms the universal elements of compassionate behavior. This particularly applies to people who may be in crisis, transition, or status change, or incarcerated. Students could choose a group of people who seem vulnerable in terms of their human rights, for example, migrant workers, and identify the tension between their rights and their reality. Then they would pay special attention to the inclusion of children in this picture—are their rights attended to or ignored? The fifth cluster of rights relates to these basic questions of health and welfare.

5. Basic Health and Welfare

Although some countries have been slow to implement the Convention, others have streaked ahead and given us examples of ways conditions for children can improve. Examples include the "child-friendly" city of Pistoia discussed above, the decision of the Jamaican government to pattern its child welfare services on the Convention, and the Norwegian decision to make physical punishment illegal under all circumstances, including parental discipline. Discipline continues to be controversial in many countries, including the United States, where parents see their freedoms as preeminent and superior to those of children (Germain, 1995).

The Convention provides an incentive to consider major pieces of social policy legislation such as "welfare reform" through a wider, global lens. For example, Link, Bibus, and O'Neal grounded their research with an idea encountered during exchanges of students and faculty in Slovenia, India, Mexico, and the United States. This idea is that children, together with their families and caregivers, regardless of their current plight, have a right to identify the way services affect them and ways they can be improved. In the United States, by far the largest number of people in receipt of welfare are children, and whatever the impact of welfare reform, it is visited most directly on children. Focus group questions were developed with this in mind. Even though the researchers learned later that the parents did all they could to shield their children from the harsh impacts of sanctions, they still realized that they cannot always "buffer" them. In an introduction to Article 27, concerned with the standard of living of children, the IFSW manual for social work and the rights of the child states:

> Many people with whom social workers work suffer social exclusion as a result of poverty. They have no realistic hope of securing paid employment and their life chances are blighted by a subsistence existence characterized by malnutrition, poor education and destitution. Breaking into the cycle of poverty requires concerted action at international, national, regional and local levels using the resources of people themselves in self-help initiatives such as cooperatives. It requires resource commitment from national governments and a shift from those policies of structural adjustment that pay little regard to human consequences. (IFSW, 2002, p. 36)

As a result of debate surrounding implementation of the Convention, the structural adjustment policies of the International Monetary Fund are recognized as pressuring already poor communities to focus on exports rather than food, on repaying national debt rather than building schools, and on restricting social welfare payments, particularly in the United States through sanctions, rather than expanding supports. Welfare reform in the United States is another form of structural adjustment, as the country juggles a massive increase in its military budget at the expense of social programs and health coverage.

In the UK, legislation requiring health visitor connection to every infant born in the country is an example of universal access. Families neither have to prove their need, nor go through lengthy admission procedures to be assigned a health visitor. The child is born; the health visitor for the address is assigned. This ease of access is considered to be one of the determining factors in high rates of immunization. Even in areas of high mobility and population density, children's well-being is central to budget allocation and health plus social service policy.

It is encouraging that rights to "well-being" were reinforced in the *State of the World's Children 2003* report. This report identified goals which have since been translated into UNICEF millennium development goals for 2015 for all:

> United Nations Member States have pledged to eradicate extreme poverty and hunger, achieve universal primary education, promote gender equality, empower women, improve maternal health, reduce child mortality, combat HIV/ AIDS, malaria and other diseases, ensure environmental sustainability and develop a global partnership for development. (UNICEF, 2003)

Bibus, Link, and O'Neal recently wrote:

> Lest these goals seem less relevant to the affluent United States, families in the Phillips neighborhood of Minneapolis have low rates of health insurance, an

outbreak of measles recently threatened the lives of immigrant children, and hunger is the main reason agencies such as Southside Family Nurturing Center offer meals at regular family night. (Bibus, Link, and O'Neal, 2005)

6. Education, Leisure, and Culture

The sixth cluster relates to education, leisure, and culture. Article 31 rather poignantly includes the right to rest: "State Parties recognize the right of the child to rest and leisure, to engage in play and recreational activities appropriate to the age of the child and to participate freely in cultural life and the arts." One of the most striking problems of the twenty-first century is the sharp divide between countries of the Global North, where resources are plentiful, and the Global South, where there is scarcity, famine, and child labor.

In a passionate plea to students his own age, Craig Kielburger, the Canadian child labor activist and author, called students to educate themselves about "two worlds"—one of lavish material goods and waste and the other of the constant struggle to keep food on the table (Kielburger and Kielburger, 2004). Kielburger became interested in child labor when he first read of the assassination of a 12-year-old boy who was organizing protests in Pakistan. The protests concerned exploitative employers and the practices of chaining children to looms and forcing them to work long hours without breaks, nutrition, or education. His work has focused on educating people in the Global North to realize that they depend on the whole world—no rubber, coffee, or tea grows in North America, and yet they are staples of the day there. Kielburger's work assists the process of recognizing how vital global interdependence is—that none of us can survive without collective action and cooperation.

7. Special Protections

The seventh cluster relates to special protections, including acute poverty and the trap of being born into whole geographical regions of devastation, famine, or structural unemployment. In addition to disparities between regions, this cluster draws attention to risks for children crossing borders and exposed to the aftermath of political and social upheaval or war. Continuing the discussion of social exclusion defined earlier, the focus here is the common human conditions and geographic realities surrounding children rather than their individual assets or deficits.

An example of practice that is attentive to geography is the English "patch system" instituted with the Seebohm Report in the 1970s. In this system social work teams were located in neighborhoods, which the social workers studied and came to know well. They walked the streets and mapped resources, meeting the local police and leaders, and came to know the family groups, working to empower communities as well as working with the individual case focus. This "patch" concept has been adopted in Australia and in Iowa (Adams and Nelson, 1992). As a school social worker in North London at the time of the implementation of the "patch" system, the author of this book (Link) took very seriously the expectation that every child on the streets after schooltime, every runaway or laboring minor should be invited to hear about opportunities for support and offered time to discuss their safety and their family supports. Relationships were established with the police department's "juvenile bureau," and children coming to the attention of either department were referred and discussed at monthly reviews but without children's participation. In retrospect, social work has strengthened its practice in terms of focusing on solutions and participation, and at times these encounters may have seemed paternalistic. These services were prior to the Convention. Since the 1980s, the UK has ratified children's rights, an ombudsman for children has been established, and "social exclusion" units of the Blair administration have focused their work on the well-being of children and families enduring poverty. These goals are now part of the UK policy to expand family centers and ensure the "inclusion" of children and their families in community development and decision making.

Connected to the awareness of children in terms of geography is the question of national borders and human trafficking, particularly minors, across borders. Article 35 states: "States Parties shall take all appropriate national, bilateral and multilateral measures to prevent the abduction of, the sale of or traffic in children for any purpose or in any form."

Trafficking in human beings is included in the European Penal Code, and cases of abduction and sexual exploitation have posed complex problems for service providers, particularly in creating agreements with neighboring countries. The European organization EQUAL is well documented by the organization KLJUC (Center for Fight against Trafficking in Human Beings), supported by the United Nations Human Rights Commission. Countries may be classified as places of *origin*, places of *transit*, and places of *destination* for trafficking in human beings (THB)—especially children:

> Slovenia is classified as belonging to all three categories. In its role as a country of destination, Slovenia provides a market mainly for adult females and females who are legally still minors, who come from Eastern European Countries and the Balkans. (KLJUC, 2005)

Now that the Convention exists and countries are asking questions about the vulnerability of minors and the means to prevent abduction, recognition of this universal problem is emerging. Trafficking in human beings is not limited to a few countries; it is worldwide and lacks the human awareness that could impede its growth (www.freethechildren.com). The KLJUC organization speaks to the levels of work that are involved, including fostering international cooperation, raising awareness of the risk population, increasing knowledge of both the expert community and lay public, and increasing creativity in working with vulnerable groups. One of their innovative projects stood out in a summer 2005 presentation in Ljubljana. The project involves circulation of a small "dictionary" to victims and young people in bars and vulnerable circumstances. Indeed the book begins with translations of words from Slovenian to English; then by page 15 it states:

> If you are a victim of human traffickers you can get help and protection now. . . . Traffickers in human beings are often part of criminal gangs that operate in several countries. They work by gaining your trust in your home country, before you leave, and later, once you are in a foreign country, they begin to threaten and abuse you so that you are so frightened and confused you feel you have no choices . . . [but] now you can get help. (KLJUC, 2005)

The United Nations Human Rights Commission has coordinated work in implementing the Convention on the Rights of the Child and has supported such publications relating to human trafficking in a number of countries, including Afghanistan (Samar, 2005).

8. Implementation

Regarding implementation, the eighth cluster of articles of the Convention, it is recognized that no society has a monopoly on the solutions, and that all share to some degree the challenges and goals identified in the Convention. Articles 42 and 43 are explicit in the macro-level approach of each state and its administration:

> States Parties undertake to make the principles and provisions of the Convention widely known, by appropriate and active means, to adults and children alike. For the purpose of examining the progress made by States Parties in achieving the realization of the obligations undertaken in the present Convention, there shall be established a Committee on the Rights of the Child, which shall carry out the functions hereinafter provided. (United Nations, 1989)

As we note the progress in implementing the Convention in a range of countries, we can see from the UNICEF *State of the World's Children* reports that children's supports are widely acknowledged as crucial (UNICEF, 2004). Infant mortality is decreasing in countries with access to immunizations; national health and children's ombudsman services give voice to a wide variety of needs from Norway to Costa Rica (IFSW, 2002; www.unicef.org; ENOC, 2005). The committee for implementation has encouraged a holistic approach to legislation that affects children, and examples include the policy in Jamaica and Slovenia to utilize the Convention as a template for all child welfare services (www.varuh-rs.si). At a visit of U.S. social workers to the children's crisis center in Celje, Slovenia, the staff presented their ideas about empowerment and youth participation. The question was asked by a U.S. student: "Do you use the Convention on the Rights of the Child in your work?" The instant response, "Of course," surprised the U.S. listeners, and they detailed their approach to children's participation in planning their futures, the group norms, and the permission from youth that they seek when approaching parents (University of Ljubljana Summer School, July 2005).

In New Zealand, a central office of coordination has established a children's commissioner and has overseen major progress in sustaining indigenous Maori culture. Since adverse international reaction to the treatment of two 10-year-old boys who committed murder in the UK in 1999, that country has also now established an ombudsman for children's office. Also, the former Blair administration established social exclusion units that identify whole areas of economic deprivation, where families are trapped in cycles of poverty, where school leavers (legal at 16 years) and "dropouts" have few opportunities, and where rates of teenage pregnancy are high. These units continued under Prime Minister Gordon Brown. Additional government funds were made available for community initiatives that benefit children and their families, and these are often delivered through the extensive network of family centers and NEWPIN (New Parent Infant Network) services (Stones, 1994).

The International Labour Organization (ILO) continues to deliberate on the concept of social exclusion in implementing policies, referring to it as "multi-dimensional, focusing on exclusionary forces . . . both who and what is responsible for processes of impoverishment and marginalization" (Figueiredo and de Haan, 1998). For many children experiencing poverty, a sense that society has excluded or dropped them rather than its being their choice to drop out inhibits their ability to survive. Arjan de Haan's definition of social exclusion—"the process through which individuals or groups are wholly or partially excluded from full participation in the society within which they live"—invites discussion of ways to include children and seek their participation. One example of participation is the practice of "children's parliaments" now spreading in Europe and welcomed by the United Nations (Slovenian Association of Friends of Youth, 2002).

Certainly for some countries, it has been a natural extension of their nonpunitive approach to people experiencing poverty to expand their policies to nurture and protect, as well as offer opportunities for participation of children. Norway, Jamaica, New Zealand, and Slovenia are some of the countries referred to in this chapter that join others in standing out in their detailed attention to the Convention. The recent increase in opportunities for participation affect social work in many ways.

This chapter identifies practice that incorporates the Convention on the Rights of the Child as a tool to guide social development and social work at all systems levels: from macro (largest systems of global relationships), exo (national organizations), and mezzo (more local community action), to micro (individual relationships that implement larger ideals). The mechanisms of implementation identified in the Convention assist the actual application of the concepts through channels that include expert committees, support for research, and encouragement of community, national, and international dialogue. The example of Pistoia illustrates a combination of the community or mezzo and macro approaches to children's rights (GNP Media, 2002). In New Zealand, the Maori tribal languages are now being cherished and strengthened through the development of language "nests" in schools and communities across the nation. This idea of "nesting" to preserve language and culture has reverberations in different parts of the world, including Native American communities, Wales, and Italy. Similarly in Slovenia, the concern is to coordinate childrens services in dialogue with neighboring countries, and to "lay new foundations for its child and family policy," which meets standards of international research in the Convention (Slovenian Committee for UNICEF, 1995). These examples of implementation are opportunities for social workers worldwide to bring their practice into the luminous expectations of the Convention—expectations that simply speak to making real our commitment to children.

SUMMARY

In recent years, the Convention has been implemented across the globe and is now recognized for the dynamic instrument it offers us in coming to grips with the complex needs of children. Carol Bellamy states that this is a "giant step" from the harsh labor and exploitative conditions for young people at the beginning of the twentieth century to the current documentation and ratification of a wide array of rights that children need in order to thrive (Bellamy, 1998). When we pause to value this remarkable living document we realize that it offers many layers of support to human service. The Convention does the following:

Gives countries a goal to reach for in their services and welfare policies;
Identifies the various elements of children's well-being that need attention;
Identifies these wide ranging elements and thus offers a framework and checklist for service development;
Gives legislators information and examples to argue and lobby for change in their own countries;

Provokes dialogue between countries and raises standards and expectations;

For U.S. "welfare reform" in particular, reminds us of the narrow interpretation
and restrictions put on services which increasingly have a marketplace emphasis in their programs and delivery;

Raises questions of who is at risk when economic supports are restricted (when
adults are experiencing poverty, children are the first to suffer);

Demands that children be allowed their childhood and not be pressed into pre-
mature roles as earners, soldiers, or adult prisoners; and

Compels attention to the overrepresentation of children in all poverty statistics,
and most particularly children of diverse culture for the U.S. and the UK
(list generated in SWK 230 undergraduate course Augsburg College, spring
2005).

Thus the Convention on the Rights of the Child has become social work's
template for meeting the human rights of people under 18 years of age. While
countries openly acknowledge that they have policies to debate and to amend
in order to meet the best interests of the child as stated by the Convention,
there has been obvious progress. For the United States this progress relates
to the decision that no child be put to death for crimes committed and that
their rehabilitation to society be the focus of policy and practice. For many
countries, the concern about children's identity has reached the consciousness of social workers, and there is new attention to the processes of adoption
and scrutiny of processes for incarcerated women who are pregnant (IFSW,
2002). The United Nations has led the way in helping children to participate
in their futures and has celebrated their abilities to speak and be heard. In
their summary of the Convention, the International Federation of Social
Workers challenges social workers across the world (even if their country is
still working on ratifying the document—we are global citizens and global
practitioners): "Rights are meaningless if citizens do not know they have
them. Article 42 requires states parties to widely disseminate information
about the Convention to children and to adults" (IFSW, 2002). As of 2004,
the Convention had been ratified by 192 countries, "Only two countries have
not ratified: the United States and Somalia, which have signaled their inten-
tion to ratify by formally signing the Convention" (www.unicef.org). In a
positive sign, during his presidential campaign Barack Obama stated that the
failure of the United States to sign the Convention was an embarrassment and
vowed to review the decision (reported at blogs.amnesty.org.uk/blogs_entry
.asp?eid=2808).

The rights of children are no longer a pipe dream. Certainly there are children this morning, today, and tomorrow who are picking through garbage
in Mexico and sweating over a loom in California and India. However, the
picture on the 1997 *State of the World's Children* report of a small child of

six or seven asleep over the softballs he is sewing, has been replaced by images of young girls in the 2004 version who are telling the stories of their part in education, in village public life, and in health projects across the globe (UNICEF, 1997, 2004). Social workers have a key role to play in supporting children's rights and to keeping society attuned to who is hungry and who is suffering. The Convention on the Rights of the Child demands that we keep our practices focused on a better journey for all children, where they do not just survive but thrive in an atmosphere of peace without discrimination. These are real goals, and the UNICEF call for us to accomplish them in the next 10 years is in our grasp.

As soon as people have rights enshrined in law, however, these rights seem to be absorbed into the fabric of society (such as the right of women and people over 18 to vote). It is as though the rights always existed, and then the enfranchised risk being taken for granted or even ignored; and this especially relates to the lives of children. Even as children's voices are accepted at the adult table, social workers, in particular, are in a position to ensure that children maintain their place and are not only represented adequately, but offered expanded opportunities for participation. Thus the role of social work practice in relation to the Convention on the Rights of the Child is multidimensional. It includes at least the following layers of work:

Social workers educate themselves in the goals and expectations of international policy instruments.

Social workers alert their social work organizations and agencies to the implementation requirements of these policies.

Social workers question practices that do not meet the principles, in this instance of the Convention on the Rights of the Child.

Social workers keep the articles of the Convention a priority within the social work profession in accordance with the agreement of the International Federation of Social Workers and the International Association of Schools of Social Work.

The 2015 UN commitment to eradicate absolute poverty is something we are all responsible for. Living as we do in this spectacular period of technology and economic growth, there may be some evening out of the playing field in terms of access to information and outsourcing of jobs and the sprouting of Internet cafes in isolated neighborhoods. Yet we are still beset with the simple task of making sure children everywhere have enough to eat, loving adults around them, school to attend, and a future to live. The Convention on the Rights of the Child helps social workers address this task and is indeed a "luminous" document (Annan, 2003).

STUDENT ASSIGNMENT

Bengt Morten Wenstøb suggests in the case history textbox 3.2 that the history of Norway since World War II has assisted their policymaking in relation to children so that they have public commitment to the rights of the children and to human rights. Select a country and explore the reasons why they have or do not have a high level of commitment, as demonstrated in the office of the Ombudsman for the Child.

Chapter Four

Values, International Ethics, and Their Role in Social Work Practice

Never doubt that a small group of thoughtful committed citizens can change the world. Indeed, it is the only thing that ever has.

—Margaret Mead

Ethical behavior requires constantly using our imagination to think through alternative ways to put social work values into practice where both culture and human rights are in synchrony. Ethics involves norms that are believed to be universally beneficial to all. They set standards by which actions can be evaluated (Powell, 2006). Thus, while exploring the common human condition, ethics becomes an integral part of our attempts to understand human behavior. This means we need to focus on self-reflection through an examination, analysis, and deconstruction of specific oppressed groups within a multicultural context (Sisneros, Stakeman, Joyner, and Schmitz, 2008). This will help in grasping how different living conditions affect oppressed, vulnerable, and minority groups differentially, enabling the practitioner to fine-tune the social work intervention strategies. According to the recent Educational Policy and Accreditation Standards (EPAS), competency-based education is based on performance outcome, based on the social work profession's pedagogy: "Signature pedagogy represents the central form of instruction and learning in which a profession socializes its students to perform the role of practitioner. Professionals have pedagogical norms with which they connect theory and practice" (p. 8).

Social work, an applied profession, helps students connect the theoretical and conceptual contribution of the classroom with practice experience. Nevertheless, what Neil Postman has suggested is very germane: that is, increasingly innovative technology has outstripped the human ability to think through the consequences of our actions (Postman, 1992). The opportunities offered by genome mapping, for example, seem at first glance to outweigh the risks. But on second scrutiny, we can imagine how such mapping will play out according to who has health insurance and what the "preexisting" condition clause contains. Suddenly the advantage of mapping depends on whether you live in a country with universal health care access that focuses on prevention and public health, or one where health administration and delivery are about profit. Health providers can be dedicated and talented, but their insurance companies and diagnostic regulators will determine whom they get to see.

In the twenty-first century we have nanotechnology and microcameras that can be fed into our arteries, to spare us invasive surgery. The ear, nose, and throat specialists are working together with brain surgeons to perform brain surgery through the nose. Conjoined infants can more often be separated safely to live separate lives. However, along with these extraordinary medical advances, we are struggling to stay abreast with the ethics, for example, of separating conjoined twins when one may die; recognizing sentient beings other than bipeds; maintaining persons on life support when their disease is inevitably killing them; deciding who should receive the highest technology treatment and who should go without. There used to be controversy about differential treatment of the elderly or developmentally delayed, but advances in technology have made decisions much more complex. Skarnulis writes about quality-of-life decisions, or quality-adjusted life year, for infants born with multiple challenges as a formula for medical personnel in their decision making about interventions (Skarnulis, 2004).

This chapter explores steps in using our imagination for ethical decision making in social work assessment and human behavior. The "Seedhouse Grid" is applied and reinforces the systems-level thinking introduced in chapter 1 (Seedhouse, 1989; see figure 4.1 in the next section). Ethical behavior can never be taken for granted. All of us should continually scrutinize our professional behavior, dual roles, potential conflicts, and end-of-life decisions, and it has become especially important to think through the implications of our technological progress. Following a definition of social work ethics, different approaches to ethical decision making in various parts of the world are reviewed, the International Federation of Social Workers' *Statement of Principles* is presented, and steps for ethical decision making in a global context are identified. Case examples in relation to developmental disabilities, gerontology, medical practice, and credit for the poor help to illustrate this narrative.

DEFINITION OF SOCIAL WORK ETHICS

In *All Our Futures*, Link writes, "The study of ethics means the turning of a searchlight on our behavior and how our actions fit with the well-being of others. The bright light that causes us to constantly pause and consider the impact, moral and social, of our actions lies at the core of social assessment" (Ramanathan and Link, 2004, chapter 5). Social work is one of the key professions in terms of conscientious application of ethical decision making that enhances human functioning. This refers to the clear recognition that a solution to a problem, such as patient discharge to home or institutional care, or placement of an abused child outside the home in a culturally less aligned environment, or provision of health or credit services, may not have an absolute right or wrong answer, but can be carefully weighed for the opportunities and risks involved with the full participation of the people affected—whether they are patients, clients, or whole communities. Čačinovič Vogrinčič identifies the many layers involved in such decision-making:

> The social work relationship—every project with working points and concrete steps for action, is based on the definition of the problem: the agreement, the understanding, the consensus co-created, investigated, interpreted together with the clients. . . . If we take the paradigmatic "together with the clients" seriously, then we need to add the special constructionist contribution: knowledge for what Lynn Hoffman calls "the ethics of participation." In my understanding that means to replace the objective observer (social worker) with the idea of collaboration, where no one has the final word, no one needs the final word, what we need is a conversation that can be continued. (Čačinovič Vogrinčič, 1997, p. 2)

The continuing conversation about ethical behavior in social work and assessment clearly identifies a "relativist" perspective in ethics. Although some philosophers have identified good and bad, and also truth and falsehood in absolute terms, the reality for social workers is a more relativist perspective, where reasoning depends on taking into account many points of view. Even this statement is reflective of a tension for social workers. The IFSW recognizes the Declaration of Human Rights, which gives the profession universal values to refer to. However, as social workers we are also reaching beyond the twentieth century of dominance of social work education by Western views. Colleagues in the Global South expect more respect of cultural norms (Gray, Coates, and Yellow Bird, 2008). This live tension flows through contemporary debates and should not be underestimated (Healy, 2008).

In his study of ethics and health care in Europe, David Seedhouse suggests that both ethics and health-services work "are beset by the problem that people in complex societies have different values and beliefs amongst each other . . . [and] there are no clear-cut solutions" (Seedhouse, 1989, p. 9). In the Terri Schiavo case in the United States, politicians entered the very human dilemma that arises when an individual no longer has the capacity to care or make decisions for themselves: namely, who decides when they are ready to die. In Minneapolis a kidney transplant was reported in the local newspaper involving a 22-year-old European American man and a young Hmong woman, who was a friend of his family (*Minneapolis Star Tribune*,

August 30, 1997). The young woman would have died without the transplant, but her family had long opposed it for cultural reasons as well as objections to the intrusive nature of Western medicine. The Western doctors expressed frustration that she kept going back to her family to discuss decisions and, in their view, delayed needed action (Ramanathan and Link, 2004, p. 71).

Within the study of ethics there is also a historic tension between the absolutist (or cognitivist) position that actions are either morally right or wrong in themselves and the relativist (noncognitivist) position that actions are inextricably linked to their consequences. In many countries there is the added and often unconscious contradiction that individuals may clearly recognize that an act such as killing another human being is morally wrong. At a societal level, however, these same individuals participate in a system that permits capital punishment or "death by legal intervention" (*Accident Facts*, 2006). The cognitivist (absolutist) school of thought holds that it is feasible to "reach conclusions about right and wrong and that ethical principles are true or false" and that noncognitivists (relativists) think it is impossible to find absolute moral principles, so "that we can only have an opinion or preference" (Reamer, 1995).

Loewenberg and Dolgoff identify two schools of philosophical thought that are precursors to cognitivism and relativism: the deontologist school and the teleologist school. The deontologist school "stresses the over-riding importance of fixed moral rules . . . [so] an action is inherently right or wrong, apart from any consequences that might result . . . [and] ethical rules hold under all circumstances" (Loewenberg and Dolgoff, 1992). In this vein, a social worker "always tells the truth to their client" or always makes their role explicit. In contrast, the teleologist school recognizes the context and the consequences of decisions. In a Western courtroom, the professional judge will base his or her work on absolutes of right and wrong, truth and lie. For social work, the professional role is one of restoring or building relationships and therefore, the circumstances of the situation always play a part in the decision making. For social work, a code or declaration of ethics implies a set of guidelines based on experience and carefully considered decisions.

Later in this book, we explore human rights and the Declaration of Human Rights, which asserts an absolute stand on how we should treat fellow human beings; these are an agreed set of standards to live by. It is part of the complexity of social work, however, that we may adhere to the Declaration of Human Rights in relation to agreements made on our behalf by the United Nations (for example that everyone has the right to be free from harm and torture) and are therefore being absolute in our commitment. Simultaneously however, we recognize that we sometimes make decisions with families based on the best available assessment of opportunities over risks. This process of balancing opportunities and risks is the relative approach. Despite these contrasting messages, social workers across the world can strive to be consistent in their orientation and ethical practice in these ways:

- Search for the "objectively good." One might pursue some ultimate value or ordering of values in relation to human rights and dignity.
- Search for a set of professional rules or a code of practice to provide a committed basis.
- Appeal to the law of a country or international policy instruments and laws.
- Adopt a relativist position with reference to cultural beliefs and frameworks in the public domain. (adapted from Seedhouse, 1989, p. 9)

The "Seedhouse Grid" reveals the kaleidoscope of elements for consideration (see figure 4.1). This framework comes from the health field and captures the imagination for ethics in social work. It identifies a central place to begin, expecting "respect for persons equally," "respect for autonomy," "creation of autonomy," and "service to needs before wants." This last goal, identifying needs before wants, has sometimes been the domain of the professional; in

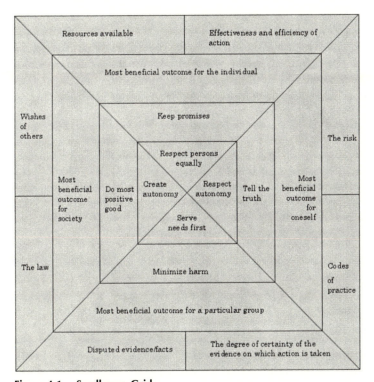

Figure 4.1. Seedhouse Grid

this ethical context it is the social worker's task to ensure that the client and community identify their needs, with the social workers as an ally rather than the professional who is taking charge (Link, in Ramanathan and Link, 2004). Moving outward from the center of the grid, the additional layers of ethical considerations become increasingly complex. For example, "truth telling" is a key stressor in terms of the individual's right to know a medical diagnosis. The attempts of doctors to estimate length of life have been much criticized, while attitudes toward telling the truth about a diagnosis vary widely from culture to culture (Lewis, 1986; Hirshberg and Barasch, 1995; Parry and Shen Ryan, 1995). It is particularly noteworthy that this grid includes dialogue about the "increase of social good" and reminders to keep looking at a situation from the micro level to the widest lens possible. The outer layer also includes recognition of legal rights and makes reference to codes of practice as one segment of a very complex process that varies from place to place but contains some essential commitments for social workers internationally.

ETHICAL DECISION MAKING IN DIFFERENT PARTS OF THE WORLD

Since the 1990s, the *International Code of Ethics for the Professional Social Worker* and then the 2004 *Statement of Principles* published by the International Federation of Social Workers (IFSW) (www.ifsw.org) have been reminders of worldwide efforts to think through the universal and distinct aspects of ethical decision making. The IFSW reminds us that

> Social work originates variously from humanitarian, religious and democratic ideals and philosophies and has universal application to meet human needs arising from person-societal interactions and to develop human potential. Professional social workers are dedicated to service for the welfare and self-fulfillment of human beings; to the development and disciplined use of scientific knowledge regarding human and societal behavior; to the development of resources to meet individual, group, national and international needs and aspirations; and to the achievement of social justice. (www.ifsw.org)

The result of four years of dialogue, from 2000 to 2004, was a groundbreaking agreement with the International Association of Schools of Social Work (IASSW) and the IFSW, which have published the following definition of social work:

> The social work profession promotes social change, problem solving in human relationships and the empowerment and liberation of people to enhance well-being. Utilising theories of human behaviour and social systems, social work intervenes at the points where people interact with their environments.

Principles of human rights and social justice are fundamental to social work. (www.ifsw.org)

Until 2001, the International Code had many similarities to the U.S. Code of Ethics and other Western instruments, such as the British Code of Ethics, but it was quite different from the Indian Declaration of Ethics. The International Code "formulates a set of basic principles which can be adapted to cultural and social settings" and adheres to the Declaration of Human Rights.

Dialogue between member countries, the IASSW, and the International Federation of Social Workers generated a *Statement of Principles* that includes a preface on the agreement that "ethical awareness is a fundamental part of the professional practice of social workers" all over the world. The innovative aspect, however, is the emphasis on broad principles that all social workers can agree to and the recognition that there are "particular cases" and situations that relate to individual nations. All social workers now are asked to work in a context that respects and utilizes the United Nations and its conventions. The IFSW lists some of the key human rights declarations and conventions that "form common standards of achievement and recognize rights that are accepted by the global community." This is a very helpful distinction: we have some human rights that are globally recognized and there are some social and cultural conditions that are nation-specific. As a result of their vital dialogue, the IFSW now lists individual national codes of ethics and is itself content to identify the broad principles and global policy instruments of key interest to practice at all levels.

The IFSW incorporation of diverse approaches to ethics is borne out by the Indian social workers who have questioned the relevance of clinically orientated Western codes for Indian community development and prefer the term "declaration of ethics" for people-centered work in their country (Desai, 1998). This is a crucial discussion, since the emphasis in some Western codes seems weighted in favor of interaction between social workers and the individual "client" rather than community or group. Also, the social work profession in any country needs to have a system of implementation, accountability, and assessment if it uses the term "code" and some countries do not currently have the resources of boards and organization for this work.

For U.S. social work, the Code of Ethics clearly adopts a relativist approach for all aspects of intervention from individual to family to group and community:

Ethical decision making is a process. There are many instances in social work where simple answers are not available to resolve complex ethical issues. Social workers should take into consideration all the values, principles, and standards that are relevant to any situation in which ethical judgment is warranted. . . . Instances may arise when social workers' ethical obligations conflict with agency policies or relevant laws or regulations. When such conflicts occur, social workers must make a responsible effort to resolve the conflict in a manner that is consistent with the values, principles, and standards expressed in the NASW Code. (National Association of Social Workers, 1999, p. 3)

The U.S. Code of the National Association of Social Workers, similar to the IFSW, refers to six spheres of behavior, presented in textbox 4.1: toward the client, toward colleagues, toward the practice setting, as professionals, to the social work profession, and to the broader society.

It is a significant reflection of the nature of North American social work, however, that the broader society and world receive the least narrative attention in the six areas of decision making. In the early 1900s, the history of U.S. social work reflected an emphasis that included community work through the Settlement House movement as well as the clinical focus on individual clients. The profession gained recognition and status however through its work in clinical settings, and only recently has there been a renewal of attention to community work and social and economic development (Midgley, 2000).

Community work and "conscientization" have always been the hallmark of social work in Mexico. Mexican social workers are involved in traditional Western roles of practice in prisons, schools, and hospitals, but many are also involved in radical political struggles, working with communities to achieve human rights. Community work is frequently central in Mexican social work because workers assist in the organization of cooperatives (such as Luz y Libertad, mentioned in chapter 2) and labor, addressing the ethical issues of rights to clean water, land use, women's labor rights, and health (Whitaker and Federico, 1997). There is constant debate about key factors in people's lives, including inflation, the extent of poverty of indigenous people, and the mobility of maquiladoras. This tension is encapsulated in the term "conscientization," which refers to the process of understanding the gap between what we are told and what is, and between what is and what can be (Ramanathan and Link, 2004).

The essence of ethical work is clearly at the heart of "conscientization." This concept involves observation, action, and reflection in a dynamic cycle termed "praxis" by Paulo Freire (1989). Social workers engaged in community action in Central and South America often place themselves at risk for their lives in the interests of freeing people from poverty. In the film *In Her Own Image* (Media Network, 1991), women in Bolivia talk of their cooperative marketing and the resistance, discouragement, and lack of social support from powerful people who run the banking community. Recently, the women who joined together to form Luz y Libertad in Cuernavaca found the power of their collective work. Increasingly social workers are becoming involved in creative ways to support community access to resources. The classical model is the Grameen Bank, established in Bangladesh in order to provide small

---

Textbox 4.1.   Excerpt from the Code of Ethics

Includes

- Mission of the Profession
- Value Base of the Social Work Profession
- Purpose of Code of Ethics (includes identifying core values; providing standards of assessment and practice; socializing to the profession; invoking cooperation)
- Social Workers' Ethical Responsibilities to Clients
- Social Workers' Ethical Responsibilities to Colleagues
- Social Workers' Ethical Responsibilities in Practice Settings
- Social Workers' Ethical Responsibilities as Professionals
- Social Workers' Ethical Responsibilities to the Social Work Profession
- Social Workers' Ethical Responsibilities to the Broader Society

MISSION OF THE PROFESSION

- To enhance human well-being and help meet the basic human needs of all people
- To be attentive to the needs and empowerment of people who are vulnerable, oppressed, and living in poverty
- To focus on individual well-being in a social context and the well-being of society
- To pay attention to the environmental forces that create, contribute to, and address problems in living

WHAT SOCIAL WORKERS DO

- Social workers promote social justice and social change with and on behalf of clients.
- Social workers are sensitive to cultural and ethnic diversity and strive to end discrimination, oppression, poverty, and other forms of social injustice.
- Social workers engage in direct practice, community organizing, supervision, consultation, administration, advocacy, social and political action, policy development and implementation, education, and research and evaluation.

---

loans to women setting up craft industries. It has been immensely successful and challenges the unethical practices of traditional banking that refuses to make loans to individuals without equity.

Students in Link's class at Augsburg College brainstormed over the differences between traditional and innovative banking as a case study in the ethical

Table 4.1.   Alleviation of Poverty: The Ethics of Traditional Banking

Traditional Banking Characteristics	Micro Credit Banking Characteristic
Credit report	Everyone has access
Personal history	No history
Education/literacy	All educational levels
Down payment	No collateral
Proof of ability to pay, e.g., employment	Team commitment
Cosigners	Friends and neighbors collaborate
Collateral	Trust
Residency	Community member
Gender bias toward men	Embraces women and men
Suspicious until proven reliable	Inviting
Promotes individual wealth accumulation	Promotes reinvesting in community well-being

Source: Augsburg College, SWK 230 Peace and Global Development, student discussion, spring 2006.

distribution of wealth. Their discussion gave them a critical understanding of the discrepancies and injustices of traditional methods and gave them insight into to the "worldwide" aspects of social work ethics (see table 4.1).

The work of the Grameen Bank, inspired by Muhammad Yunus, has been a catalyst across the world in taking understanding to action. Yunus established the Grameen (meaning "rural") Bank in the 1970s in response to the abject poverty he saw in the villages of Bangladesh. He recognized that "in a major way economics is responsible for the world that we live in" (Walljasper, Spayde, and the editors of *Utne Reader*, 2001, p. 133) inspired him to lend money to bamboo stool makers and with this step he began his path to the Nobel Prize. Since this innovation, the traditional banking system continues to flourish, but numerous alternative and cooperative systems of financing thrive, including the Foundation for International Community Assistance, or FINCA (www.villagebanking.org), which focuses on loans to women with children. It is a matter of ethical behavior when society continues to promote men to the role of chief executive officer of all manner of banking institutions and blame women for their children's poverty. The work of Yunus shows us that people should not be dying of hunger. It is within our power to change and it is within our ethical obligation as social workers to recognize the ways:

> Grameen Banks works in thirty-six thousand villages in Bangladesh; has 2.1 million borrowers, 94% of them are women, and employs twelve thousand people. The bank completed its first billion dollars in loans in 1997. A bank that starts its journey giving twenty-seven dollars in loans to forty-two people and comes all the way to a billion dollars in loans is cause for celebration. They felt good to have proven all those banking officials wrong. (Collopy, 2000, p. 75–77)

Yunus's ideas have been adopted in a number of cities in the United States. "In a Chicago project initiated by two young women, Connie Evans, an African American, and Susan Matteucci, an Anglo American. Their clients were low-income women, many of whom were on public assistance. The theme remained the same as that of the Grameen Bank, but the process was modified to fit American conditions" (Elliot and Mayadas, 2004).

Although there are myriad interpretations of ethical behaviors, there are common themes of justice, access to resources and loans, protection of children, and human rights to well-being that relate to global society. The *Statement of Principles* from the IFSW and IASSW has been revised several times, and it is acknowledged that it will never be complete. New dilemmas confront us, such as the spread of child "soldiers," torture, identity theft, and other crimes and tensions as a result of the opportunities afforded by the ongoing anguish of war plus strides in technological invention (Barash, 2000).

Technology throughout the world is racing away at such a pace that "privacy" has become increasingly controversial and easily breached. The speed of communication is often an asset, but this means that people hear of disasters and acute episodes via CNN or satellite images before they realize that they relate to them.

The indelible images of the bombings in New York, in Bali, in Jakarta, in Baghdad, and in London have created ethical issues in terms of who has access to acute human experiences of loss. Suddenly, private grief becomes public property. The day of the London bombings, one of the authors of this book was about to engage a class of Slovenian students in discussing children's rights and was derailed by the thought of her own young daughter working in central London. People become traumatized without the opportunity to process the realities of loss of safety, privacy, and trust; social work is sometimes overwhelmed. Alissa Hoven, one of the author's students, writes: "My agency cannot work with all the homeless migrants and refugees coming through our doors . . . [and] if they are undocumented we are not supposed to work with them . . . but when they are children, relatives, what can we do?" The study of ethics has taken on global proportions that all of us are involved in, across borders and across cultures; the challenge for us is to find the common ground.

STEPS FOR ETHICAL DECISION MAKING
IN A GLOBAL CONTEXT

The International Federation of Social Workers (IFSW) combines both principles for social work decisions and ethical practice, plus attention to global policy instruments and international conventions. The principles guide our work, the statements on professional conduct remind us of the various spheres of action, and together they provide us with steps for our work. The *first* step is to review the principles and apply them to our work. The *second* step is to address each statement on professional conduct and sphere of work in turn. The *third* step in a wider approach includes acknowledging the global elements that are understood through policy elements, and the *fourth* step is to summarize this wider lens on the process of ethical behavior. The principles include many of the United Nations approaches to human rights and are summarized in textbox 4.2. Chapter 3 on human rights offers the case example of international adoptions as an illustration of children's rights as well as the illuminating case history of unethical behavior at an international adoption agency where these policy instruments and international agreements were ignored (Shukovsky, 2003).

The IFSW has taken bold steps to integrate human rights and attention to contemporary issues, such as terrorism, into its statements and principles. Social workers are reminded throughout the document that they are often at

---

Textbox 4.2.   International Code of Ethics

1. Preface
   Ethical awareness is a fundamental part of the professional practice of social workers. Their ability and commitment to act ethically is an essential aspect of the quality of the service offered to those who use social work services. The purpose of the work of the IASSW and IFSW on ethics is to promote ethical debate and reflection in the member organizations, among providers of social work in member countries, as well as in schools of social work . . .
2. Definition of Social Work
   The social work profession promotes social change, problem solving in human relationships, and the empowerment and liberation of people to enhance well-being. Utilising theories of human behavior and social systems, social work intervenes at the points where people interact with their environments. Principles of human rights and social justice are fundamental to social work.
3. International Conventions . . .
4. Human Rights and Human Dignity . . .
5. Professional Conduct
   It is the responsibility of the national organizations in membership of IFSW and IASSW to develop and regularly update their own codes of ethics or ethical guidelines.

Source: Excerpt from IFSW (2004). *Ethics in Social Work: Statement of Principles.* Bern, Switzerland.

the front lines of societal values and norms, often caught between being the helper and controller.

There is no simple solution or prescribed way to achieve ethical practice, but a review of the standards of work in different social groupings (such as colleagues, clients, community) may be helpful. The following narrative uses the IFSW principles and expectations of professional conduct.

IFSW Ethics Statement on *professional conduct*: This section begins by confirming that it is "the responsibility of the national organizations in membership of IFSW and IASSW to develop and regularly update their own codes of ethics or ethical guidelines." It reminds social workers to take the necessary steps to communicate effectively, "to develop and maintain the required skills and competence." More boldly than in any earlier document, IFSW states that social workers "should not allow their skills to be used for inhumane purposes, such as torture or terrorism" (IASSW/IFSW, 2004). Also, social workers act with integrity and must "not subordinate the needs of people who use their services to their own needs or interests" (IASSW/IFSW, 2004). In practice, this may mean seeking cultural leaders and interpreters to clarify the situation. This section reminds social workers to know their own limitations, to uphold the profession, and to use their skills and knowledge fully while constantly clarifying the social needs of the client.

Ethical standards toward individual clients are the primary focus for the national codes, unlike the IFSW principles. However, in the IFSW statement there is reference to upholding social justice, as well as the client's right to a relationship of trust, privacy, and confidentiality. Confidentiality is something social workers often have to role-model in interdisciplinary teams, reminding their colleagues that people have shared their personal information with the expectation that it will be treasured and fully respected while solutions to the ethical problem or challenge are sought. It is a central component of social work that we "help the client—individual, group, community, or society" to achieve self-fulfillment. In this context the IFSW takes us to the conceptual expectation that a "client" may be any system size, including a "society."

The IFSW principles remind social workers of the steps that need to be taken to "bring to the notice of their employers, policy makers, politicians, and the general public situations where resources are inadequate" or unfairly distributed. The entire section 4.2 addresses social justice issues in more depth than earlier "codes" and reminds social workers of the constant re-sponsibility "to promote social justice" (IASSW/IFSW, 2004). This section assumes that the worker will take initiative to change policies that prevent service or are outdated, which may bring a clash of expectations. For ex-ample, an agency may help migrant workers find housing, but some come without documentation. Where policies are unjust, social workers "have an obligation" to challenge them.

Ethical behavior in relation to colleagues and the overall standards of the profession are integrated into the large section 5 on professional conduct and section 4.1 on human rights and human dignity. This latter section focuses on increased attention to human rights and "treating each person as a whole." This expectation of professional cohesion and support for one another is clearly a key issue when social workers are trying to be nonviolent or when surrounded by war.

This revised set of principles reminds social workers of their larger commitment to the profession both in their country of practice and in the global context of, for example, the International Federation of Social Workers, the International Association of Schools of Social Work, and the United Nations.

SYNTHESIS OF STREAMS IN
ETHICAL SOCIAL WORK THOUGHT

(An earlier version of this section appeared in Link, in Ramanathan and Link, 2004, chapter 5.)

National boundaries have always been artificial in regard to environmental health, the spread of disease, and the flow of clean air and water. In the domain of professional ethics, it is similarly artificial for any one country to rely on its code as discrete or adequate by itself. Currently, practitioners and agencies that have access to sophisticated technology have increased tools to fight injustice, poverty, and oppression. However, simultaneously, there is the tension created by the presumption that people without these contemporary trappings are less capable or are lacking in creativity. As Mother Teresa has taught us, we learn humility by being with people who survive without, rather than by our vulnerable information systems. Similarly in India, Emma Bhatt founded and organized the largest women's organization in India—perhaps in the world: the Self-Employed Women's Union (Hill Gross, 1992). Without personal computers, she managed to engage a mass movement in social justice. Is it ethical for social workers to become technology-bound in a way that distances them from clients and client reality? Are we carried on the tide or making choices? How often do we pause and reflect on these processes? One such reflection is portrayed in textbox 4.3.

The tension for the social work profession is constantly to seek to define the implications of ethical questions—their context, reality, and relationship to the larger environment—before taking action. Statements of principles and codes of practice often miss the wider context of ethical issues in terms of human rights, with regard to such essentials as health, clean water, and sustainable development of communities now and in the future. The most helpful elements of codes of practice are the way they prompt questions for

Textbox 4.3.   Personal Professional Journey

Rosemary Link

MEXICO

A day in the foothills near Tepotzlan stays with me forever. We had driven into the campo to visit families who may be willing to receive students for home-stays. I am invited to spend a day to be part of a family's activities. The journey takes us along dusty roads; we stop at a vegetable and fruit market. Neat pyramids of every color bean are set out on mats beneath tarpaulins, strung with baskets, flowers, beads, herbs. Many fruits and foods are new to me as I look in wonder at the colors and absorb the vibrant life. So many new discoveries to feast my senses. We travel on slowly, behind carts and donkeys laden with sugarcane. Our destination is a mile or so uphill, beyond the track's end. I am hot and aware of my heart rate as I notice my Mexican colleague striding up this spectacular terrain.

My Spanish is halting at best, but I am welcomed warmly and offered frescoes and a seat in a white-walled courtyard with bare earth, jasmine, and much activity. My colleague settles in for a few hours of conversation over recent events. Government officials have been visiting to talk about putting up a soccer field for the local youth, despite the villagers' urgent call for roadways and water. The talk is of the people's priorities and the economic choices and ethics of the current government, who try to buy people's votes with soccer fields instead of water supplies. As I gather confidence to try my ideas in my newly acquired vocabulary, I am drawn in and my colleague leaves.

Two sons arrive on horseback; a daughter lights a fire in the wall, striking sticks for a spark. I watch her, mezmerized as she pats and flips a tortilla so expertly, chatting and laughing with a grandparent, who is smoking and swaying watchfully from his hammock (no word for nursing homes here). I am aware of his inquisitive gaze and I feel gawky, out of place; for heaven's sake, don't expect me to show my fire-lighting, horse-tending, hog-catching, culinary skills. I have a brace on my front teeth; it suddenly feels like an emblem of strange priorities. It also makes it very difficult to bite hard food. I am offered a corn cake and struggle politely, not wanting to offend; it tastes wonderful after my too early breakfast, but is like iron. Quietly, I slip it into my sundress pocket. Foolish city person. A piglet speeds out of the house, scuffles for a moment with a sibling, then shoots her nose in the air. Corn cake! Quick as a flash she is diving in my pocket and my hosts are laughing as I struggle away, the cake still concealed. Their mirth and relaxation as they prepare for the *comida* are infectious. How often do I miss lunch in my usual pelting routines? What more am I missing?

(*continued*)

> I am invited to eat and follow the daughter's example of washing her hands in a stone bowl to the side of the yard. We pour water on our hands; it flows through the central outlet into a spiral groove round the stone stem. Chicks cluster to drink at the base; the remainder flows through onto a wild profusion of herbs in a garden patch. Why did it take me 50 years to appreciate water—to think about how every drop is used and the ethical consequences of denying our right to turn on a tap?

detailed facets of a decision and for the various groups of actors as well as the way they lead us to frameworks for decision making. Loewenberg and Dolgoff have identified a nine-step sequence or "screen" for thinking through an ethical decision, which connects readily to the International Code of Practice. The early focus on clarifying societal values is a key reminder of the complexity of an absolute or relativist social context and the implications of this for the worker, the client, and the community:

1. Identify the problem
2. Clarify the society values
3. Establish goals
4. Identify alternate targets
5. Assess and weigh possible outcomes
6. Identify and rank order ethical principles involved
7. Select the most appropriate option
8. Implement the option
9. Evaluate the results for subsequent intervention. (Loewenberg and Dolgoff, 1992)

As we seek to identify steps on the journey to increased critical thinking in ethical decisions, we recognize that this will always be an unfolding process of great complexity. Dialogue with colleagues in a variety of countries confirms that ethical considerations are a universal component in social work. The particular form or emphasis an ethical review takes reflects the history and socioeconomic and cultural context in which social work has developed. For example, the recent emergence of Eastern European countries from strict socialist regimes has led to a concern for individuality and the focus on a person's "right to reality" to be "listened to, to be heard and to be taken seriously" (Čačinovič Vogrinčič, 1997). In Latin America, the tension between people in poverty and the wealthy has prompted a broad-scale political interpretation of ethical considerations in the language of conscientization. In countries such as the United States, the detailed codes of ethics may be reflective of a more legal tradition reflected in the current wave of diagnostic regulations and the form of service delivery known as "managed care."

When the approach to ethics is explored in a world context, beyond our usual national frame of reference, many universal principles are identified. Some of these are outlined in the code of the International Federation, and others represent the universal challenges and principles for social workers who seek social and economic justice. In this book, these principles fall into four categories:

1. Widest perspective for assessment
   - Before acting, review personal value, history, and cultural bias and ask the question "How am I influenced personally and professionally by this question or problem?"
   - Review the value base, history, culture of the other(s) concerned with the ethical question.
   - Question geocentrism and the impact of the location of people involved. What would be different if this dialogue were happening elsewhere in the world and why?
2. Inclusion of the service user in dialogue and decisions
   - Discuss the "right to reality" of service users and their family or community; spend time defining this reality;
   - Acknowledge the power of the professional;
   - Attend to the use of clear language;
   - Consider the question of conscientization. To what extent is the immediate ethical tension reflective and part of wider societal and global issues?
3. Reference to International Policy Instruments
   - Which are the relevant policy instruments for the question at hand?
   - Review the IFSW/IASSW professional conduct guidelines.
   - See international examples of similar situations (especially occurring in the medical field for organ transplant, separation of conjoined twins, treatment of rare diseases such as SARS).
4. Joint evaluation
   - Was the outcome lasting in its resolution of the ethical questions in both the workers' and service users' view?
   - Which actions of staff worked best?
   - Which actions of the service users worked best?
   - Did all members feel included and respected?
   - What would be different in a future instance of this ethical decision?

It is clearly a considerable task for the International Federation of Social Workers to gather these varying perspectives for us all. Their cooperation with the International Association of Schools of Social Work has role-modeled the global dialogue that characterizes social work in the first and second decades of the twenty-first century. To synthesize these streams and to learn from one another across the globe are key to helping the profession toward deeper understanding and effective action in this ever more complex domain.

STUDENT ASSIGNMENTS

1. When are we acting in a way that reflects the deontologist school of philosophy and when are we acting in a way that reflects the teleologist school? How separate are these streams of thought? Give examples of your thinking. How adequate are these two streams of theory in characterizing ethical issues globally?
2. Trainer, in his book *Developed to Death* (1994), states that the hunger of millions of the world's children is a question of ethics. What does he mean? Outline the current situation for children in relation to world hunger (a place to start would be the UNICEF report *The State of the World's Children 1997*); identify the ethical questions raised; discuss your own approach and identify the theoretical base you are using. To illustrate his perspective, Trainer writes: "Millions of hungry people live near the Pacific coast of South America, but fishing boats from the developed countries take almost all the fish caught there. Western cats could not live so well if we did not have access to these regions" (Trainer, 1994).
3. How does a professional's respect for the client's "right to reality" become evident in our practice? Give an example of application at an individual or community level.
4. Does your country of practice have a code of ethics? How can we relate the International Code of Ethics with a country code? What are the universal principles? In what ways does a country code differ? How would you add to the International Code bearing in mind that it is under constant scrutiny?
5. Review this case study for India and apply this approach to ethics to the country where you practice (A version of this case study appeared in Ramanathan and Link, 2004, chapter 5.):

Ethical Issues and Value Dilemmas in a Global Economy:
An Example of Occupational Social Work

Chathapuram S. Ramanathan

Occupational injury rates are generally alarming in nations of the Global South. In a global economy, expansion of multinational corporations in developing nations, particularly Asia, is inevitable. Unfortunately there is an inverse relationship between increased economic activity due to multinational investment and the health and safety of workers in these countries. Occupational social workers in multinational corporations in Asia can benefit workers by advocating for standards similar to those mandated in legislation in the United States through the Occupational Safety and Health Act and Federal Coal Mine Health and Safety Act legislation, in order to ensure similar safe and healthy work environments. Given that workers in the Asian countries are more vulnerable in their health and wellness, social workers have an ethical obligation to raise social justice issues and actively advocate on behalf of these workers in multinational subsidiaries (Ramanathan, 1994).

Roles for occupational social workers may arise in response to the legislative requirements. For instance, in Indian industries where there are more than 50 women employees, employers are mandated to provide and to maintain child care assistance, or "creche," for children six years and under. These centers are to be staffed by child care workers (Srivastava, 1967). The 1976 amendment of the Factories Act of 1948 mandated employers to provide child care assistance if they employ 30 women. This is stipulated by the Indian Factories Act of 1948 as amended in 1976 (Srivastava, 1988).

Indian Factories Act Se. 48 Creches "(1) In every factory wherein more than thirty women workers are ordinarily employed there shall be provided and maintained a suitable room or rooms for the use of children under age of six years of such women. (2) Such rooms shall provide adequate accommodation, shall be adequately lighted and ventilated, shall be maintained in a clean and sanitary condition and shall be under the charge of women trained in the care of children and infants. (3) The Provincial Government may make rules—(a) prescribing the location and the standards in respect of construction, accommodation, furniture and other equipment rooms to be provided, under this section; (b) requiring the provision in any factory of free milk or refreshment or both for such children; (c) requiring that facilities shall be given in any factory for the mothers of such children to feed them at necessary internals" (Factories Act Sec. 48, as quoted in Srivastava, 1988).

Further, the report of the royal commission on labor explicates that the employer provide short periods of absence from work at necessary intervals to nursing mothers. Existence of these kinds of legislation in the host countries affect the role of occupational social workers. Also occupational social workers have an ethical role to help industries to increase their corporate social responsibility regarding both health and safety of their workers and the communities in which these industries are located. The absence of the latter is still very clear in our minds regarding the Union Carbide incident in Bhopal, India, where thousands of people died, and several thousand were permanently affected due to the poisonous gas leak from the Union Carbide factory, triggered by acceptance of lower levels of safety standards, as opposed to Union Carbide factories in the Global North (Ramanathan, 1992). Also, the extent of compensation provided to the families of the dead and injured was very minimal, thus implicitly conveying that the value of human life varies in different parts of the globe.

Chapter Five

Cultural Competence in Local and Global Relationships

... diversity makes for a rich tapestry, and we must understand that all the threads are equal in value no matter what their color.

—Maya Angelou

This chapter explores the role of culture and the goal for social workers to be culturally aware with competent skills in all their relationships and assessments. Just as we assert a "common human condition" in chapter 2, we also recognize the need for individual and group identity established through culture. Even as we seek to understand our common humanity, we respect local uniqueness and indigenous traditions as pieces of a giant puzzle that contribute to our richly woven universe.

Culture is a universal phenomenon, that is, something everybody has. Multicultural education begins with everyone understanding his or her own roots and culture. Such an understanding gives a sense of grounded identity from which to learn and value others. Culture is an inclusive terminology, because everyone has a culture. Each of our families is a subculture of the larger community culture (or reference group—such as religious affiliation, professional group, geographic community, and so on), and every individual, group, family, and community has unique qualities based on their culture.

One cannot aspire to have a grounded understanding of diversity without adequate awareness of global interdependence. In order to be effective social work practitioners and researchers, we need to focus on cultural awareness as well as cross-cultural transactions. This awareness of global interdependence is critical, whether the professional social worker is engaged in social work assessment, intervention, or evaluation. The grounded understanding of diversity must take into account issues concerning mobile populations, cultural norms that pertain to power, hierarchy, gender status and its relevance in society, family functioning,

99

religion and identity, related group politics, and so on. Thus, in our judgment, it is not an "either/or" proposition in social work when we seek global community to appreciate both cultural diversity and cultural uniqueness. These aspects of our humanity are sides of the same coin—we are all humans sharing a planet that is becoming more accessible through technology. We have traditional roots that give us our sense of identity in a local context and a sense of other when we meet new cultural traditions. These differences can enhance our lives if we seek to respect and understand each other peacefully. One of the greatest dangers facing the earth is the readiness to stereotype and dehumanize people who seem threatening, given to desperate acts, or different from "us" in their approach to life than the state we happen to live in. George Orwell spoke of this long ago when he referred to the dangers of nationalism:

I mean first of all the habit of assuming that human beings can be classified like insects and that whole blocks of millions or tens of millions of people can be confidently labeled "good" or "bad." But secondly—and this is much more important—I mean the habit of identifying oneself with a single nation or other unit, placing it beyond good or evil and recognizing no other duty than that of advancing its own interests. (Orwell, 1953)

This chapter defines then both the realities of *culture*, the dangers of denying it to others, and the reach for skills that can be termed communication with *cultural awareness and competence*. Affirming the social work core values of human dignity and individual uniqueness is critical as we aspire to increase our cultural awareness and competence. Although each individual is unique, inclusive of cultural differences, there is a lot in common within the human race, such as interrelatedness and interdependence, or quite simply, as the retired Professor Emerita Marilyn Belgum explains—"laughing and crying in the same language" (Belgum, 2000).

Eastern philosophy, including Hindu philosophy, has systematically emphasized the uniqueness of individuals and common bonding of the human race, as they pertain to interrelatedness and interdependence, which are reflected in those cultural traditions. This philosophical underpinning of the human spirit is reflected in the following passage of the *Upanishads*:

It is great and self-effulgent; and its form is unthinkable. It is subtler than the subtle. It shines diversely. It is further away than the far off; and it is near at hand in this body. Among sentient beings, it is perceived as seated in this very body, in the cavity of the heart. (*Munduka Upanishad*, 3.1.7)

Similarly, Mahatma Gandhi's philosophy of life and humanity espoused over eight decades ago yet still very pertinent today: in nature there is fundamental unity running through our lives.

Thus in order to begin our journey to effective cross-cultural communication, we address theoretical aspects and definitions of culture and cultural competence; awareness of our own culture and the impact of our behaviors especially in relation to stereotyping through a case example of Asian American experiences in the United States; and forms of assessment and dialogue and opportunities that enhance our social work skills in cultural efficacy.

DEFINITIONS AND THEORETICAL PERSPECTIVES

Theorists such as Terry Cross identify elements of competence in a cycle from incapacity, also known as racism, to advanced insight and action for social justice. In this book, we acknowledge that we can rarely become fully competent in another culture, but we can seek to understand. Cross's (1986) conceptual work can be used both to increase individual awareness and to expand agency self-awareness (see textbox 5.1).

Textbox 5.1.   Cross's Conceptual Work

Cultural Incapacity: "The capacity to help people from other cultures is lacking. People are denied access to their natural helpers and healers" (Cross, 1986). People with diverse cultures are not valued; a paternal posture is assumed toward "lesser" cultures, or "second" languages. Ignorance and unrealistic fear of other cultures exist and are allowed. There are different expectations of colleagues/clients from other cultures. Students can identify examples.

Culture Neutral: (Cross uses the concept "blind," but our blind students protested.) Services are provided with the philosophy of being unbiased. There is a belief that color and culture make no difference and we are all the same. An ethnocentric helping approach is applied to all. Cultural strengths are ignored and assimilation is encouraged.

Cultural Precompetence: Affirmative action is used to include culturally diverse people. The focus is external, outward, focused on "them." There is some attention to learning how different cultures affect social work practice.

Cultural Competence: Acceptance and respect for difference exists. Careful attention is paid to the dynamics of difference. Effort is made to understand the meaning of a person's behavior (high or low context for example). There is ongoing gathering of cultural knowledge and resources. Services are adjusted to meet a variety of cultures.

Advanced Multicultural Competence: There is a focus on cooperation and communication across communities and agency services. Social workers anticipate and welcome working in a multiethnic and diverse workplace; "there is conscious work to share power and focus on client empowerment and self-determination," plus transparent communication. Diversity is highly valued and recognized as part of our human condition—perhaps the most valuable part.

Source: Brief summary drawing on T. Cross's (1986) continuum.

Community examples help to illustrate these concepts, including Amrita Patel's appeal to the men of the Indian Milk Marketing Board for gender parity, to encourage their sisters in their work. Another example is the police force in Willmar, Minnesota, United States, who learn Spanish and respond thoughtfully to the overarrest rate of migrant workers. These illustrations are presented in the chapter. In order to engage people in challenging cultural incapacity or discrimination, there needs to be conversation concerning the definitions of culture.

The concept of culture is defined in a variety of ways, and for our initial discussion we use Carter and Qureshi's definition of culture as a "learned system of meaning and behaviors that is passed from one generation to the next" (1995). We recognize that this always relates to processes of socialization and usually to geographical boundaries. In their development of a global model of ethnic diversity, Mayadas, Elliott, and Ramanathan studied six aspects of culture that can lead to conflict: race/ethnicity, values/beliefs, art, language, rites/traditions, and religion (Mayadas, Elliott, and Ramanathan, 1999). Culture can be defined from an individual perspective or from a collective perspective that focuses on the community generated by shared culture. Figure

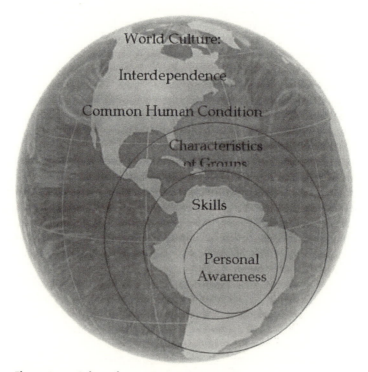

World Culture:

Interdependence

Common Human Condition

Characteristics
of Groups

Skills

Personal
Awareness

Figure 5.1.   Culture from a Systems Perspective

5.1 (Link and Bill, 2005) illustrates the elements of the concept of culture that are taken into account by social workers and that build layers within the context of "shared systems of meaning" (Carter and Qureshi, 1995).

Ann Aguillar Lutterman (2005) introduced American students to Hall's (1976) theoretical idea of high- and low-context cultural exchange. In high-context environments, people take time to socialize, to greet one another, and to generate trust before they embark on decision making (in author, Link's, class at Augsburg College). Often community comes before individual and ideas are developed in circular discussion and reflection (Hall, 1976). In low-context cultures, people "go straight to the point" and cut out the social exchange; often, thinking is linear and based on individual approaches to responsibility.

Tiong Tan similarly suggests that cultural awareness and conflict negotiation are built from an understanding of high- and low-context communication (Tan and Rowlands, 2004). For people who are socialized to be precise, time pressured, and goal oriented, with little time for ritual and spirituality in the workplace, conflict will be negotiated differently from those socialized in a high-context environment. In high-context cultures, people expect to hear one another in a variety of ways, including verbal and nonverbal, actual and spiritual. In a video exchange between Augsburg College students in Minneapolis and students from the National University of Singapore in 2004, Tan invited students to compare the adversary model of conflict negotiation that corresponds with low-context culture with a restorative and mediation model termed "Qing, Li, and Fa" that is more the norm in Eastern and native cultures.

CULTURE AS CHARACTERISTICS OF PEOPLE

Culture is most often thought of as the characteristics of a group of people passed down from generation to generation in social behaviors, language, dress, customs, dance, song, food, and social groupings, and often considered unique to that group. As the term "culture" comes to life in its complexity, our understanding of what is involved in communicating effectively becomes more layered. One of the authors of this book (Link) was admiring the intricacy and beauty of lace made in Idrija, Slovenia, and commented to a colleague that it reminded her of the lace she had seen in Cuernavaca, Mexico. The Slovenian colleague immediately commented that this lace is unique to the region and could not be similar; it was part of their cultural heritage. The author realized that while she had intended to refer to the sharp juxtaposition of acute poverty and maintained loveliness demonstrated in the ability of women in impoverished circumstances to transcend their deprivations, and to cherish and maintain their artistic skills, the compliment sounded as though

their art were being reduced to "sameness." The identity of the women in Idrija is invested in their lace, as it is for the domestic workers in Cuernavaca;
the resilience displayed in their work and art is the common human condition,
while the details are spectacularly unique.

The example of demeaning someone's culture by misunderstanding the
significance of artwork can be more easily retrieved than the demeaning
characteristics of culture in circumstances of war. Recently, the U.S. army
has been criticized for a lack of cultural competence in Iraq. Brigadier Nigel
Aylwin-Foster, the second-most senior British officer responsible for training
Iraqi security forces has made "blistering" attacks on the U.S. army for being overly nationalistic with an aggressive style of greeting and interrogation
that undermines efforts to work with local Iraqis. Aylwin-Foster identifies
the U.S. strategy as "to kill or capture all terrorists and insurgents: they saw
military destruction of the enemy as a strategic goal in its own right; the U.S.
army has developed over time a singular focus on conventional warfare, of
a particularly swift and violent kind" (Aylwin-Foster, 2006). The debate is
a reflection of the difficulty in moving past the destruction and devastation
of traditional warfare of the twentieth century to conflict management that
includes strategic planning for peace and cross-cultural engagement of the
community. Cross-cultural engagement includes respect for culture.

The paradox of war means that in order to kill, soldiers are trained to dehumanize their victims—they deliberately ignore cultural characteristics. In
order to establish peace, that same person has to invest humanity and cultural
awareness into dialogue with the "enemy." The task is unfolding before us,
seemingly out of reach, while dehumanization and cultural incapacity are
the styles of interaction. For soldiers and social workers alike, the first step
to peace is to pay attention to valuing all people, without exception and discrimination.

A less violent and smaller scale example of policing demonstrates that it
is vital to move from stereotyping and demeaning to recognition and respect
in order to engage in community building. In the 1990s criticisms were being leveled at the police force in a U.S. Midwest town that was struggling to
incorporate the most recent migrant workers, now labeled in the U.S. Census
as "New Americans." Mexican American workers are a group whose work
is vital to the local farmers and seasonal trades in Minnesota. However, tensions were gathering over the high arrest rates of Spanish-speaking youth as
well as fights among school students, late night parties, and noise. Following
town hall forums and citizen dialogue, in part facilitated by local teachers,
priests, and police officers, the local police made a profound change that
represents a leap forward in terms of their cultural competence skills. They
agreed to change their hiring practices to include Spanish-speaking recruits
and encouraged officers to learn another language. The community also

voiced and listened to the stories of their cultures—people from Mexico and hot countries generally rest at midday and go to bed later. In the cold Midwest of the United States people go to bed early (before 10:00 p.m.) and rise early. These essential differences become sources of aggravation for a community integrating newer members, until these cultural characteristics are accepted for what they are.

Immigrants and refugees who arrive to the United States from non-European countries bring personal mores and behaviors, cultural patterns, and religious rituals that may be unusual at a time when there is so much emphasis on assimilation by eradication of differences (Mayadas, Ramanathan, and Suarez, 1999). Therefore, it is critical that as social workers we guard ourselves against the societal biases that may influence our thinking in assessments and interventions. Specifically, a three-dimensional cultural interface model proposed by Mayadas, Ramanathan, and Suarez (1999) guides social work practitioners to be more effective in the field of mental health and other fields of social work practices. When social workers in the field of mental health assess and treat mental health problems, they need to focus on (1) the culture of the group at risk; (2) societal attitudes, cultural sensitivity, and tolerance of differences; and (3) openness of the practitioner to new concepts and willingness to respect and move toward a multicultural mapping system.

CULTURE AS PERSONAL AWARENESS OF TIME, PLACE, VALUES, BELIEFS, SELF, AND OTHER

Cultural awareness and competence essentially mean that we are able to identify our own affiliations to culture and can recognize and respect differing traditions of culture in others in ways that influence our styles of communication and expressions of respect. However, this definition implies deep understanding of the layers of ourselves that are built through our cultural heritage and that we carry as "norms" of behavior. A student comments that it is not "normal" for families to offer sacrifices. What is normal for a European American is different from what is normal for a Hmong family who have survived great trauma in refugee camps and "sacrifice" their hair to give thanks. Norms may not be shared by people in parallel cultures, and so our word "normal" becomes a trap for judging others. In contrast a review of the source of a norm (such as patterns of sleep and work) can lead to a natural connection with people who, despite their differences, are recognized as fellow humans.

Dolores Norton (1997) speaks of theoretical concepts of *sustaining and nurturing* aspects of culture and invites us to map our nurturing systems as

the source of our norms—the places where we feel most recognized, welcomed, and unconditionally loved (see texbox 5.2). An overarching system
is the sustaining environment of our workplaces, our judicial institutions, our
educational establishments, our health resources, and larger political systems.
In some localities, people of similar language and faith also work together and
there is a congruence of norms; for example, in a particular location everyone
celebrates Good Friday and eats fish and this synchrony is affirming. In other
localities, people work together from a wide variety of experiences, beliefs,
languages, appetites, and faiths, and more effort is needed to recognize each
other's "norms" and find common ground. For example, people who have
a very different faith tradition and festive observance, such as an important
Hindu festival, may have different food habits and observe specific customs
during these festive times. Specifically, strict vegetarian food is eaten, during Ganesha Chaturthi, or Ganesha Festival, a day on which Lord Ganesha,
the elephant-headed son of Shiva and Parvathi, is widely worshipped as the
supreme god of wisdom, prosperity, and good fortune. This festival is also
known as Vinayaka Chaturthi or Vinayaka Chavithi in Sanskrit, Kannada,
Tamil, and Telugu, or in Konkani (Indian languages), and as Chauthi and as
Chathaa in Nepali Bhasa (language spoken in Nepal). It is celebrated as the
birthday of Lord Ganesha. The festival is marked in the Hindu calendar (based
on the lunar calendar) and is calculated as the fourth day of the waxing moon.
Typically, the day usually falls between August 20 and September 15.

For social work, we expect to work with people of many cultures, and it is
part of our mission to extend ourselves and become thirsty for knowledge of
cultures different from our own. It is easier to be thirsty for cultural knowledge when our well-being or safety is not being threatened. Differing levels
of access to power and resources are often superimposed on cultural groups
with the result that conflict becomes a conflation of culture and circumstances. Intercultural communication may be a celebration of arts or sports,
as in the Olympics, but when the content of communication is access to clean
water or oil, the cross-cultural tension is greater and more prone to misunderstanding. Sen discusses this in his article, "Civilizational Imperatives" (Sen,
2002). On the surface, honoring the point of view of another sounds like a
reasonable and attainable aspect of civilization. However as Mahatma Gandhi
realized, civilized earth remains out of reach when one group considers itself
"more" civilized than another.

Social workers see conflict daily as part of their work. For cultural competence to become a reality it is necessary to accept conflict or different ideas
and approaches to situations; however, this is always in the context of peaceful communication rather than physical violence. Finn and Jacobsen point
out that the Spanish word for courage—*coraje*—combines courage and rage:
"Social justice work calls for the expression and honoring of anger and frus-

---

Textbox 5.2. The Dual Perspective by Dolores Norton

Students are asked to identify the characteristics of their *nurturing* environment—the place we feel most loved and nurtured and the people and groups who help to create that place. Then we identify the *sustaining* environment, where we work and sustain ourselves economically and in formal systems such as health, courts, and education.

We draw circles for each and see how far they overlap or have gaps. The larger the gaps the more need for dialogue and storytelling and the higher the potential for conflict. For example, one Somali student in Minneapolis has come to the United States not for a "good life" but to "save her life" following conflict in her home country. She misses her nurturing environment—the family, the home, the food, the music, and the traditions, and is trying to settle into a new sustaining environment. The two circles barely touch. However, her fellow student from a town in Minnesota with Scandinavian heritage finds the environment of a small Lutheran college very familiar, and the two systems reinforce one another.

---

tration, rather than their containment. Working effectively with difference means allowing for anger and engaging with conflict as a valid and valued part of the work" (Finn and Jacobsen, 2002).

Social workers have a responsibility to create communities and services that establish the most productive, creative, safe, and energizing environments possible for all clients, employees, customers, and the wider community while accepting opportunity in conflict. Changing identities means changing interpretations, such as when countries of Eastern Europe join the European Community; as students from India move to the university opportunities in Singapore; and as immigrants from Africa move to the United

---

Textbox 5.3. Case Examples

In Bristol, UK, there have been racially motivated attacks, for example, on a shop run by a British-Pakistani family. The SARI (stand against racial incidents) project is a neighborhood organization where neighbors come together to tell their stories, find their strength, express their hurt, be angry safely, learn about each other's cultures, and seek ways to live together peacefully.

In Delhi, India, the Milk Marketing Board has its first woman director, Amrita Patel, who has thanked the men in the organization for supporting their sisters, mothers, wives, and daughters in working together with equal status and respect. She "co-opts" her adversaries by engaging them.

States. People are moving from country to country, and from region to region, in higher numbers than at any time in history. In order to live more peacefully we need to hear and strive to understand each other's cultural realities, methods of conflict resolution, and survival stories—these are the challenges inherent in cultural awareness and competent communication.

BUILDING CULTURALLY AWARE PRACTICE

For social workers to make effective and efficient social assessments, interventions, and evaluations, we need to be culturally grounded in a variety of ways (see figure 5.1). This cultural grounding warrants that we develop cultural competencies in multiple areas, including

- *Competency in Cultural Identity*: This involves our ability to identify ancestral heritage, national origin, and role of the cultural group in the country's history.
- *Competency in Cultural Characteristics*: This involves our familiarity with diverse attires, languages, demographics, and celebrations.
- *Competency in Cultural Stereotypes*: This requires our having knowledge of assumptions, labels, biases, and uniqueness (both negative and positive) attached to different cultural groups.
- *Competency in Communication Styles*: This involves familiarity with unique cultural behaviors, etiquette, protocols, and communication dos and don'ts.
- *Competency Regarding Religions*: This requires that we have knowledge of the religious origins of Christianity, Islam, Hinduism, Sikhism, Judaism, Buddhism, Jainism, and respective spiritual traditions, and their major holy days and observances.
- *Competency in Seminal Civil Rights*: This requires that we have knowledge of cases that pertain to culture-, ethnicity-, national origin–, and religion-based discrimination, racial profiling, and hate crime incidents.

Around the world, religiously based disparate treatment and the incidence of hate crimes continue to persist. In the current millennium, tens of thousands of people have been killed because of religion-based community riots or state-sponsored deaths based on ethnicity.

In 2008 there are desperate images of hate-based deaths in Israel, Palestine, Pakistan, Afghanistan, and Kenya, and the list could be longer. In 2002, in India, a railway compartment of Hindus returning from a visit to a holy place (Ayodhya, birthplace of Lord Rama, an important god for the Hindus) during a festive time was burned by Muslim extremists, killing 58 Hindus. The train compartment was burned near a town called Godhra. Subsequently, the state of Gujarat in India saw systematic burning of properties and killings of hundreds of Muslim minority people in a city called Ahmedabad. After this outbreak of communal tensions based on religion, several civic-minded Hindus and Muslims in India who felt deeply hurt were concerned and expressed their sentiments. One such sentiment is expressed by the poet, Indrani Kailas. The poet refers to saffron, which is a symbolically sacred color for the Hindus. Similarly, the color green is a symbolically sacred color for the Muslims.

Saffron—No Longer the Colour I Like
Indrani Kailas

Was it the colour saffron that I once liked?
So pure, sacred and divine!
The colour so very lively and bright!
Symbol of sacrifice and the sunlight.

Today seems to be intolerable!
Impure, terrible and gruesome.
My journey from Godhra to
Ayodhya through Ahmedabad.

I traveled without a ticket
Through the media with emotions.
A bloody war of colours,
Greens sparked at Godhra,
And the saffron got inflamed!

The beautiful saffron has turned red!
The colour of fire and firings,
Of violence and of killings.
Revenge and naked hatred,
Creating the injured and the dead!

This saffron now seems too ugly,
Draped with intolerance and hate
Drenched with feelings of fanatics,
It smells of violence!
This colour with its changed connotations,
Spells danger, fear and destruction.
Yet they celebrate this saffron
Cherishing its new definitions!

I feel ashamed with tears choked.
Was that the colour I liked?
I pray, Please oh God!
Take away the saffron and give us white!
Give Gujarat the dawn of peace
After a long deadly night!

Why the holy man, even now
You drew in saffron?
Please change to white!
I appeal, because I do not like the saffron!

A grieved Hindu.

In February 2009, President Obama of the United States of America, during his address on the national prayer day, underscored that faith should not be used to divide us. He referred to how we have witnessed faith being wielded as a tool to divide us from one another—as an excuse for prejudice and intolerance, resulting in waging of wars, and slaughtering of innocents, and for centuries entire religions have been persecuted, all in the name of perceived righteousness. President Obama, while acknowledging the fact that the very nature of faith means that some of our beliefs will never be the same, because we read from different scriptures, and follow different edicts, also focused on what binds each religion: the call to love one another; to understand one another; to treat with dignity and respect those with whom we share a brief moment on this earth. Thus, religion requires us not only to believe, but to do—to give something of ourselves for the benefit of others and the betterment of our world (Obama, 2009b). Ramanathan and Link (1999, 2004) explicated the importance of power of language as being central to social work practice, and yet this is not systematically explored in social work education at the macro level. They referred to consequences of using disempowering terminologies such as "third world." In January 2009, President Obama referred to the power of language regarding categorizing different faiths. He emphasized that "the language we use matters," and that "we cannot paint with a broad brush a faith as a consequence of the violence that is done in that faith's name" (Obama, 2009).

The authors of this text believe that social workers have an important role to play to enhance interfaith understanding. The authors also believe all hate crimes are an extreme form of prejudice and discriminatory behavior, arising from the stereotyping of people. Textbox 5.4 discusses the impact of stereotyping and the importance of awareness of cultural norms in interpersonal communication.

ASIAN AMERICAN SCENARIOS TO ILLUSTRATE THE IMPACT OF DISCRIMINATION AND A FRAMEWORK TO EXPAND APPROACHES TO ASSESSMENT

In order to address the complexity of challenging our own knowledge and practice in social service, we need to expand our awareness of ethnically sensitive work. To this end, reviewing the cultural "protocols" identified by

Textbox 5.4.   A Case of the United States of America

Pravina Ramanathan and Chathapuram Ramanathan

Culture, as a universal phenomenon, has tangible and objective aspects, including its components that are easy to recognize, for example, clothes, language, food, art, dance, and so on. Further, such an understanding is to include the arts, literature, history, political structures, social systems, and so forth, of various cultures.

Although having knowledge of the objective culture of a group can aid in the understanding of that cultural group, it does not prepare us for relating to people that belong to that particular culture. Judging a book by its cover without knowing the content will not be useful. Similarly the superficial knowledge of a culture without familiarity of cultural nuances does not help foster understanding. Therefore, we need to place emphasis on the subjective or deeper aspects of a culture that are not easily recognized, for example, communication styles, rituals, thought patterns, ordering of time, patterns of handling emotions, approaches to problem solving, and so on, of various cultures. Much of the subjective or deep culture is never considered or comprehended, yet these dimensions can powerfully direct our lives and actions in significant ways. Getting to know someone on a deeper level is more effective and helps to break down and overcome cultural barriers.

It is human nature to assign attributes to fellow human beings, based on their personal characteristics. Assigning of attributes is not a problem in itself. The problems start when those attributes are used or misused to facilitate allocation of resources or to deny and obstruct access to resources. In a given society, the one issue that is experienced by all the ethnic, racial, and/or religious groups, is that they are discriminated against through the use of stereotypes. Stereotypes are based on attributes we assign, or our perception of attributes assigned to these diverse groups. Thus, there can be both positive and negative stereotypes. Often, stereotypes arise because of our own insecurities due to lack of understanding of our cultural strengths and weaknesses.

Now, first let us examine the negative impacts of stereotypes, and how this is relevant to, and relates to, the discriminatory behavior toward members of these groups. Second, we present alternate ways of communication that are inclusive and respectful.

THE NEGATIVE IMPACT OF STEREOTYPES

First and foremost, we examine the etiology of stereotypes: Where do stereotypes come from? And how do we perpetuate them?

Some stereotypes are brought about by the media and education. When children watch television shows, they are strongly influenced by racial stereotypes,

(continued)

or by the portrayal of people who do not belong to the Judeo-Christian tradition as abrasive and violent people. Similarly, through the lack of representation in educational curriculums, children of color may feel that individuals of their own race are not as important to society as whites.

STEREOTYPES IN THE CONTEXT
OF THE UNITED STATES

While discussing the stereotypes of cultural groups in the United States, we address the First Nation People, African Americans, Latino Americans, Asian Americans, and Arab Americans. A special emphasis is on Asian Americans, as they form the largest minority group with the most pluralistic cultural and religious background.

STEREOTYPE NUMBER ONE

People who are a model minority, with no problems, aloof, unfriendly, secretive, and much smarter than the rest of us. They are resourceful and keep to themselves. The men are sexist and the women are subservient. They are wizards at math and science, although most of them can't speak English. They outsource our jobs to India and China.

Asian Americans

a. Model minority:
Referring to Asian Americans as a model minority is a myth. All Asian Americans are not physicians and engineers who earn very high incomes and live in huge homes, and so forth. This myth has become a burden to many Asian Americans; they do not receive many services offered by the government, because they are considered a minority that does not need any assistance. Assigning the label "model minority" not only does disservice to the Asian American community; it also incites the jealousy and hatred of other minority groups, because of the implicit portrayal of Asian Americans as superior to other racial and/or cultural minority groups.

b. Aloof and secretive:
Asian American cultures believe in building trust and then, after that, move toward the building of friendship, which takes time. They are not aloof or secretive, nor do they keep to themselves; it's cultural for them to not ask personal questions or reveal too much about themselves unless a firm friendship/trusting relationship is established. Asian Americans do not want to be considered rude by talking too much or out of turn, as it is cultural for them to wait their turn

to talk and only in appropriate situations. When talking to a person in authority or an elderly person, Asian Americans provide short precise answers to the questions asked and will not strike up a conversation without being invited to do so. This is because of the respect factor.

c. Men are sexist and women are subservient:
Asian American men are not sexist, and women are not subservient. It is cultural for both men and women to have roles in the family and adhere to the tradition in order to keep the family unit intact and cohesive. A woman, however highly educated and accomplished she may be, will look to her husband to provide a family's response to an outsider, as that is seen as a man's role. Decisions that affect the family are made only after discussing it with the woman in the household. Although the decision may have been arrived at because of the woman's input, unless the outsider is a woman, the husband will generally speak on behalf of the family.

d. Wizards at math and science:
Asian Americans place a very strong value on education; math and science are considered the core subjects and hence necessary subjects to be mastered. Asian American parents pass on those values to their children. High education is number one priority for most Asian American families; this has led to higher education rates, and hence the myth of being very smart.

e. Cannot speak English:
English is second language for many Asians. Some countries in Asia have English as their official language and hence their citizens can speak, read, and write English very well. The first generation Asian Americans will have an accent, but it does not mean that they do not know English.

f. Outsource jobs to India and China:
Outsourcing is a business practice initiated by corporations keen on increasing profits and the value of their stocks. The majority of the U.S. businesses are owned by shareholders, who are primarily Caucasians. Assigning blame of outsourcing to Asian Americans or their countries of origin is tantamount to blaming the victim. In a global economy, businesses are moving their back office operations (mostly to India and China), and to a highly skilled labor pool in Asia, as they pursue the free market, a core element of democratic societies. Yet biases that exist against Asian Americans spill over into the area of outsourcing. This happened once before in the 1980s, when the U.S. auto industry was not doing well (challenged by Japanese competition). This bias was implicated in the brutal murder of Vincent Chin, a Chinese American, in the Metro Detroit area. Ironically, the defense lawyer argued that the killing occurred due to mistaken identity, as Mr. Chin was mistaken to be of Japanese descent.

(*continued*)

STEREOTYPE NUMBER TWO

People belonging to this group are lazy and don't work and spend their government checks on booze. Their children run wild and are heathens. They are all rich from casinos.

American Indians / First Nation People

a. Lazy and spend government checks on booze:
American Indians, in the state of Michigan, for example, do not get any special money from the government. American Indians with better education and employment have better living conditions. Not all Indians are alcoholics, but some do still have a major problem with substance abuse.

b. Children run wild:
American Indians do have more placid and permissive child-rearing practices, and use a holistic approach to child care.

c. Rich from casinos:
Up until casinos were introduced on the reservations, there were no jobs and people needed to move away from the reservation to gain employment. That is why still today, 87 percent of the American Indians in Michigan live away from the reservation. There are 12 Native American tribes in Michigan, and only one pays out any substantial money from casino profits, so most First Nation People are not getting rich off casino monies.

STEREOTYPE NUMBER THREE

These people are hot-blooded and are not from here; they are undocumented and do not speak the English language. They carry knives and are lazy and welfare dependent.

Latinos

a. Hot-blooded:
Latinos are passionate about life, and many are emotional about their way of speaking and body language. Latinos use their hands a lot as they express themselves.

b. Not from here:
Latinos were living in several southern states before the American Union became a nation. In 1848, the United States took over 40 percent of the Mexican territory. That's why Mexican Americans say: "We did not come to the United States; the United States came to us."

c. Do not speak English:
There are many Latinos who speak both Spanish and English. Many of them live in the Southwest, particularly in certain parts of Texas.

d. Carry knives:
Many Latinos came to Michigan and other parts of the United States to do agricultural or slaughter-type work, and knives are the tools of the trade.

e. Lazy and welfare dependent:
Many Latinos, especially Mexican Americans, do or have done farmwork to survive. They work with their families and do backbreaking work in the hot sun on the farms, so that they do not have to be on welfare. Many in the midwestern and southern states of the United States work in construction, hospitality industries, landscaping sectors, and so forth, so as to not be dependent on welfare. Recently, as rebuilding of New Orleans began, after Hurricane Katrina, many Latinos moved to the area to work in construction.

STEREOTYPE NUMBER FOUR

They own gas stations and supermarkets; most of them are in this country illegally and don't pay taxes. They are terrorists.

Arab Americans

a. Own gas stations and supermarkets:
It is not true that all Arab Americans and Chaldeans own gas stations and supermarkets. The reason for owning neighborhood stores was due to early immigrants' language barrier. Arab Americans are attracted to finance and real estate business whether they are in the United States or anywhere else in the world. They would rather own their businesses than work for others.

b. In the country illegally:
Arab Americans are not illegal immigrants. They are American citizens either by birth or by naturalization. According to U.S. Census data, 82 percent of Arab Americans are U.S. citizens, with about 63 percent born in the United States.

c. Are terrorists:
Arab Americans are not terrorists. For this ethnic group, the media is the biggest enemy; it is biased in reporting on issues concerning Arab Americans in the United States or in the Arab world.

(*continued*)

STEREOTYPE NUMBER FIVE

Members of this group are prone to criminal behavior, are hustlers, are involved in drug usage and trafficking, and are loud, flamboyant, and colorful. They are emotional and undisciplined, and make good dancers, entertainers, and athletes.

African Americans

a. Are criminals:
According to recent data the most prevalent crime in America is drunk driving. The largest percent of offenders are not African Americans. Drug usage at the street level, in the school and homes, is higher in suburban communities than in urban areas. Because of racial profiling done by local and state and federal law enforcement agencies, the direct targeting of blacks and Latinos has resulted in disproportionate numbers of blacks' and Latinos' being sentenced and incarcerated at higher rates.

b. Are flamboyant:
African Americans are high spirited, which is reflected in their creativity in music and art. The most recent example is that of the world's infatuation with the hip-hop culture, which is urban in origin and reflective of young urban blacks.

c. Not disciplined:
The notion of not being disciplined is not supported by accomplishments of noted figures in sports, entertainment, and professions.

ETHNIC PROTOCOLS AND
POSITIVE STYLES OF COMMUNICATION

With some understanding of the importance of getting to know and relating to other cultures, let us focus on diverse communication protocols and positive styles.

Ethnic groups have different methods of communicating. What is acceptable to one group may not be acceptable to another. Hence, it is important that we be sensitive to these differences, and not inadvertently offend the people we are trying to communicate with. The central goal of communication is to build a bridge, so it is imperative that we be sensitive to the unique methods of communicating. This is an exciting time to be practicing social work. Today's workplace spans the entire globe, in terms of both whom we work with and whom we serve. The workplace encompasses people from different non-European countries and non-Western cultures that many of us never before have encountered. Globalization has opened up an entirely new world of opportunity for social work professionals. For example, while the need for courtesy and respect is universal, the ways they are expressed vary.

A SAMPLE OF GLOBAL ETIQUETTE

Gestures

Both protocols and communication styles play a major role in the lives of ethnic groups. Gestures vary from country to country, and can easily be the sources of slight misunderstandings and/or serious offenses. For example, in the Arab world and in Asia, people go ahead and cross their legs, if they so choose. But one needs to be careful that the sole of one's foot isn't facing anyone, as this would be an insult.

Greetings

Every culture has a unique greeting, and that greeting paves the way for successful communication.

An African American may use a firm handshake as a greeting, while Asian Americans may fold their hands and bow their heads. Arab Americans greet with a handshake, and this may be accompanied with a hug and a kiss among friends and relatives. In the Arab culture, some Muslims may choose not shake hands with strangers of the opposite sex, but for religious reasons, as they greet put their right hand across their heart. American Indians use a handshake more in ceremonies rather than in greetings. In the Latino American culture, a handshake and a nod will be appropriate in informal or business settings. If one is with relatives and/or friends, then, a hug and a kiss are a must.

Eye Contact

There are cultural differences in what is considered proper eye contact. African Americans use direct eye contact to show respect, trustworthiness, and sincerity, while looking away and avoiding eye contact may lead to suspicion. For Asian Americans, looking away is considered appropriate, with little or no eye contact. Having indirect eye contact with authority figures or strangers is respectful. In the Latino culture, eye contact varies among Mexicans, Puerto Ricans, and Cubans. For Mexican Americans, a quick glance in the eyes and looking downward is a sign of respect.

Personal Space

Let us discuss ways in which personal space might be a concern in certain cultures. African Americans prefer close proximity in conversations, while in

(continued)

the American Indian culture, it is recommended that you should stand a four-
to five-people space away and touching is considered an invasion of personal
space and privacy. In Asian cultures, proximity of three feet or more for conversation between men and women is important. Close friends and family members
may be allowed to step in personal space. In Arab culture, close contact is acceptable among relatives and friends, keeping in mind that in social gatherings
and religious rituals, traditional Muslim men and women may choose not to be
in the same room or not to sit next to each other. This is due to religious rituals.
In the Latino culture, the norm is close contact with friends and relatives and no
contact and some space with business and professional people.

Body Language

Use of body language varies, just as with greetings and eye contact. So it is
essential to know the importance of body language while communicating,
because each culture differs. For example, Asian Americans may have closed
body language; they may not show their emotions as freely, and may not use
gestures as often while communicating. Do you think that this might differ
from African Americans? African Americans oftentimes are more demonstra-
tive and may speak more assertively. What about personal space? Have you
ever felt that someone was standing too close or too far?
    Is touching acceptable during conversation in all cultures?

Chathapuram and Pravina Ramanathan is helpful. The cases of discrimination
mentioned below, are based on real-life circumstances, experienced by the
Ramanathans in their professional practice. The identities of the individuals are
disguised, but the cases are factually correct.

Case 1

I am an American citizen of Asian Indian national origin. I believe that I
was not promoted because of my national origin. I joined the Water and
Sewerage Department, on January 4, 1994, as an assistant engineer. I became senior assistant chemical engineer in 1996. On March 22, 2000, a new
group was created to support the management on various regulatory and
technical issues. I worked in this group with the manager and developed
various pollution prevention programs to support the industrial pretreat-
ment program. It seemed that my work was appreciated by the management.
On August 27, 2001, four supervisory positions of Environmental Specialist III were created. I interviewed for those positions in September 2001.
One of these positions was for pollution prevention group, for which I was
highly qualified. On December 25, 2001, I heard that that job was offered

to an African American from another department with less seniority and experience.

Questions

What stereotypes would you expect to come into play here?

As a social worker who is providing family therapy, what are the various steps you will undertake?

Case 2

I am a Japanese American woman and I believe that I was subjected to unfair, unprofessional treatment by the health care provider because of my nationality. I needed medical treatment. I went to the specialist XYZ, to get the medical services, and he did not provide me with proper treatment because of his bias toward me, and told me that if I am not satisfied with the care then I should go back to Japan.

Questions

You are a medical social worker, how will you respond to the client who has divulged the above information to you?

What additional information will you need?

What systemwide intervention will you want to initiate?

Case 3

I am Asian and I believe I was subjected to retaliation and ultimately discharged due to my race and national origin. I began working as a center director on February 2, 2004. On November 9, 2005, I was discharged. In a staff meeting the vice president stated that he does not want to hire any more Asians because one is too many. I am the only Asian American working for this day care center. I believe I was discharged because I informed the human resources department about the vice president's comments. Immediately after I reported the incident to human resources, I began receiving write-ups and negative evaluations.

This client has come to you, as his lawyer referred him to you for helping with the stress the client is facing.

Questions

What additional information will you seek from the client ?

What steps will you take to help this client cope with the stress of losing the job?

Case 4

I am a Muslim of Pakistani national origin. I am subjected to harassment because of my religion, national origin, and as retaliation for complaining. I was hired as the director of public services by the ABC City, in July 1998.

I have been subjected to ongoing harassment by the city manager, who is my supervisor, and employees who work for me. I filed a complaint in June 2001. Since then, the harassment has increased. I have been subjected to derogatory name-calling like "wacky Paki" and "sand nigger" and to statements like "Why don't you fire him and send him back to Pakistan?"

Questions

What stereotypes are likely to be operating here?
   What systemic interventions would you consider and why?

ADDITIONAL SCENARIOS OF DISCRIMINATION

Example 1

I am an Indian American who belongs to the Hindu religion. On September 12, 2001, my coworkers surrounded me and asked me whether I was involved in the attacks, and so on. I went to complain about this to my supervisor, who asked me where I stand on the issue of terrorism as a Muslim. I informed him that I am not Muslim; since then I am subjected to ongoing harassment by coworkers' leaving articles, cartoons, and so forth, regarding terrorism, and adding my name to a suspects list and passing the e-mail around. On November 13, 2001, I was suspended after being interrogated by the internal audit department of the company for not doing my work according to the policy. I believe it was because of my perceived religion. My evaluations up to the beginning of September 2001 were excellent.

Example 2

I am a Korean American and I have worked for the respondent for four years as office support in their sales division. Recently I applied for the sales representative job, and though I was most qualified for the job I was denied the promotion, and my supervisor informed me that the division manger was concerned that we may lose customers because of my accent.

Example 3

I am a Chinese American, and I worked for a carpet-cleaning business as office manager. A few months after I started working, the respondent owner started subjecting me to sexual harassment. I refused his advances and dating requests, but the harassment continued. On August 18, 2005, he told me that he will take me out, get me drunk, and have fun with me. When I asked him to stop harassing me he stated, "Why are you getting angry? In your culture aren't women submissive?" I quit my job on August 19, 2005, because I was very stressed and scared to go to work.

Example 4

I am an Indian American; I bought a site to construct a house in the city of XYZ.

I engaged the same contractor that was building several homes in that area. My house had a cathedral ceiling just like my white neighbor's. When I presented my house plan for approval to the city board for variance approval, the board rejected it, saying that the ceiling was too high; my white neighbor was granted variance for the same height of ceiling during the same meeting.

For non–Asian Americans reading these examples, it is clear that there is a gulf of experience for people who live their lives as the "majority" culture and those who have education and confidence but are constantly thrown into the dimension of "other" by the behaviors of their neighbors. For social workers these illustrations illuminate the meaning of increased awareness. Peggy McIntosh has introduced social workers to the concept of the "invisible knapsack" that needs unpacking as people examine their own status and privilege in society and the access it affords them without conscious thought (McIntosh, 1988). In this chapter students are encouraged to consider thinking in relation to culture and to seek stronger understanding of the impact of their behaviors and anticipated social work interventions.

The "Cultural Competency Level" questionnaire in table 5.1 is an example of ways social work students can trace their progress in increasing cultural awareness and competence.

SUMMARY

Green suggests that "becoming culturally skilled is an active process, one that is ongoing, and it is a process that never reaches an end point" (Green, 1999). As discussed in textbox 5.4, stereotyping is deeply ingrained in many societies of the world. This chapter demonstrates that we need a combination of *theoretical* understanding of culture and communication, a deeper *awareness* of our own cultural strengths and baggage and *forms of assessment, plus dialogue* and *opportunities for experience* in cultural groups other than our own

Table 5.1.   Questionnaire to Determine Cultural Competency Level

Please select a number that accurately assesses your level of cultural competency with diverse cultural groups. The scale used is a 5-point scale, where 1 is Not Competent and 5 is Exceedingly Competent.

Cultural Knowledge	Cultural Competency Level		
I can identify my own cultural identity in terms of ancestral heritage and the role my cultural group played in my country's history.	Not Competent 1 2	Competent 3	Exceedingly 4 5
I can identify cultural groups, people by characteristics, attire, language, and demographics.	Not Competent 1 2	Competent 3	Exceedingly 4 5
I can identify cultural stereotypes and cultural uniqueness.	Not Competent 1 2	Competent 3	Exceedingly 4 5
I know some key words in languages other than English to communicate better with ethnic groups.	Not Competent 1 2	Competent 3	Exceedingly 4 5
I am able to communicate and be sensitive to cultural styles and communication, behaviors, and etiquette.	Not Competent 1 2	Competent 3	Exceedingly 4 5
I am familiar with and respectful of different religions and religious practices.	Not Competent 1 2	Competent 3	Exceedingly 4 5
I am familiar with major civil rights cases and events of different cultural groups.	Not Competent 1 2	Competent 3	Exceedingly 4 5

Source: Chathapuram S. Ramanathan.

that can inform social work practice. We also add the dimension of world culture, which asks us to reach for a sense of global citizenship.

According to Oxfam, world citizens put the well-being of all people above one nation; they appreciate that their culture is part of a greater whole; they seek to know people of the earth; they commit themselves to cooperation rather than destruction (Oxfam, 2000). Margaret Wheatley (2000) has introduced us to the "Gaia" concept of an interdependent world in a universe, a world that survives when we value the ecological threads that tie us all together. Wind and water know no boundaries. As we address the universal themes in relation to culture, we end with the seven principles offered by James Leigh (1998) and ask readers to add their own principles. We welcome the ongoing nature of becoming culturally competent and finding the opportunity and catalyst in difference and commonality. Our complex, mobile world and workplace mean this process will never end, as we engage fully in these statements:

1. I accept the fact I have much to learn about others.
2. I have an appreciation of the regional and geographical factors related to people of color and contrasting cultures, how the individual may vary from the generalizations about their group, and how regional groups vary from the total group.
3. I follow the standard that knowledge is obtained from the person in the situation and add to my learning about the situation from the person before generalizing.
4. I have the capacity to form relationships with people from contrasting cultures in professional and social relationships.
5. I can engage in a process characterized by mutual respect and conscious effort to reduce power disparities between myself and persons of different culture or status.
6. I have the ability to obtain culturally relevant information in the work encounter.
7. I have the ability and actively enter into a process of mutual exploration and creative work with people of contrasting cultures and minority status in society. (Leigh, 1998)

CASE EXAMPLE FOR DISCUSSION

In what ways does the U.S. Patriot Act reflect cultural understanding and in what ways does it set up cultural conflict?

The Patriot Act

The Patriot Act was passed into law on October 24, 2001. Just 45 days after the September 11 attacks, with virtually no debate, Congress passed the USA PATRIOT Act. "There are significant flaws in the Patriot Act, flaws that threaten your fundamental freedoms by giving the government the power to access to your medical records, tax records, and information about the books you buy or borrow, without probable cause, and the power to break into your home and conduct secret searches without telling you for weeks, months, or indefinitely" (Webster, 2008)

Text of the Act as summarized by the Department of Justice:

The Patriot Act allows investigators to use the tools that were already available to investigate organized crime and drug trafficking;

The Act allows law enforcement to use surveillance against more crimes of terror. The Act enables investigators to gather information when looking into the full range of terrorism-related crimes, including: chemical-weapons offenses, the use of weapons of mass destruction, killing Americans abroad, and terrorism financing;

The Act allows federal agents to follow sophisticated terrorists trained to evade detection. Because international terrorists are sophisticated and trained to thwart surveillance by rapidly changing locations and communication devices such as cell phones, the Act authorizes agents to seek court permission to use the same techniques in national security investigations to track terrorists;

The Act allows law enforcement to conduct investigations without tipping off terrorists. In some cases if criminals are tipped off too early to an investigation, they might flee, destroy evidence, intimidate or kill witnesses, cut off contact with associates, or take other action to evade arrest. Therefore, federal courts have allowed law enforcement to delay for a limited time when the subject is told that a judicially approved search warrant has been executed. Notice is always provided, but the reasonable delay gives law enforcement time to identify the criminal's associates, eliminate immediate threats to our communities, and coordinate the arrests of multiple individuals without tipping them off beforehand.

The Act allows federal agents to ask a court for an order to obtain business records in national security terrorism cases. Examining business records often provides the key that investigators are looking for to solve a wide range of crimes. Investigators might seek select records from hardware stores or chemical plants, for example, to find out who bought materials to make a bomb, or bank records to see who's sending money to terrorists. Law enforcement authorities have always been able to obtain business records in criminal cases through grand jury subpoenas, and continue to do so in national security cases where appropriate. These records were sought in criminal cases such as the investigation of the Zodiac gunman, where police suspected the gunman was inspired by a Scottish occult poet, and wanted to learn who had checked the poet's books out of the library. In national security cases where use of the grand jury process was not appropriate, investigators previously had limited tools at their disposal to obtain certain business records. Under the Patriot Act, the government can now ask a federal court (the Foreign Intelligence Surveillance Court), if needed to aid an investigation, to order production of the same type of records available through grand jury subpoenas. This federal court, however, can issue these orders only after the government demonstrates the records concerned are sought for an authorized investigation to obtain foreign intelligence information not concerning a U.S. person or to protect against international terrorism or clandestine intelligence activities, provided that such investigation of a U.S. person is not conducted solely on the basis of activities protected by the First Amendment.

[The Act also allows federal agents to ask a court for an order to obtain business records in national security terrorism cases; ACLU, 2003.]

The Patriot Act facilitated information sharing and cooperation among government agencies so that they can better "connect the dots." The Act removed the major legal barriers that prevented the law enforcement, intelligence, and national defense communities from talking and coordinating their work to protect the American people and our national security. Now police officers, FBI agents, federal prosecutors, and intelligence officials can protect communities by "connecting the dots" to uncover terrorist plots before they are completed.

The Patriot Act updated the law to reflect new technologies and new threats and it allows law enforcement officials to obtain a search warrant anywhere a terrorist-related activity occurred. Before the Patriot Act, law enforcement personnel were required to obtain a search warrant in the district where they intended to conduct a search. However, modern terrorism investigations often span a number of districts, and officers therefore had to obtain multiple warrants in multiple jurisdictions, creating unnecessary delays. The Act provides that warrants can be obtained in any district in which terrorism-related activities occurred, regardless of where they will be executed. This provision does not change the standards governing the availability of a search warrant, but streamlines the search-warrant process.

The Patriot Act increased the penalties for those who commit terrorist crimes. Americans are threatened as much by the terrorist who pays for a bomb as by the one who pushes the button. That's why the Patriot Act imposed tough new penalties on those who commit and support terrorist operations, both at home and abroad. In particular, the Act:

- Prohibits the harboring of terrorists. The Act created a new offense that prohibits knowingly harboring persons who have committed or are about to commit a variety of terrorist offenses, such as: destruction of aircraft; use of nuclear, chemical, or biological weapons; use of weapons of mass destruction; bombing of government property; sabotage of nuclear facilities; and aircraft piracy.
- Enhanced the inadequate maximum penalties for various crimes likely to be committed by terrorists: including arson, destruction of energy facilities, material support to terrorists and terrorist organizations, and destruction of national-defense materials.
- Enhanced a number of conspiracy penalties, including for arson, killings in federal facilities, attacking communications systems, material support to terrorists, sabotage of nuclear facilities, and interference with flight crew members.
- Punishes terrorist attacks on mass transit systems.
- Punishes bioterrorists.
- Eliminates the statutes of limitations for certain terrorism crimes and lengthens them for other terrorist crimes. (Department of Justice, n.d.)

As Herman (2003) discusses, the USA Patriot Act allows surveillance of U.S. citizens even where there is no probable cause and minimal judicial involvement. For example, "roving wiretaps" extends the powers under Title III. The Department of Justice logic is that revision of existing wiretap law was necessary to keep up with modern technology in order to allow a roving wiretap that would allow conversations to be intercepted even if the person carried a cell phone, or moved from phone to phone. The authority to order a roving wiretap existed under Title III, for investigations where probable cause has been demonstrated. (The Supreme Court has not decided as to if this blanket permission to intercept a person's conversations on any telephone is a revision of a notion that a telephone is in a physical place, or a violation of the Fourth Amendment's requirement that a warrant describe a specific place to be searched.) Thus, the USA Patriot Act secretly extends this authorization of roving wiretapping to intelligence wiretaps, which is not based on probable cause. Therefore, this kind of authorization may be nationwide and the consequence of this authorization is such that if the monitored target uses someone else's home telephone other users of that telephone will automatically become subjects of continuing surveillance.

Interestingly, Herman continues, the government already had authority to order a telephone company to turn over a list of the numbers being dialed to and from a particular telephone. (This standard is less than probable cause standard.) A judge has to grant the order if the government certifies that the information sought is "relevant to an ongoing criminal investigation," even though the judge does not agree with the government's conclusion. Similarly, under this Act the government can now access lists of e-mails, both the mails that have been sent and received, as well as a list of the websites visited on a particular computer. Herman argues that in the case of the telephone example, "getting a 'pen register,' with its list of telephone numbers to and from which calls were made on a particular phone, offered no opportunity to hear the contents of those conversations. In the computer context, the information about e-mail addresses and websites evidently travels with its content. The Department of Justice promises to separate the two, and not pry into content. There seems to be no way of supervising whether this promise is kept. In addition, it seems that if a target uses a computer in a cyber café or the public library to check e-mail or visit a website, surveillance of that computer may simply continue, giving the government access to the e-mail and Internet activities of a multitude of nontargets" (Herman, 2003).

According to Herman the impact of this Act is immense on immigration. The attorney general of the United States has been empowered by the USA Patriot Act to detain and/or deport noncitizens with minimal or no judicial consideration. The Attorney General can justify his actions by merely saying that he has reasonable grounds to believe that these noncitizens endanger national security.

The Patriot Act also authorizes the attorney general and secretary of state to designate domestic groups as terrorist organizations, and the noncitizens belonging to these groups can be deported. Furthermore, the attorney general announced that he intends to eavesdrop on inmates' attorney-client conversations and announced his plans to have state and local law enforcement officials cooperate in questioning 5,000 people, whose selection appears to have been based on their ethnicity or religion. The attorney general is flexing his newly acquired power to detain immigrants, and to contract the information available under the Freedom of Information Act.

The most controversial section of the Act stems from Section 215. Section 215 allows FBI agents to obtain a warrant from a secret federal court for library or bookstore records of anyone connected to an investigation of international terrorism or spying. On its face, the section does not even refer to "libraries" but rather to business records and other tangible items in general. In summary, these antiterrorist initiatives have major consequences for individuals, societies, and nations all over the world. Consequently, human rights and civil rights are compromised (especially in the United States for people of Middle Eastern and South Asian origin), in the interest of national security, even in democracies.

STUDENT ASSIGNMENTS

Questions for class discussions based on textbox 5.4.

1. What is the impact of stereotyping?
2. What effects do these stereotypes have on members of these cultural groups?
3. How do we challenge prejudice and stereotyping?
4. What is an appropriate response to someone who makes such a stereotyping comment? What has worked for you?
5. Are there ways that we can prevent stereotyping?
6. Do we need to systematically explore these questions and develop an individual plan of action?
7. How do changes in the economic climate play a role in stereotyping and resulting discrimination and hate crimes?
8. Is touching acceptable in conversations in all cultures?

Chapter Six

Migration and the Borders That Divide Us

Everywhere immigrants have enriched and strengthened the fabric of American life.

—John F. Kennedy

In this chapter two countries, the United States and India, are used as case studies in the discussion of migration, with additional reference to global statistics on the movement of labor and refugees.

Although this chapter's focus is on the migration of people across national boundaries, and its resulting consequences, we acknowledge the fact that migration within nation-states has its own set of consequences. For instance whether it is the economic motive that propels people to move from Bihar (a state in the Indian Union) to Assam (another state in the Indian Union), or the post-hurricane movement of people for safety, and survival, from the state of Louisiana to Houston, Texas (in the United States), conflicts do occur between the established locals and the new arrivals.

Understanding migration, its impact on families, and its relationship to social and economic development is central to social work assessment and practice. Returning to the concept set out in chapter 1, this part of our "journey through the globe" addresses the "south" in our concept map (see figure 8.1), which refers to the elements of our understanding and skills for inclusive practice with mobile populations. The impact of migration on local communities is also a reflection of cultural awareness and community attitudes to difference, discussed in chapter 5. Although migration has been occurring since time immemorial in the pursuit of sustenance, in this period of our history it has become most contentious and threatens our ability to build peaceful coexistence.

IMMIGRATION ISSUES: UNITED STATES

The United States, known as a land of immigrants, has a long history of immigration laws. The Immigration and Nationality Act (INA) of 1952, with some changes, continues to be the basic immigration law of the country. The most significant amendment to the INA, enacted in 1965, abolished the natural origin provisions and established a new quota system. For INA purposes, an "alien" is any person who is not a citizen or a national of the United States. There are different categories of aliens: resident and nonresident, immigrant and nonimmigrant, documented and undocumented ("illegal").

The U.S. Congress has total and complete authority over immigration. The power of the president is limited to policies on refugees. Unless the issue concerns the rights of aliens to constitutional protections, the courts have rarely intruded. The need to curb illegal immigration prompted Congress to enact the Immigration Reform and Control Act (IRCA) of 1986. The IRCA toughened criminal sanctions for employers who hire illegal aliens, denied illegal aliens federally funded welfare benefits, and legitimized some aliens through an amnesty program. The Immigration Marriage Fraud Amendments of 1986 sought to limit the practice of marrying to obtain citizenship.

The goals of limiting illegal access in immigration policies are achieved by granting or denying visas. There are two types of visas: immigrant and nonimmigrant. Nonimmigrant visas are primarily issued to tourists and temporary business visitors. Nonimmigrant visas are divided into 18 main categories. Only a few categories of nonimmigrant visas allow their holders to work in the United States. Immigrant visas permit their holders to stay in the United States permanently and ultimately to apply for citizenship. An alien who has an immigrant visa is permitted to work in the United States. Congress limits the overall number of immigrant visas, and many immigrant visas are also subject to per-country caps.

SALIENT ISSUES IMPACTING IMMIGRATION

Since 2001 in the United States, the challenges of terrorism have been at the forefront of politics and even earlier in those parts of the world struggling with terrorist acts, including Jakarta, Indonesia; Iraq; Sri Lanka; Bali; London; Mumbai; and New Delhi. Refugees and migration are the direct consequences of war, terrorism, and conflict. Social workers must pay adequate attention to the processes of migration, both voluntary (often for economic reasons) and involuntary as refugees of conflict. Fariyal Ross-Sheriff gave a vivid account of her research with women from Afghanistan who get caught up in a seemingly endless cycle. These mothers pick up their children and leave for the safety of Pakistan; when the situation seems calmer they return to Afghanistan to the debris and shock of reintegration, then leave again when hostilities are renewed (Ross-Sheriff, 2004).

In contemporary times oppressed people around the globe struggle to meet basic needs for food, clothing, shelter, and emotional and economic security. From a social work paradigm of *person in environment* transactions, this is the human challenge to transact with their environment regardless of political borders. According to Rappaport (1995) and others, migrants experience educational, political, and economic exclusion because of their demographic characteristics, rather than their individual characteristics. This is yet another example of why we need to address "group rights" when we address "human rights" issues. In this context, consider Mahatma Gandhi's words: "If I could produce all my country's wants by means of 30,000 people instead of 30 million, I should not mind it provided that the 30 million are not rendered idle and unemployed" (cited in Rao, 1982). Mahatma Gandhi preferred people to work locally, within their own local and natural resources, than be put at risk through unemployment and migration for work.

In this chapter migration is addressed from the personal or *micro* to the global or *macro* levels of interaction, beginning with an overview of some of the current data and then moving to (1) the current reality in terms of global migration, (2) the documented experience of migrants; (3) the role of local agencies, (4) the political role of nation-states in relation to the UN, (5) the global level of the UN and its role, and (6) a review of the task of social workers as they address discrimination and exclusion in the communities they serve locally in the larger, global context of cooperation with neighboring countries and regions, learning from one another in their approach and practice.

The population of the world is more mobile than at any documented time in history. The U.S. Census Bureau reports that "one in five Americans speaks a language other than English at home . . . and 11.9 million people live in linguistically isolated homes," meaning nobody in the home 14 or older knows English very well, up 54 percent from 1990 (U.S. Bureau of the Census, 2003). In India, Tamil refugees seek refuge on the subcontinent of India from the continuing strife in Sri Lanka. The 2007 riots of socially excluded Africans in France were compelling to watch unfold considering that this is a country that experienced revolution in search of equality and human dignity.

In terms of migration, the flow of people seeking safer lives may be between countries or within countries, and especially in relation to rural and urban opportunities. The pressure of rural to urban migration spurred the development of nongovernmental organizations (NGOs) in India, even before the NGO movement became popular globally. We have argued elsewhere in this book that some of the key corporate leaders in India have systematically focused on the need for societal development as an integral part of advancement of technology and growth of corporations. In this vein, the author Ramanathan in his case study of Larsen and Toubro (see textbox 1.3) highlights the fact that

India is going through rapid developments, with the information technology explosion confined primarily to the educated urban class.

THE CURRENT REALITY IN TERMS OF MIGRATION: CASE STUDY INDIA

According to Mr. Ramalingam, board member of ECOMWELL, a registered nongovernmental organization in the southern state of Tamil Nadu, the intellectual capital created by the visionaries and political leaders of a free India has enabled India to forge a place at the top in the information age with software exports.

India is a nation of nearly 634,321 villages (Census of India, 2001). The state of Tamil Nadu has a population of over 63 million, with nearly 17,000 villages (Census of India, 2001). Mr. Ramalingam, after his retirement as the chief engineer of the Madhya Pradesh Electricity Board, has been an active volunteer through NGOs. While he was chief engineer of Madhya Pradesh, he exercised his leadership in moving Madhya Pradesh toward achieving 100 percent rural electrification (Ramanathan, May 2007). Madhya Pradesh is known as the "heart of India" both because of its location in the center of the country and because it is the home to the cultural heritage of Hindhuism, Buddhism, Jainism, and Islam. The population of Madhya Pradesh is over 61 million, with over 55,000 villages (Census of India, 2001).

Ramalingam has dedicated himself to calling on India's president Abdul Kalam to implement a strategy called Providing Urban Amenities in Rural Areas (PURA). Ramalingam asserts that until the changes are evenly spread and equitably distributed especially in rural areas, one cannot call it "development." As a consequence of the information technology explosion, various state governments in India end up giving a large portion of their land to urbanization. As a consequence there is large-scale migration of the rural population, with their children, to urban slums in search of livelihood. One consequence of this rural to urban migration is the proliferation of illiteracy; migrant children grow up as street children because their families cannot afford schooling. Ramalingam passionately argues that the time has come to stop and even reverse this trend of urban migration.

The National Rural Employment Guarantee Act (NREG Act) is a pro-people policy, enacted in April of 2005, which invested in economically backward districts from 2006 to 2007 with an allotment of Rs.16,000 Crore (about 400 million U.S. dollars).

Andhra Pradesh is a state in southern India with a population of approximately 77 million, and 28,000 villages (Census of India, 2001). In a small block of Palamaner in the Chittoor District of Andhra Pradesh, the NREG Act has provided employment to 4,063 Job Card holders (families) and paid Rs. 107.14 lakhs (250,000 U.S. dollars) as wages, deposited into their savings accounts in post offices or banks. No cash was disbursed, so as to eliminate misappropriation. In addition, it has provided essential food (rice, lentils, beans, and oil) to all these families as an interest-free credit and enabled them to repay it in monthly installments. This has limited the migration flow to urban areas to those who do not want to perform manual labor. The NREG Act is an enabling act and pays a minimum wage to men and women equally (Ramanathan, May 2007).

The Policy on Opening Air Waves as a public property in February 2007 has given birth to community radio (CR), which serves as a means to access information, and to propagate knowledge, guiding the rural people in matters of health, disease outbreaks, and maternity care, and offering open-air classes for adults, which impart training in handicrafts and handweaving, setting up small enterprises, creating opportunities for entertainment by their own innovations and artists, and so forth. The farmers can be guided on type of crops; the availability of seeds; watering required for "More Crop per Drop," or water conservation; the fertilizers required for the crop; any pesticides required; and so forth. The sky is the limit. What cannot be aired is specified in the license. ECOMWELL proposed setting up a pilot CR at Kotur in the Palamaner block in the Chittoor District of Andhra Pradesh. The CR would be run and operated by the people themselves. The initial cost of setting up the CR would be handed over to those volunteering from the village to operate and run the CR, and would be about Rs.10 lakhs (about 20,000 U.S. dollars). The NGO, ECOMWELL was applying for the license on behalf of the community, and funding the project all by private donation.

In the context of economic development schemes, community radio could help immensely. Every morning at an appointed time, the places at which work is available, and the number of adults (daily wage agricultural labor) required can be announced, instead of villagers' walking several miles only to find out that more workers showed up than were required, and that those who were not hired will have to walk back without an opportunity to earn. In addition, the names of all those who were marked present on the previous day in the muster roll can also be announced to avoid any complaint and to be transparent with regard to employment in government-funded projects. This can help investigation of complaints at any later date by public expenditure "watchers." Records of all broadcasts were to be preserved for six months before being sent to a library (Ramanathan, June 2007).

We expect that the readers of this book will be very familiar with the thirty-fifth U.S. president John F. Kennedy's appeal to U.S. citizens: "Ask not what your country can do for you, ask what you can do for your country." Similarly, at the NASSCOM (National Association of Software and Service Companies) 2007 India Leadership Forum on February 7, 2007, in Mumbai,

India, Nobel Laureate Amartya Sen voiced a powerful sentiment intended to conscientize computer software professionals. Professor Sen said,

> Given what the country has done for Indian information technology, it is not silly to ask: what specially can the industry do for India? This seems to me to be right, but I would also like to emphasize that historical reciprocity is not the only—perhaps not even the most important—reason for being interested in social obligations of the industry. Many considerations arise there.—Negligence of the suffering of others is sustainable, given human interest in justice and equity, only if we know little about their suffering. More information in itself goes a long way to breaking that chain of apathy and indifference.—Can there be a group initiative in any of these fields? (2007)

We now review the task of social workers as they address discrimination and exclusion in the communities they serve locally in the larger, global context of cooperation with neighboring states and regions learning from one another in their approach and practice. Similarly, we can encourage reciprocity and cooperation between and among social workers globally, in our efforts to reach common ground and foster a common human condition that can help us to move toward a just world.

In terms of contemporary migration the persistent structural issues are the following: What is prompting people to move? How are they surviving the journey? How are they being received after they move? All of these questions are the domain of social work. Recently the increase in human trafficking from Mexico to the United States, and from Eastern to Western Europe, has raised the alarm in terms of treatment of minors left alone when their abductors are apprehended. The KLJUC organization in Ljubljana, Slovenia, has recently included social workers in their dialogue and innovative practices, which include a "Dictionario" that appears to be a working dictionary but actually contains a central section listing emergency and help resources, plus statements that the victims are not alone.

The United Nations Declaration on Human Rights affirms the right of people to move; everywhere however, there are politically drawn geographical boundaries. Texas is a particularly harsh arena, where frequently "immigrants are found dead" (Yardley, 2002). Migrants to the United States are a major resource for Mexico. After oil, money sent back by laborers in the United States is the second largest source of income; however, Mexico is ambivalent at best in terms of valuing this rich source of income. In Europe, from Spain to Scandinavia, there is a political leaning to the right as politicians play on anticrime, anti-immigrant sentiments—a phenomenon that is being described as neofascist. Concerns about outsourcing, domestic and international issues, employment, and the economy are addressed in the next section in terms of their impact on social work.

India wants the United Nations to focus on promoting teamwork among nations to maximize the benefits of international migration while reducing its negative effects. In the debate on "globalization and interdependence," we concur with Indian delegate Anil Basu's assertion that we need to recognize the inevitability of international migration (Basu, 2006). The increased demand for specialists in developed countries can be matched by their availability in developing countries; at the same time developed countries also need to be more receptive to enhanced market access. As Basu points out, the World Bank's *Global Economic Prospects 2006* report notes that a rise in migration from developing countries raises incomes of natives in high-income countries. With regard to immigration in a global economy, in spite of the significant contributions that are made by the immigrants, immigrant populations face tremendous prejudice in North America and Europe. At the same time, immigrants with lower levels of skills undertake their migrant journeys in very inhumane conditions, and many of them die in their journey toward economic opportunities. For instance, a local paper in 2002 records:

In Houston, Texas, two men were charged with murder this early morning in the deaths of two undocumented immigrants who were found dead inside a truck after a sweltering 12-hour ride that immigration officials said left at least 13 others hospitalized on a day when temperatures neared triple digits.

Immigration officials said up to 40 people, including at least 5 children, were crammed into a truck loaded with medical supplies, leaving little room. The truck grew so hot on the trip from the Mexican border to the Dallas area that the people inside tried to cut a hole in the roof but failed. Each passenger had paid $1,500 to $2,000. "For all intents and purposes, there was no ventilation," commented Lynn Ligon, a spokesman with the Dallas office of the Immigration and Naturalization Service. "In an air-conditioned car, it would be a long drive. In a non air-conditioned, crowded, smelly 18-wheeler with no water, you can imagine how unbearable it would be." The drivers, Troy Dock, 30, and Jason Sprague, 27, were each charged with one count of murder. The deaths are a reminder of the risks that people south of the border often take to reach the United States. Since 1998, more than 1,300 immigrants have died trying to cross the border, often on foot. Most of them have been found collapsed in the baking deserts near the Rio Grande. Thirty-three people have died this year. Trucks driven by people known as coyotes are often used to transport undocumented immigrants directly from the border to large cities, where the demand for cheap labor is high. (Yardley, 2002)

THE DOCUMENTED EXPERIENCE OF MIGRANTS

Globally, anti-immigrant mentality and treatment take many forms. The anti-immigrant sentiments and treatments have differential effects on those immigrants with low levels of skill sets, and those with higher levels of skill sets. First, legislative initiatives (as seen in Britain's Highly Skilled Migrants Program) restrict free movement of workers from an economically challenged region that has a labor pool with high levels of skill sets (like from the subcontinent of India), which lays greater emphasis on earnings.

According to a 2006 Bank of England report, one in five of the immigrants in the UK was born in the European Union, one in five from the Indian subcontinent, and one in four was born in Africa or the Middle East. The report points out that nearly half the immigrants with university degrees are likely to work in hotels and restaurants. Although some of them, according to the report, get better jobs, the numbers are not encouraging, as the majority continue to work in elementary occupations (*Deccan Herald*, January 30, 2007). It is disheartening that these discriminatory practices occur. Even when the immigrants are more educated than their British-born counterparts, they are more likely to be working in low-skilled jobs (*Deccan Herald*, December 11, 2006).

Anti-immigrant sentiments are also seen in educational admission policies in the United States of America that hold students of Asian descent to higher admission requirements, as compared to Caucasian, African American, and Hispanic American students. The Asian-descent students who are held to these standards also include Asian American students (Golden, 2006).

People with lower levels of skills and/or people engaged in manual labor who want to migrate to economically advanced countries are often exploited by miscreants, who charge huge sums of money for bringing them across the borders, to the countries in the European Union, Israel, and/or the United States, Canada, and so forth. In 2006, 12 youths from Punjab, duped by travel agents on the pretext of sending them to Germany, Spain, and other countries, were trapped in the jungles of Algeria for more than a year and were subjected to atrocities by residents of the area. Some Sikh youths in the group also alleged that they were forced to cut their hair and were beaten up by locals when they protested. The youths also mentioned that they were left with no other option but to go begging. Narrating a similar tale, Jagjit Singh, father of Khushwant Singh from the state of Punjab in India, said a travel agent had promised them that Khushwant would get a highly paid job in France. "After spending Rs 9 lakh (equivalent to U.S. $20,000), Khushwant took a flight to France, but even after nineteen months he is yet to reach the country. The families state that they have suffered financial loss, and now this news that his hair was forcibly cut has shocked them," according to Jagjit Singh. Men belonging to the Sikh religious background, for religious reasons, do not cut their hair (Sharma, P., 2006).

Popular backlash against open borders leads to discrimination (Erlanger, 2002) at a time when migration is primarily a product of safety to avoid war zones plus access to social and economic opportunity.

Since 2008, people of Asian Indian origin have increasingly become targets of racist behaviors including acts of violence perpetrated against both Asian Indian immigrants and students who have come to Australia to pursue higher education. In fact, Australia's former defense force chief, General Peter Cosgrove, is asking his country to confront racism, and has stated that the attacks against Indians is a "major problem," and due to the nature of these attacks, in Melbourne, Australia, concluded that they were racially motivated (Cosgrove, 2010).

Managing the movement of people means being aware of the resource base. Social workers are intimately connected with issues of family poverty and unemployment. Asking the larger questions of why people are displaced or uprooting themselves leads to a more preventive and creative approach to social work than the purely reactive stance of dealing only with the end result of economic disruption, namely, poverty. Many studies have investigated the different effects of international migration on income inequality, and the ultimate impact on family relationships when there is a lack of income (Ramaswami, 1968; Rivera-Batiz, 1982). According to the literature, the focus on personal income levels in host countries is partly because of the underlying assumption that migration is a personal rather than family-based decision (Stark and Bloom, 1985). Immigrants to Britain may be better educated than some of their British-born counterparts, but are more likely to be working in low-skilled jobs. According to the report from the Bank of England cited above, the proportion of foreign-born residents aged between 16 and 64 in Britain rose from 8 percent in 1995, to 11 percent in 2005. Around a fifth of migrants were born within the European Union, while a further one-fifth were from the Indian subcontinent, and a quarter were from Africa or the Middle East. Of those who had immigrated within the past two years, nearly half—45 percent—arrived with a university degree, compared to just 17 percent of British workers. The report, however, said that despite those higher education levels among immigrants, they were still more likely to be working in hotels or restaurants. The Bank of England said that while some might eventually use their qualifications to get better jobs, and others could return to their homelands, the overall picture was unclear. Thus, the new immigrants were more educated than both previous waves of immigrants and those born in the UK, but they were more likely to be working in elementary occupations, the report said (*Deccan Herald*, December 11, 2006).

Some politicians make statements that could have an unintended consequence of negative impact by reducing the size of a talented and highly skilled labor force, as well inciting bias in the general population. Therefore, the consequences could be both in terms of immigrants returning back to their countries of origin, as well as those who have decided to stay in the United States facing prejudiced and discriminatory behavior patterns exhibited toward them by the general population. For example, as the debate over H-1B workers (nonimmigrant visas to work in the United States) and skilled immigrants intensifies, the United States will no longer be the only land of opportunity. These immigrants, who fueled innovation and economic growth, now have options elsewhere. Immigrants are returning home in greater numbers. According to Professor Wadhwa of Harvard Business School, new research documents the fact that the immigrants are returning to enjoy a better quality of life, better career prospects, and the comfort of being close to family and friends (Wadhwa, 2009). World-renowned economist Jagdish Bhagwati (professor, Columbia University) has argued that the provision to restrict hiring of H-1B visa holders would deprive the United States of the best global talent. Others, like the deputy chairman of the Planning Commission of the government of India, view these policies as the beginning of irreversible protectionism (Ahluwalia, 2009).

U.S. Senator Sanders (from Vermont) argues: "While we are suffering through the worst economic crisis since the Great Depression, the very least we can do is to make sure that banks receiving a taxpayer bailout are not allowed to import cheaper labor from overseas while they are throwing American workers out on the street" (*Express India*, 2009).

Workers of Indian origin account for a majority of those with H-1B visas, which are issued to nonimmigrant skilled workers for up to six years. So there is apprehension in the Asian American community in general, and among Indian Americans in particular, that this prejudice in the labor market will contribute to discrimination toward Indian Americans and permanent residents of Indian origin, because of their unique sounding names that do not have a Judeo-Christian flavor. This kind of bias is more of a concern in light of a comment made by a Texas legislator. In a puzzling move, a Texas lawmaker Brown (although she apologized later due to demands from the Asian American community), while she insisted it wasn't about race, said in House testimony that "Asian Americans should change their names to ones that are easier for Americans to deal with. Can't you see that this is something that would make it a lot easier for you and the people who are poll workers if you could adopt a name just for identification purposes that's easier for Americans to deal with?" (Byrne, 2009).

Yet immigrants and naturalized citizens and racial minorities continue to be targets of violence, and in turn contribute to continued violence. For example, in Oldham in the UK, race-based rioting left at least 20 people hurt in the country's worst outbreak of racial violence in years. The clashes followed an attack by a gang of white youths on a home in a neighborhood whose population comes largely from the Indian subcontinent (Associated Press, 2001). These experiences leave the racial minorities to really wonder why the society is conveying that they do not belong. Another issue that makes immigrants question where they belong is the sudden changes in immigration policies. For example, in the United States of America, the work- or employment-based visa program (H-1B), supported and championed by high-tech superstars like Bill Gates, Andy Grove, and Scott McNealy, has become a lightning rod of controversy over immigration policy. Significant numbers of computer scientists and programmers moved to the United States for employment reasons, to fill the increased numbers of available jobs to address the anticipated problems pertaining to Y2K. At that time nearly half a million of these immigrants were caught up in the labyrinth of immigration laws, dynamics of organized labor and high-tech industries, and congressional politics, all in order to fulfill the dream of becoming permanent residents of the United States of America. Although they felt pretty much at home working with Java computer programs or managing C++ projects that American businesses needed, they were not sure which end of the earth they could call home—United States or India (Wayne, 2001). These are some of the challenges of contemporary immigrants who are playing by the immigration law.

On the other hand, consider immigrants of yesteryears. Like people of other ethnicities, the Chinese immigrated to the United States for better lives. Before 1900, their work included farming, mining, and building railroads. Men sent money home to their families in China. But American laborers resented the Chinese because the latter were willing to work for cheap wages. Americans accused the Chinese of monopolizing jobs. Stiff immigration laws were passed. Many Chinese immigrants were forced to prove they had a husband or father who was a U.S. citizen or be deported. From 1910 to 1940, Chinese immigrants were detained and interrogated at Angel Island immigration station in San Francisco Bay. U.S. officials hoped to deport as many as possible by asking obscure questions about Chinese villages and family histories that immigrants would have trouble answering correctly. Men and women were housed separately. Detainees spent much of their time in the barracks, languishing between interrogations. The immigrants expressed their fears and frustrations through messages and poems written or carved into barrack walls. Some poems are still visible at the museum today. Immigrants were detained weeks, months, sometimes even years. Historically, earlier immigration policy such as the so-called Chinese Exclusion Act prohibited Asian people from immigrating to the United States; this included people of Asian Indian origins in addition to Chinese. Eventually this law was repealed.

It is evident that human migration is a natural human condition.

While the American dream may not become a reality for everyone who settles in the United States, it continues to act as a powerful attraction for people who are unable to find freedom or prosperity at home (UNHCR, 1991). For over 200 years, the United States of America has been built on the strength of immigrants, who have chosen to arrive here seeking refuge from socio-political, religious, and economic persecutions, experienced in their countries of origin. From the new settlers, to almost the end of the 19th century, the majority of immigrants had one unifying characteristic, i.e., they came from the United Kingdom, and continental Europe. Their national and ethnic differences were superseded by their common "Caucasian race." The experiences of other groups of immigrants inclusive of the Indo Americans were quite different. (Mayadas, Ramanathan, and Suarez, 1999)

Historically, according to Chandrasekhar (1982), the first recorded presence of an Asian Indian in the United States of America was in Salem, Massachusetts, in 1790. Yet only in the latter part of the nineteenth century did Asian Indians start immigrating in large numbers. Indian immigrants came mostly from the Punjab, and settled in California. Most of these immigrants were agricultural workers. At that time, only male immigrants were allowed into this country, and bringing spouses and/or family was prohibited. Hence, most remained single or married Mexican women (Hart, 1998).

Asian Indians were denied citizenship between 1923 and 1946. After the passage of the Immigration Act of 1946, immigrants from the Indian subcontinent were able to immigrate legally to the United States. However, there was an annual quota of 100 immigrants. Presently, Asian Indians are the fastest growing immigrant group in the United States. The Asian Indian population increased dramatically after the passage of the Immigration and Naturalization Act of 1965, and after the immigration quota of 100 people was abolished. The Asian Indians who immigrated to the United States can be grouped over time as Punjabi farmers; scholars who came as graduate students and subsequently pursued economic opportunities in the United States; professionals in science, medicine, nursing, engineering, and other fields; Asian Indian refugees from Uganda; Caribbean Island Indians (Balgopal, 1997); and computer software engineers inclusive of the Y2K immigrants (software engineers who immigrated to address computer problems due to the turning over to the year 2000). In spite of their long residence in the United States of America, and significant numbers, Indo-Americans remain peripheral in mainstream discussions of American culture, racial discourse, immigration experiences, and history. They are viewed as a marginal minority, and are also marginalized (Hess, 1976). Twenty-five years after Hess's work, the situation, unfortunately, was not very different. The recent changes in the demography of Indo-Americans, however, provided new perspectives and opportunities. According to the 2000 Census, Indo-Americans form the third largest Asian American group.

In 1967, there were 199 million people in the United States, and in 2007 well over 300 million people, making it the third most populous nation in the world with China having 1.3 billion, and India having 1.1 billion people. It is startling that in the most powerful democracy, 46 million Americans have no health insurance. Also, 48 percent of middle-income people in the

United States had no health insurance in 2005 (Gupta, 2006). Nevertheless, there is more anger toward the immigrants and undocumented persons for the economic challenges as opposed to holding the government accountable in order to address systemic issues. This is a clear indication that social work educators, practitioners, and social work students must work together to have a cumulative impact as advocates on behalf of the vulnerable population that do not have health insurance.

In the United States of America, as highlighted in chapter 5, as jobs are outsourced by corporations, there is rampant prejudice against people of Asian Indian descent. For example, an Indian American technology worker has filed a suit in a federal court in Texas against a U.S. firm alleging daily incidents of racial harassment and discrimination because the company outsourced work to India. The lawsuit by Neelima Tirumalasetti, a senior IT analyst in quality assurance, says that after her company Caremark announced in December 2003 that it would be outsourcing work to IBM India, she became the target of widespread anti-Indian harassment (Rediff India Abroad, 2005). Her coworkers repeatedly called her "brown-skinned b****," "dirty Indian," and other insults, accused her of coming to the United States to take their jobs, mocked her accent in team meetings, and excluded her work projects. Hoping for some relief, Neelima, who is a U.S. citizen, reported the harassment to her manager, her manager's direct supervisor, human resources, two vice presidents, and even Caremark's ethics hotline. But the reports made matters worse, she says. Caremark removed her team-leader responsibilities on a large project, isolated her from prime work assignments, began auditing her work daily, denied her pay, and blocked her access to leave.

THE ROLE OF LOCAL AGENCIES, EMPHASIS ON MENTAL HEALTH

There are key skills that social workers use when working with people who have migrated or who are refugees. Voluntary migration may mean that families and individuals have maintained a sense of control and choice over their lives; however, they still have to negotiate new environments, different languages or dialects, new social norms, and, as discussed in chapter 5, discrimination often based in lack of knowledge and fear in the receiving community. For refugees the situation is often even more complex. At Southside Family Nurturing Center in Minneapolis, staff have worked with families who are reluctant to speak of their experiences and who display the symptoms of post-traumatic stress. In one instance, a four-year-old child had dangerously low weight and was given the label "failure to thrive." Doctors and social workers viewed this child's inability to accept nutrition as a direct result of the trauma and tension of the family journey from camp to camp and eventually to the relative safety of the strange U.S. city. In a poignant essay explaining the circumstances of his migration as a child and "boat person" from Vietnam and eventually to the United States, Phu Tai Phan described the dislocation and complex feelings of loss and depression that both accompany the leaving of family and known places and then later the revisiting and reconnecting (Phan, 1994).

Often people in the United States are caught up in the pressure of too many tasks and not enough time to accomplish them. Recently a student of one of the authors of this book interviewed women settling in the United States from Somalia. One of the respondents commented that one of numerous shocks she experienced on arrival in Minnesota from Somalia was the emphasis on speed, particularly when eating. A local pizza parlor advertises "Eat in 15 minutes or free slice" and "All you can eat in an hour." The woman commented, "In Somalia, time is always coming to us, it is not lost or missed, it is coming" (Maria, 2003).

For social workers there are many approaches to working with people in distress; however there are some key and essential elements to working with migrants and refugees:

- Make time to hear the story as far as the teller chooses;
- Accept and invite teaching of elements that are new to the listener, that is, the professional social worker; for example, the need for a mother to sacrifice long-treasured hair if an infant survives the Mekong River crossing, when so many drowned;
- Differentiate the impact of voluntary migration status and involuntary migration, asylum, or refugee status;
- Identify the level of felt or experienced safety when leaving, when arriving, now;
- Engage in immediate tasks for safety as experienced by the migrant;
- Support resource search and longer-term planning of the individual and his or her family;
- Maintain a clear attitude of acceptance concerning plans and even seemingly unrealistic plans for family reunification while engaging in the broadest array of solutions; and
- Most central to the entire social work encounter in this context: conscientization—a critical awareness of the complex reality of what we experience, what we are told by governments and people in power, what we observe around us.

Consider the clinical case of Vasu, an immigrant and naturalized citizen (Citizen of the United States by Naturalization—after staying for five years in the United States, an immigrant who has been admitted into the United States with an immigrant visa is eligible to apply to become a citizen of the United States. When that applicant meets several immigration criteria, which include clearance by the Federal Bureau Investigation, Centers for Disease Control, and so on, and is qualified to take the citizenship test, and when the test is successfully passed, the Citizenship Oath is offered).

Vasu, an Asian American woman of Asian Indian heritage, after moving to the United States was experiencing cultural schizophrenia. In this real-life case situation, Vasu, a Hindu American woman who had spent most of her life in the United States, became addicted to alcohol, and attempted to commit suicide on a few occasions.

Vasu's relationships with her mother and grandmother in India and her husband and teenage sons in New York revealed profound conflicts between her traditional upbringing and her personal and professional aspirations, and life in a Western society where there are many diverging value systems in operation. Her internal psychological struggles, and the family dynamics, were realigned as Vasu and her family participated in both individual and family therapy sessions. The interventions helped her to regain her life without alcohol, and the family adapted to a Vasu who was sober, and made changes by which both Vasu and her family began to experience higher levels of satisfaction. Vasu completed her graduate degree with the emotional support of her family, and maintained sobriety, and became a very successful educator and administrator at the university level (Krishnan, 1990).

POLITICAL ROLE OF NATION-STATES WITH REFERENCE TO POST-9/11 UNITED STATES AND THE UNITED KINGDOM

Managing the movement of people means being aware of the resource base. Social workers are intimately connected with issues of family poverty and unemployment across borders. Asking the larger questions of why people are displaced or uprooting themselves leads to a more preventive and creative approach to social work than the purely reactive stance of dealing only with the end result of economic disruption, namely, poverty. "Several studies have examined the different effects of international migration on income inequality" and the ultimate impact on relationships of lack of income (Ramaswami, 1968; Rivera-Batiz, 1982; Stark and Bloom, 1985) It is not just a question of the economic drivers however. The ever-present stressors and damage of war are constant sources of refugees and migrants, and countries vary immensely in their response.

It was in the post-9/11 ethos that a very limiting legislation, namely, the Patriot Act, was passed in the United States. This legislation adversely impacts the civil rights of some citizens of the United States, and some who are permanent residents of the United States, and others who are visitors to the United States from other countries. In the United States of America, in October 2006, the Bush administration repealed habeas corpus and the Geneva Convention for noncitizens in one fell swoop in passing the Military Commissions Act of 2006. So foreign nationals and permanent resident aliens residing in the United States are advised to remember the admonishment of former White House press secretary Ari Fleischer, "to watch what they say, watch what they do" (Kelkar, 2006). For example, Akhil Sachdeva, an accountant from India, a Hindu, who immigrated to Canada, and was a Canadian citizen, was seized at gunpoint by U.S. agents and held for months along with hundreds of foreigners in the months following the 9/11 terror attacks. He was chained to a bench at the FBI's Manhattan office on December 20, 2001; federal agents demanded to know his religious and political beliefs, asked whether he had taken flying lessons, and sought his personal views about the suicide hijackers, he said in an interview to an international news agency. Sachdeva wondered as he spoke to the reporters about the lawsuit (Bernstein, 2009) he had filed. "Maybe because of my skin color? I am an Indian and I look like any person from Pakistan or an Arab country," he said after completing depositions in Toronto taken by lawyers representing the U.S. government in the suit. "First of all, I want an apology," Sachdeva said by telephone from his home in Brampton, Ontario. "One day I have everything, the next day they destroyed my life and I was not even charged for anything—had done no crime. I understand that there was a need of national security then, but how can they treat people that way?" (Sharma, M., 2006)

Similarly, in the United Kingdom, some recent immigrants of South Asian and Middle Eastern countries, living in a post-9/11 ethos, are struggling with ensuing challenges, specifically due to prejudice. For example, in recent times, the British government has drawn up a plan to ask lecturers and university staff across the country to spy on "Asian-looking" and Muslim students (*Deccan Herald*, October 17, 2006).

SUMMARY

Human migration is a naturally occurring human condition. Migration of people both within and between continents has been occurring throughout the history of *Homo sapiens* and Neanderthals. Migration patterns have been both voluntary and involuntary in nature. These patterns have differential impact on social work practice and the policies that guide those practices.

Depending on the nature of the migration pattern, the intensity and magnitude of the impact vary. For instance, the occurrence of involuntary migration because of religious, economic, or ethnic upheaval is often met at country borders with oppressive responses. Voluntary migration, for example from Europe to the Americas, was interpreted as adventure and exploration in a pioneer spirit. In the United Kingdom, people rarely think of the Romans as pioneers; they have always been classified as an invading army. That same classification has rarely been applied to European arrivals in North America and sometimes for the Spanish arrival in Central America in the sixteenth century.

There are key skills that social workers use when working with people who have migrated or who are refugees. Social workers also need to be sensitive to changes in immigration policies and the general sentiment toward immigrants during challenging economic times and their impact as they pertain to prejudice and discrimination and their consequences on the bio-psycho-socio-spiritual well-being of immigrants and refugees and their families. The International Federation of Social Workers, by offering a universal statement on ethics, asks social workers to increase their cooperation and share strategies, such as the "Dictionario" of the KLJUC organization. Similarly, social workers are seeking a stronger presence at borders both as advocates and as protectors of human rights and children's rights. Earlier in this chapter a list of skills was offered that included slowing down as a social worker and making time for the story, differentiating the experience of the individual and his or her family, and engaging in various tasks. The final point was a key one: attending to the process of conscientization.

The English word "conscientization" is introduced in chapter 2 in relation to social work in Mexico and is a translation of the Portuguese word *conscientizacao*, which is also translated as "consciousness raising." The word was coined by Brazilian activist-educator and theorist Paulo Freire in his 1970 work *Pedagogy of the Oppressed*. During the time when dictators ruled many South American countries, Freire began teaching the poor and illiterate members of Brazilian society to read when literacy was a requirement for suffrage. "Conscientization" is a term that students and social work educators have been using in many countries, including India, since the 1970s. For example, as part of the Indian Students' Union activities in 1977, one of the authors of this book (Ramanathan) and his colleagues used the intervention technique of conscientization, while working with slum youth. In urban India, the technique of conscientization was replicating Freiri's strategy in a totally different cultural ethos, which had a totally different geopolitical consideration. The common base, however, whether it was applied in rural Brazil, Mexico, or urban India, was to increase critical awareness among the poor. Thus, this intervention technique was used to increase critical awareness among slum youth, as it pertained to analyzing the number of buses that serve the slums, and the frequency of those buses, as opposed to the affluent parts of the city. Similarly, calculations and analysis regarding per capita use of water taps were also used to increase awareness of slum youth. These interventional strategies were used prior to encouraging the slum youth to familiarize themselves with the Constitution of India, and the criticality of exercising one's voting rights. Conscientization proceeds through the identification of "generative themes," which Freire identified as producing vast representations that have a powerful emotional impact in the daily lives of learners who are in abject poverty. In this way, individual consciousness helps end the "culture of silence" in which the socially dispossessed internalize the negative images of themselves created and propagated by the oppressor in situations of extreme poverty.

North American students have encountered the idea of "conscientization" in Mexico as they volunteer their services and begin to understand the structural reasons for acute rural poverty (Center for Global Education, 2006). Thus, conscientization also means to become more fully aware of meaning and social reality: the source of a definition, the bias, the inclusion and exclusion of information. As another example, the northern border of the United States with Canada is less tightly maintained and monitored than the border between the United States and Mexico, for reasons that are open to critical thought and action. Migration is an eternal phenomenon and one that offers both opportunity and despair. Social workers are poised for greater collaboration across national borders. International debates and conferences are just beginning to realize the potential of our working and learning together across the globe.

RELEVANT WEBSITES

www.un.org
www.unhcr.org
www.newint.org
www.guardian.co.uk
www.oxfam.org
www.cpag.org.uk
www.ilo.org
www.iom.int

STUDENT ASSIGNMENTS

1. Why is the understanding of cross-national legal immigration and within-nation migration important?

2. Are there similarities and differences between cross-national legal immigration and within-nation migration?
3. When global movement of people is guaranteed by the United Nations Charter, why is there so much resistance in many parts of the world toward immigrant populations?
4. What policy and program initiatives would you suggest to your agency directors and/or the board to serve also immigrant and refugee populations?
5. Does the U.S. Constitution have different rights when it comes to citizens and legal immigrants?
6. What difference if any do you see between minority populations based on culture or race, and legal immigrants and refugees?
7. Do some policies initiated affect differentially the legal immigrants and refugees compared to the general populations?

Chapter Seven

Planet Earth and Sustainable Life

We did not weave the web of life; we are merely a strand in it. Whatever we do to the web, we do to ourselves.

—Chief Seattle

Planet Earth is a precious being and the satellite images that frequently cross our computer screens show her to be a jewel of blues and greens in space. The sense of our joint stewardship of this life-giving habitat has existed for centuries but has been heard differently among nations and cultures. Currently in the postindustrial (Europe, North America, parts of South America, and Oceania) and industrial (India, China, Africa, Central and South America, and other parts of Asia) world our collective effort has been subdued by rapid globalization of trade, industry, and labor (Singer, 2004). Asian nations like India and China, and South American countries like Brazil and Argentina, contest the above "industrial" classification. We consider it important to remember that when economic development gets linked with environmental emissions, the United States and the European Union ask these countries to reduce dependence on coal, and these countries tend to point out that the United States and Europe were industrialized before the current limits were imposed on economically developing nations. Nevertheless, after the environmental summit in Copenhagen in 2009, a non-legally-binding accord was agreed to by nation-states. In early 2010, Brazil and South Africa signed this accord, and it is anticipated that China and India will do the same (*Deccan Herald*, 2010).

For social workers it is second nature to think in terms of interacting systems, but sometimes we stop arbitrarily with the systems we know best—family, local community, nation—rather than embracing the world in all its complexity and different patterns of growth. In this chapter we address the impact of global ecological systems on human well-being. The question is asked: What is the role of social work in relation to preservation of basic resources, protection against toxins, and survival of the earth's ecosystems? The chapter answers this question by addressing (1) the concept of stewardship as part of collective well-being; (2) the impact of toxic environments on children and families; (3) the role of corporations in creating and dumping waste and implications at the local and global level; (4) the impact of war and terror on the environment and human life; and (5) the role of social work. Included in these discussions is the backdrop of global warming. There is broad acceptance that climate change, particularly increasing sea levels as a result of warmer oceans, will have disastrous consequences for many communities (Singer, 2004). Simultaneously, there is increasing awareness that humans can make an impact for good with even seemingly small steps, such as recycling, using public transport, and promoting alternatives to use of oil such as wind power, wave power, and solar energy. The social work profession recognizes both the threats to human well-being and the steps in community organizing that can have a positive effect. For example, with global warming, viruses and tropical diseases are marching northward to unprepared localities, and health crises are expected.

Recently the SARS outbreak spread quickly through air transport from Singapore to Toronto. Following the outbreak, public health measures became a model for future responses by community workers, medical staff, and social workers. Based on this experience, the researcher Tiong Tan has laid out a crisis management approach to public health threats that are universally applicable and are discussed in the final section of this chapter on the role of social workers (Tan, 2004). Similarly, the new swine flu cases are caused by an influenza strain called H1N1, which seems to be easily passed from person to person (Bradsher, 2009). According to the World Health Organization, as of January 17, 2010, worldwide more than 209 countries had reported laboratory-confirmed cases of pandemic influenza H1N1 2009, which included at least 14,142 deaths (WHO, 2010).

Scholars such as Tiong Tan (concerned with preparedness in response to health crises), Mary Rogge (concerned with the impact of lead paint in schools), and Golam Mathbor (natural disaster response planning) are identified throughout this chapter. Also case studies are shared that help unravel the twenty-first-century challenge to humanity to become better stewards of the earth for the good of humankind and the universe.

THE CONCEPT OF STEWARDSHIP AS PART OF COLLECTIVE WELL-BEING

"Taking charge of our own lives" is a universal element in social work throughout the world. Certainly the various approaches, concepts, and cultural context of the "helping" profession changes, so that "own lives" will

---

Textbox 7.1.   World Health Meeting Focuses on Epidemics

Geneva:

The 59th World Health Assembly began on a somber note on Monday following the death of the director-general of the World Health Organisation, Dr Lee Jong-wook, hours before the inaugural session.

But health ministers said they remained focused on major challenges in the international disease and health environment, especially the threat of bird flu and escalating HIV/AIDS and TB epidemic in poor countries.

"I am sorry to tell you that Dr Lee Jong-wook, director-general of the WHO, died this morning," said Elena Salgado, Spain's health minister and the chair for the 59th WHA. Dr Lee, 61, died after surgery. . . . He took office as the head of WHO three years ago when SARS (Severe Acute Respiratory Syndrome), the infectious respiratory disease began to threaten parts of Asia.

"Under his leadership, the WHO has been strengthened and has been able to give an effective response to world (health) problems," the Spanish minister said. The annual session, which was briefly suspended for 30 minutes, will end on Saturday. Anders Nordstrom, currently assistant director-general, will head the global health body until members found a new chief.

Indian concerns:

"India has some major issues to be addressed during the six-day Assembly," Dr Anbumani Ramadoss, health minister, said.

"India wants easy movement of health professionals—both doctors and nurses—to countries that are in dire need," he told *Deccan Herald*. "Basically, the issue of health, human resources and services is a management problem but there are some hurdles which need to be removed," the health minister said.

Besides, India wants proper allocation of funds for countries suffering from public health emergencies such as HIV/AIDS, tuberculosis, and malaria.

More importantly, developing countries, led by Kenya and Brazil, have moved a resolution calling on the rich countries and global pharmaceutical companies in prioritising research and development in developing countries to address the poor man's diseases such as communicable diseases and malaria.

So far, big pharmaceutical companies are invested heavily in diseases such as cardio-vascular or cancer-related diseases but not in tackling the age-old diseases.

US health secretary Michael O Leavitt said Washington was concerned about the deadly spread of H5N1 virus, pointing out that the Bush administration was convinced that a pandemic will happen.

"We are already building the stocks for tamiflu (which is the only medicine to target bird flu) and we want governments to show greater transparency as well as share information for grappling with avian flu." A senior US health official said rigid "treaties" are not a solution to address the so-called Type 2 and Type 3 diseases in poor countries, implying that these issues must be left for the pharmaceutical companies to decide.

Source: From Kanth, D. R. (2006, May 22). *Deccan Herald News Service.*

Textbox 7.2. Silent Valley National Park

(A version of this case study appeared in Ramanathan and Link, 2004, chapter 3.)

Chathapuram Ramanathan

Silent Valley, a national park in Kerala, India, is situated in the Kundali Hills of the Western Ghats, at the southwestern corner of the Nilgiri Hills in the Palghat District (county). The nearest town, the location of park headquaarters, is 40 kilometers by road to the south. Originally declared a national park in 1980, Silent Valley was supposed to be excluded as the site of a proposed hydroelectric project. The same area was originally constituted reserved land under Section 26 of the Forest Act in 1888. The park is bounded by Attappadi Reserved Forest to the east, and the vested forests of Palghat Division and Nilambur Division to the south and the west, respectively. Silent Valley is an integral part of the ecosystem of the region. Although the specific area where the dam was to have been constructed is believed never to have been settled, there are indigenous tribal people living in the area (Rahmani, 1980). There are settlements, two kilometers southeast of the area, and five kilometers southwest.

The Silent Valley forest, locally known as "Sairandhrivanam" and considered by many to be one of the last representative tracts of virgin tropical evergreen forest in India, became the focus of India's perhaps fiercest and most widely publicized environmental debate in the late 1970s, when the Kerala State Electricity Board decided to go ahead with a hydroelectric project in the valley (Agarwal and Narain, 1985).

The project was expected to generate 240 megawatts of electricity and to irrigate some 100,000 hectares of land in the relatively "less developed" Palghat and Malappuram districts.

Four main types of vegetation are recognized in the park: tropical evergreen forest, which forms extensive dense stands along hills and valleys; subtropical hill forest between; temperate forest, popularly referred to as "sholas" and characterized by unrelated evergreen species with a dense closed canopy; and grasslands (Unnikrishnan, 1989). Faunal diversity is very high and includes a number of endemic and threatened species (Zoological Survey of India, 1986). Regarding the flora in the area, 966 species belonging to 134 families, and 559 genera are thriving. Also, 110 plant species of importance to Ayurvedic medicine (indigenous medicine), a pest resistant strain of rice, and other economically valuable plant species contribute to the area vegetation (Nair and Balasubramanyan, 1984). Twenty-six species of mammals (not including bats, rodents, and insectivores), such as Asian elephants, tigers, leopards, 120 species of birds, and 19 species of amphibians, have been recorded (Balakrishnan, 1984; Jayson, 1990; Mathew, 1990).

A task force of the National Committee on Environmental Planning and Coordination, under Dr. M. S. Swaminathan, the then secretary of agriculture of the government of India, and several nongovernmental conservational organizations, including the Bombay Natural History Society, Kerala Sastra Sahitya Parishad (Kerala Science and Literature Society), and the Indian Science Congress, urged the government of Kerala to abandon the scheme, but to no avail. Further, the government of Kerala refused to endorse the joint committee's findings (Agarwal and Narain, 1985). The dispute became highly politicized, and innumerable state and national organizations, as well as international organizations such as World Wildlife Fund, became involved in the "Save Silent Valley" campaign. In order to appease conservationists, the government of Kerala created a national park in December 1980, which excluded the proposed project site from the area. In November 1983, the hydroelectric project was finally shelved, and the present national park declared a year later, in deference to the weight of public opinion and to the sentiments of the then prime minister, Mrs. Indira Gandhi.

RESEARCH INITIATIVES

A significant amount of research has been conducted in Silent Valley, such as environmental impact assessments, generated by the controversy over the hydroelectric project (Vijayan and Balakrishnan, 1977; Nair and Balasubramanyan, 1984), and vegetation studies (Basha, 1987). The flora has been examined by the Botanical Survey of India (Manilal, 1988) and the fauna by the Zoological Survey of India (1986). Additionally, several ecological studies have been conducted by the Kerala Forest Research Institute (1990).

be viewed as a collective in some regions and more individually in others (Ramanathan and Link, 2004). In the "Silent Valley Project" for example, groups of concerned citizens were protesting construction of a large dam to be funded by the World Bank in Kerala, India. Although the central and state governments had authorized the plan, the people's movement (including the work of community organizers and activists) challenged this on the basis of negative consequences for the environment and social displacement of individuals and families. The case study illustrates how individual people take charge of their lives both personally (that is in micro terms of individual accomplishment) and socially (in their external mezzo and macro relationships with communities, institutions, and governments).

This case study illustrates family, group, and community systems in action to protect their habitat. Although not all family members are living together, they still encourage, reinforce, and support the cause of the Silent Valley through their natural family networks. There are numerous examples of similar actions to the Silent Valley in communities worldwide. For example, the Texas protest against nuclear waste dumping (see student assignment at the end of this chapter). At the mezzo level, not only is the individual's job at stake, but also it affects the group of people as a whole when the community has to be uprooted or is deprived of its natural resources, habitat, and continuity of the familiar niche. At the family level, children witness that their parents and relatives, through active participation in the life of the community, are able to stand up for principles they believe in and to powers that may seem overwhelming. Thus, the children have a good role model of parents acting as stewards of the earth for their own struggles.

The deeper meaning during such family and community effort is a sense of empowerment over their destiny. This has implications historically in terms of ancestral and heritage issues, in the present in terms of livelihood, and continued feelings of being connected with their community, and futuristically in terms of the positive impact on the future generations' feeling of power and experiencing the fact that people can take charge of their lives and legacy.

The self-esteem for people fighting the Silent Valley Project is a key element. In the process of organizing, individuals came to believe that they had a powerful voice. It has been well documented that there is a direct relationship between control over one's life and consequent self-esteem (Berk, 2004). In the Silent Valley Project, individuals came together with their neighbors and families and eventually made a major impact on the larger macroenvironment. This process included responding to their initial fears of loss of livelihood by mobilizing their internal resources including belief in self, ability to speak out, and the power of positive thinking, all despite massive structural challenges that they encountered from powerful institutions.

At the macro, or larger system level, the Silent Valley Project has policy ramifications in terms of how international banking industries need to work in synchronization with nongovernmental organizations in planning, designing, and implementation of such a project (Nair and Balasubramanyan, 1984). Also, it is very telling that policies formulated with a Western perspective, without adequate sensitivity to local issues, can ensure that the project fails. These local issues include a tradition of farmers' rights to land ownership according to the Indian Land Reform Act; another local issue is the connection and sensitivity of people to their environment. Children learn at an early age the importance of and reverence for the nature that surrounds them. In direct contrast to this respect, people who were far removed from the spiritual and meaningful connections to the habitat of these people planned the dam.

Both the lack of corporate connections to people's reality and the promise of economic gain facilitated this World Bank project. The funders, architects, and engineers primarily operated from a Western economic perspective without adequate attention to community sustainability of this "developmental initiative." Also in the context of macro issues, there are policy ramifications in terms of connection between international policies that might favor the Global North and their negative consequence in the Global South.

A parallel example of the Silent Valley Project is the controversy of U.S.-owned companies along the Mexican border with the United States, known as "maquiladora" plants (Prigoff, 2000). These businesses are criticized for

benefiting from cheap labor without due attention to improving working conditions or clean water supplies to communities ("Chasing Mexico's Dream
Takes a Toll," *New York Times*, February 11, 2001, pp. 1–6,). Water is the
key to healthy communities in preventing infant mortality, maintaining sanitation, personal cleanliness, irrigation, and adult health, and avoiding famine.
The structural goals of a project or investment may be driven by the rationale
of Western approaches to increase access to energy or sources of labor, while
the local needs of people who have traditionally been considered without
power are trampled. Furthermore, there is connection between poverty in the
economically advanced countries and poverty in economically challenged
countries in that the faces of undernourished children without access to immunizations or clean water are the same the world over.

Both "recognizing sense of place" and "resilience" were human behaviors
displayed in the Silent Valley Project. It has been suggested that the difference between an immigrant and a refugee is that the immigrant sends his or
her spirit ahead to a new place and the body follows; a refugee sends the
body and the spirit remains. In the Silent Valley people fought and overcame
imposed displaced-person or refugee status and became true stewards of their
earth. Along the Mexico-U.S. border, families are still struggling for clean
water. As we become more conscious of the precious quality of this life-giving liquid, we may become better stewards of water channels and the earth's
rivers and streams ("Chasing Mexico's Dream Takes a Toll," pp. 1–6).

Recently, President Obama of the United States, on April 13, 2009, in a
speech in Strasbourg, France, referred to a meeting he had with Prime Minister Singh of India:

> I was meeting with the Indian Prime Minister yesterday after the summit
> (G-20)—a very good and wise man, Prime Minister Singh—and he was talk-
> ing about how Indian growth rates have gone up 9 percent every year. They
> need to grow at that pace in order to bring hundreds of millions of people in
> their country out of abject poverty, desperate poverty. They have to grow at a
> rapid pace. Now, he actually is committed to working towards dealing with the
> climate change issue, but he made a very simple point, which is a point that I
> understood before the meeting and all of us should not forget—and that is that
> you cannot expect poor countries, or relatively poor countries, to be partners
> with us on climate change if we are not taking the lead, given that our carbon
> footprint is many times more than theirs per capita. I mean, each one of us in
> the developed world, I don't care how environmentally conscious you are, how
> green you are. (Obama, 2009)

President Obama's perspective encourages social work students, practitioners, and academics in economically advanced countries to focus on the
common human condition, and makes a direct linkage to "the concept of

stewardship as part of collective well-being." This view helps us to move away from blaming the victim and asks of us to inculcate an empowering demeanor, as we view and interact with citizens from economically challenged nations.

The American Recovery and Reinvestment Act (ARRA) contains $787 billion of investments and tax cuts. Of this sum, over $70 billion is directed to green activities. This includes increasing energy efficiency and conservation, electricity grid modernization, renewable energy, mass transit and high-speed rail, and environmental cleanup in rural areas including water and waste disposal and cleaning up former weapon production and energy research sites, along with energy efficiency programs including alternative fuel trucks and buses, transportation charging infrastructure, smart and energy efficient appliances, grant funding for the manufacturing of advanced battery systems and components and vehicle batteries produced in the United States, and weatherization assistance program. "This is a historic and unprecedented investment in clean energy, green jobs and green infrastructure," is how Melinda Pierce, Sierra Club's lead advocate for the bill and deputy director of national campaigns, reacted to the bill (Reed, 2009). Thus, budgetary allocation to green technology at this level documents the operational commitment of the Obama administration actualizing a philosophy of pursuing green (environmentally friendly) technology to reducing the carbon footprint of the United States, and thus is a testimony to "the concept of stewardship as part of collective well-being."

THE IMPACT OF UPROOTING FAMILIES AND TOXIC ENVIRONMENTS ON CHILDREN

The sense of connectedness with the community demonstrated in the Silent Valley reflects what Powell considers spiritual intimacy: "Spiritual intimacy is created through the shared revelations of faith, beliefs and insights into spiritual matters," which can help "to create a common bond, a context of belief in which understanding and trust can be fostered" (Powell, 1988). Our sense of spirituality and connectedness with surroundings becomes most clear when we are expected to leave the place of our ancestors. American Indian history is a devastating reminder of the impact of this process of uprooting children and families and is vividly illustrated in Chief Seattle's message written in 1854. This speech was made to mark the transfer of ancestral lands to the U.S. government and speaks directly to the concept of stewardship of the earth:

Chief Seattle's Message 1854

The great Chief in Washington sends word that he wishes to buy our land. The Great Chief also sends us words of friendship and good will. This is kind of him, since we know he has little need of our friendship in return. But we will consider your offer. For we know that if we do not sell, the white man may come with guns and take our land.

How can you buy or sell the sky, the warmth of the land? The idea is strange to us.

If we do not own the freshness of the air and the sparkle of the water, how can you buy them?

Every part of this earth is sacred to my people. Every shining pine needle, every sandy shore, every mist in the dark woods, every clearing and humming insect is holy in the memory and experience of my people. The sap which courses through the trees carries the memories of the red man.

The white man's dead forget the country of their birth when they go to walk among the stars. Our dead never forget this beautiful earth, for it is the mother of the red man. We are part of the earth and it is part of us . . .

So, when the Great Chief in Washington sends word that he wishes to buy our land, he asks much of us. . . . So we will consider your offer to buy our land. But it will not be easy. For this land is sacred to us.

This shining water that moves in the streams and rivers is not just water but the blood of our ancestors. If we sell you land, you must remember that it is sacred, and you must teach your children that it is sacred, and that each ghostly reflection in the clear water of the lake tells of events and memories in the life of my people. The water's murmur is the voice of my father's father.

The rivers are our brothers, they quench our thirst. The rivers carry our canoes, and feed our children. If we sell you our land, you must remember, and teach your children, that the rivers are our brothers, and yours, and you must henceforth give the rivers the kindness you would give any brother . . .

This we know. The earth does not belong to man; man belongs to the earth. This we know. All things are connected like the blood which unites one family. All things are connected.

Whatever befalls the earth befalls the sons of the earth. Man did not weave the web of life, he is merely a strand in it. Whatever he does to the web, he does to himself . . .

One thing we know. Our God is the same God. This earth is precious to him. Even the white man cannot be exempt from the common destiny. We may be brothers after all. We shall see. (Excerpt from *The Power of the People*, ed. by Cooney and Michalowski, 1987)

These behaviors and responses in taking away or trying to preserve ancestral land do not arise in a vacuum. Individuals are constantly interacting in the context of their cultural environment at all ages and stages of the family, group, and village life to protect their future well-being. Nobel Prize winner Wangari Maathai spoke to a group of students about her childhood in Kenya (Maathai, 2006). She remembered running to the stream near her village, bathing, washing clothes, carrying water for cooking. Today those same waters are polluted. As a direct result of seeing this degradation of her village life, Maathai is taking a stand that the world has heard, to increase education about the impact of toxins, soil erosion, and agribusiness, and more hopefully to increase the planting of trees.

Wangari Maathai is an example of someone with imagination. She knows that individual self-esteem, cultural identity, and structural change are always interacting and can result in cooperative or conflictual human behavior. It is a powerful reminder of the constant cycles of human behavior in common conditions of challenge or deprivation, when we see the parallels of Chief Seattle's experience in the 1850s with Wangari Maathai's contemporary work.

The prescient message from Chief Seattle has become true. We are "defiling our bed." This first decade of the twenty-first century we are experiencing water stress, differential access to potable water, polluted air, soil erosion, and overfarmed land. There is a shocking new concept: *dead zones*, concentrated area of toxins where nothing grows (UNEP, 2003). In Bill Moyer's film *Earth on Edge*, we hear farmers discussing the pollution of the Mississippi, which has resulted in a dead zone in the Gulf of Mexico. More encouraging, the farmers identify ways they currently contribute to these toxins and ways they can reduce pollution of runoff from their fields. Also filmed are community organizers in South Africa, engaging neighborhoods in cutting nonindigenous trees to enhance water quality. The effort of local volunteers in the Cape of Good Hope is having immediate impact and giving them a sense of empowerment (Moyers, *Earth on Edge*). The film shows water-guzzling nonindigenous trees (introduced by early colonists who wanted shade and were ignorant of the disruption of the local ecosystem) being felled and streams beginning to flow again.

Education about clean hands and transfer of disease is common in schools worldwide, while education about the disruption of ecosystems and the impact of toxic water is less well identified. There are encouraging innovations in oral rehydration and ways to make water potable, but still, lack of access to clean water is a giant killer. The *State of the World's Children* report connects infant mortality rates directly to lack of access to potable water (UNICEF, 2006). Even if children survive drought, the International Labour Organization has been highlighting the plight of young children in hazardous and exploitative work conditions (www.ilo.org). Child work may be inevitable in countries plagued with poverty, but access to clean water is a child's right (UN, Convention on the Rights of the Child, 1989). The distinction is made here between *child work* that is age appropriate and necessary for family economic survival and that does not prevent education, in contrast to *child labor* where the child is exploited, out of school, and in danger. In his article "Making Trinkets in China, and a Deadly Dust," Kahn quotes International Labour Organization research, which indicates that 386,645 Chinese workers of all ages died of occupational illnesses in 2002 and child work plus labor is commonplace (Joseph Kahn, "Making Trinkets in China, and a Deadly Dust," *New York Times*, June 20, 2003).

In addition to clean water, people benefit from education about our natural habitat and balance in ecological systems. However, the earth is beset with the paradox of increasing markets for natural wood, which leads to overlogging and the resulting loss of rainforests that are needed for a healthy atmosphere that in turn maintains biodiversity. Biodiversity contributes to the well-being of us all in direct ways. There is current controversy in Surinam concerning logging. The forests are being destroyed and their timber exported. However, a rare periwinkle blossoms there: this precious flower contains ingredients for the drug Tamoxifen, helpful in the fight against cancer. Suddenly the ravaging of these forests takes on a more common human meaning.

Families and children are both the actors and victims in terms of the earth's habitat. As seen in the Silent Valley and recently in Nigeria, women and children can have great power. The article "Nigeria's Oil Wealth Flows Out, Not Down" describes a group of women community organizers in Ugborodo. They came together at dawn to cross the river between their poverty-stricken village where the fish no longer flourish to the new-age power plant of ChevronTexaco:

> Only a creek separates this village from the vast ChevronTexaco oil terminal deep in West Africa's great Niger Delta, but most of the village women who raided it one day in July had never crossed over before. Just after sunrise, hundreds of unarmed women commandeered a boat and infiltrated the terminal, fanning out across the docks and the airstrip, entering office buildings. . . . On their side of the creek these women live in shacks with no phones or indoor plumbing. To see inside Chevron amounted to an epiphany. 'The Bible describes paradise as a beautiful place where there is everything . . . we could not imagine what we would find.' (Onishi, 2002)

Where larger structural systems have control, particularly in the form of transnational corporations, women and children are often the first to suffer. However, in the instance of Ugborodo, the women took matters into their own hands and are continuing to try to negotiate water and employment, with limited success. They came to realize that transnational corporations have power even over national governments and are hard to reach.

THE ROLE OF CORPORATIONS IN CREATING AND DUMPING WASTE

Although the earth's natural resources are under strain because of the actions of all of us, the role of corporations is clearly a key area for change. The

New Internationalist (www.newint.org) brought attention to dead zones (also identified in Bill Moyers film *Earth on Edge*) through its discussion of intense fertilization of banana crops by giant corporations. This has occurred in a number of countries but is particularly acute in Nigeria, where oil pollutes fishing areas, and Honduras, where even mosquitoes do not survive on some former banana plantations (Martin, 1999). Women lose their menstrual cycle, and respiratory diseases increase when laborers are exposed to the toxins of oil seeping into the groundwater and chemical sprays in the air.

Why is social work concerned with "dead zones" and the well-being of the planet? As with all aspects of systems, the human system is closely interconnected with the global system. There are questions of health, justice, and sheer survival for humans caught up in a web of camouflage rather than well-being. Clean water is our lifeblood, but children are dying from dehydration in many parts of the world (UNICEF, 2006). Most people do not realize that giant corporations make a grave impact on our environment. Dole, Chiquita, and Del Monte dominate the banana trade in ways that lead to dead zones, oppression of rural laborers, and a lack of transparency to consumers. Recently the Koch refinery in Minnesota, United States, accepted Environmental Agency fines for polluting the groundwater (Wolters, 2009). They have changed their name to Flint Hills and sound more like a golf course than a cloudy corporation, but the glittering waters of the Mississippi lie directly in their path. There are corporations choosing a more earth-friendly route, including the Body Shop. Anita Roddick, the founder of the Body Shop, has encouraged natural processes, transparent trade routes, and open access to the manufacturing base plus its locality (Glenndinning, 2007).

It takes imagination for us all to make the connections: polluted groundwater seeps into major waterways, affecting drinking water, and influencing health and well-being. The social work profession is impacted by these ecological conditions in ways that traditionally focused on public health or were not connected to the daily lives of people struggling with sick children or tired adults (*Global Warming: The Signs and the Science*, www.pbs.org). The book *Water Wars* provides a vivid depiction of these connections and represents the future for all of us in terms of common human needs for water, shelter, and food that is not tainted by chemicals (Shiva, 2002). Currently, Lake Superior water is being sold to Arizona, where urban growth is outstripping resources; deforestation is negatively affecting farming in Brazil; and the loss of oak forests is leading to landslides in India (Shiva, 2002).

When natural resources decline in quality, people either move and become migrant workers or refugees, or they stay and struggle with the result. Recently in Brownsville, Texas, there has been an increase in the number of babies born with deformities. Now the water quality is being questioned, with the realization at a community level that water polluted in Mexico knows no

---

Textbox 7.3. *Deccan Herald*

Deccan Herald (12/11/05) » News Update » Detailed Story
Bhopal Gas survivors battle it out in US courts for damages New Delhi, PTI:

Twenty-one years after the Bhopal gas tragedy claimed over 2,260 lives and affected about two Lakh [hundred thousand] people, the survivors are still battling it out in US courts for compensation and removal of hazardous waste from the Union Carbide's factory closed since December three, 1984.

In their latest move, the survivors have filed an appeal in the Second Circuit Court, New York against a District Court order rejecting their suit for damages against Dow Chemicals, the present owner of Union Carbide Corporation (UCC).

"We are confident that the Court of Appeals will vindicate the rightness of our position and reverse the decision of the lower court in whole or in part," survivors' US attorney H Rajan Sharma told PTI in an e-mail interview.

In an e-mail reply, Dow Chemicals' Accountability Network Coordinator Diana Ruiz said the company was aware of the appeal.

After a six-year battle in the American lower court, Justice John F Keenan rejected the suit, observing, "the court will not grant relief where it happens to be impossible and impractical."

"UCC now has no claims or connection with the property and has not had any control over it for several years. Ordering remediation by the defendants would be ineffectual as they have no means or authority to carry it out," he added.

Hasina Bi, one of the survivors, alleged in her suit that her well got polluted due to the leak of hazardous chemicals from the UCC factory.

---

borders. The worst irony is that U.S.-owned companies, often without the knowledge of their customers, have sought countries like Mexico and India as less expensive localities for operations. The definition of expensive is complex however as illustrated in textbox 7.3. The birth of a child without limbs or with developmental challenges presents costs to the individual, the parents, the community, the health and education systems, and ultimately to us all.

THE IMPACT OF WAR AND TERROR

Terrorism has occurred throughout history for numerous reasons. Its causes can be historical, cultural, political, social, psychological, economic, or religious—or any combination of these. Some terrorists are motivated by very specific issues, such as opposition to legalized abortion or nuclear energy, or the championing of environmental concerns and animal rights. In broad terms, the causes that have commonly compelled people to engage in terrorism are grievances borne of political oppression, cultural domination, economic exploitation, ethnic discrimination, and religious persecution. Perceived inequities in the distribution of wealth and political power have led some terrorists to attempt to overthrow democratically elected governments.

Corporations have at times aided or enlisted terrorists. For example, in March 2007 it was reported that the well-known and market-dominating banana company Chiquita Brands International "has agreed to a $25 million fine after admitting it paid terrorists for protection in a volatile farming region of Colombia. The settlement resolves a lengthy Justice Department investigation into the company's financial dealings with right-wing paramilitaries and leftist rebels the U.S. government deems terrorist groups . . . [and] prosecutors said the company made the payments in exchange for protection for its workers" (Apuzzo, 2007). Similarly, national governments have at times aided terrorists to further their own foreign policy goals. So-called state-sponsored terrorism, however, falls into a different category altogether. State-sponsored terrorism is a form of *covert* (secret) warfare, a means to wage war secretly through the use of terrorist surrogates (stand-ins) as hired guns (Nelson-Pallmeyer, 2004).

Terrorism dominated the media in 2008, but Arun Gandhi urged students to understand that "the culture of violence seeps into every part of our lives, the media, relationships, entertainment and it is a learned behavior" (Gandhi, 2007). As such, it can be unlearned. In order to "learn non-violence we need to face violence" and recognize how we inflict violence on our environment in the ways we destroy the forests and rivers in the ways we overconsume (Gandhi, 2007). As we begin to recognize the complexity, we are open to recognizing the steps of self-recognition and community restoration that are involved in Arun Gandhi's grandfather's life of "satyagraha"—or the soul force of being truly nonviolent and peaceful in our lives. Mahatma Gandhi's grandson encouraged listeners to accept that nonviolence and forgiveness is the most hopeful way for humanity. This remains a major challenge for the U.S. government.

The events of September 11, 2001, have no precedent in the history of terrorism. On that day 19 terrorists belonging to bin Laden's al-Qaeda organization hijacked four passenger aircraft shortly after they departed from airports in Boston, Massachusetts; Newark, New Jersey; and Washington, DC. In 2006, a series of bombs exploded on seven commuter trains in Mumbai, India, killing hundreds of people (Rai and Sengupta, 2006).

Arun Gandhi reminded his audience that the world stood still in shock and shared the grief with the United States with an outpouring of condolence and goodwill, "but we squandered the good will, [and] instead of finding ways for the terrorists to learn, especially through our forgiveness we offered like with like" (Gandhi, 2007). As a response to the heinous acts of the attack on the World Trade Center of September 11, 2001, the United States along with its allies went to war to topple the Taliban regime in Afghanistan. Then, as a result of policy changes initiated by the United States, and the "coalition of the willing" in several parts of the world, we began to witness the consequences of war on terrorism transcending and creating terrors of war. In this context, we agree with Jeffrey Sachs, a renowned economist, that the war against want is no less important than the war against terror. If President Bush, and now President Obama, Prime Minister Brown (United Kingdom), and the coalition of the willing spent more time and money on Weapons of Mass Salvation (WMS), in addition to combating Weapons of Mass Destruction (WMD), then, we can be optimistic, and may be make this planet more safe and hospitable. The Bush administration has spent more than $400 billion for war, yet the United States was unwilling to spend more than .1 percent of that in 2007 on the Global Fund to Fight Aids, Tuberculosis, and Malaria.

Between 1994 and 1998 Vietnam, Malaysia, Brunei, the Philippines, and Singapore imported more than $5.4 billion in major conventional weapons. Further, acquisitions were made of diesel submarines, anti-submarine helicopters, and an assortment of supersonic anti-ship missiles by the Chinese People's Liberation Army Navy (PLAN). PLAN has ambitions to extend its influence throughout the waters surrounding Southeast Asia. Also, in Asia, India is increasing its military expenditure to counter Chinese military power and in turn Pakistan increases its military expense. There seems to be recognition that Weapons of Mass Destruction (WMD) can kill millions and fall into the hands of terrorists. In contrast, Weapons of Mass Salvation (WMS), are life saving vaccines, medicines, food and farm technologies, and avert millions of deaths each year in the wars against disease, drought, and famine. Around the world, inequality is increasing, while the world is further globalizing. Half the world, i.e., nearly three billion people live on less than two dollars a day. The GDP (Gross Domestic Product) of the poorest 48 nations (i.e., a quarter of the world's countries) is less than the wealth of the world's three richest people combined. Nearly a billion people entered the 21st century unable to read a book or sign their names. Less than one percent of what the world spent every year on weapons was needed to put every child into school by the year 2000 and yet it didn't happen. (UNICEF, 2006)

Global terrorism has to be addressed; however, there is a link between poverty, desperation, feelings of subjugation, and terrorism. Besides addressing precipitators and consequences of terrorism, we believe that we need to address poverty, a human-made disaster, along with the effects of natural disasters on the human condition. Therefore, we need to be attentive to rights within the wealth-producing process. A significant proportion of wealth comes from natural resources, and those are primarily in the economically impoverished world—the Global South. If the Global South refuses to work those mines, cut those forests, pump that oil, drive those trucks, or load those ships, the powerful nations will have no choice except to negotiate in good faith. If half the expenditures on arms turned to world development, humanity could eliminate poverty and terrorism. It is critical that sustainable social development be rooted in economic democracy (Smith, 2006, 2009).

After the inhumane and criminal acts of September 11, 2001, racial and religious profiling and stereotyping of people became rampant. We have witnessed increased strife and communal violence based on religious differences. In this ethos, it is useful to remind ourselves of the saying of an enlightened Hindu spiritualist, Swami Vivekananda, on the record of religion, over 110 years ago:

> No other human interest has deluged the world in so much blood as religion: at the same time nothing has built so many hospitals and asylums for the poor . . . as religion. Nothing makes us so cruel as religion, nothing makes us so tender as religion. All religions seem to be susceptible to the disease of fanaticism. Each religion brings out its own doctrines, and insists upon them as being the only real ones. (Cited from the discourse on "The Ideal of a Universal Religion" by Swami Vivekananda, January 12, 1896, Hardman Hall, New York).

President Obama in Turkey in April 2009 stated "We do not consider ourselves a Christian nation or a Jewish nation or a Muslim nation. We consider ourselves a nation of citizens who are bound by ideals and a set of values" (Harnden, 2009). This is a very important mind-set, because when secular democracies pursue such a perspective, we will be attending to the need of the hour, which is to focus on religious pluralism and understanding and to counter religious marginalization. Further, whether it is religious and/or racial marginalization of human beings, as social work educators and practitioners we need to recognize and undertake interventions based on the fact that multicultural education begins with everyone understanding his or her own roots and culture; this understanding gives a sense of grounded identity from which to learn and value others. We need to acknowledge that each of our families is a subculture of the larger community culture (or reference group—such as religious affiliation, professional group, geographic community, and so on), and every individual, group, family, and community has unique qualities based on their culture. It is therefore crucial that social workers be culturally aware, with competent skills in our relationships and assessment in order to promote sustainable development and conflict resolution.

The challenge is to understand our common humanity, and convey respect for local uniqueness and indigenous traditions that contribute to our richly woven universe. One cannot aspire to have a grounded understanding of diversity without adequate awareness of global interdependence. This awareness of global interdependence is critical, whether the professional social worker is engaged in assessment, intervention, or evaluation, and is illustrated in this book through a variety of case studies. The grounded understanding of diversity must take into account issues concerning mobile populations, cultural norms that pertain to power, hierarchy, gender status and its relevance in society, family functioning, religion and identity, and related group politics.

It is not an "either/or" proposition in social work when we seek global community to appreciate both cultural diversity and cultural uniqueness. One of the greatest dangers facing earth is the readiness to stereotype and dehumanize people who seem threatening, given to desperate acts of terror, or different in their approach to life than the state we happen to live in.

Hindu philosophy and First Nations' values, for example, have systematically included the uniqueness of individuals, and the common bonding of the human race as it pertains to interrelatedness and interdependence is reflected in those cultural traditions.

In order to be successful in our journey of promotion of sustainable development and peace, we need to be effective in cross-cultural communication. In this context, we must be reflective practitioners, and be able to transcend *awareness of our own culture* and the impact of our behaviors, especially in relation to *stereotyping*, to be *culturally competent professionals.* Therefore, we will have to focus on cultural *assessment* tools, and design and implement interventions that integrate *cultural efficacy skill sets*, so that we are systematically engaged in the promotion of sustainable development and harmony. So, in October 2006, when the Bush administration repealed habeas corpus and the Geneva Convention for noncitizens in one fell swoop in passing the Military Commissions Act of 2006 (Kelkar, 2006), we as social workers should have asked, "What interventions and steps would Jane Addams have taken?" and been inspired and acted. In this context, it is a paradox that nine days after 9/11, President George Bush delivered a speech to a Joint Session of Congress, in which he uttered the now famous words that "they hate our freedom . . . our freedom (to) disagree with each other. . . . Every nation, in every region, now has a decision to make. Either you are with us, or you are with the terrorists." Yet democracies around the globe are fighting terrorism and have antiterrorism laws, and have not repealed habeas corpus. People of color are likely targets of profiling. Despite these backlash reactions, people of color are loyal to their countries of citizenry, as reported in a recent study by the Institute for Public Policy Research: in Britain, Asians and African/Caribbean descendants feel more British than whites. The study found 51 percent of Asians and African/Caribbean descendants describe themselves as British compared to 29 percent of whites. This could be because the white population fragments into English, Scottish, Welsh, and Irish identities

(Stone and Muir, 2007). So one has to ask if legal and political identity structures are superseding cultural identities, and is this by design by the dominant
culture or minority culture, and we need to look at the related ramifications
for social policies.

THE ROLE OF SOCIAL WORK

Perhaps later we will see the first decade of the twenty-first century as a time
when social work came to recognize and act on the interdependence of global
networks, especially relating to our habitat and well-being. For example,
the impact of toxic environments on child development has been identified
by researchers as crucial in brain development but has taken time to filter
through to citizens, teachers, and social workers in terms of their practices
and workplaces (research in Glasgow, Scotland, in Burningham and Thrush,
2001). Mary Rogge presented a conference paper in 2002 on community
collaboration to rid schools of lead paint, and part of the dialogue included
the role of social work (Rogge, 2004). Jane Addams, 100 years ago, lifted
her skirts and picked up garbage to dump on the steps of the legislature as a
protest about the threat to public health of the refuse in the streets surrounding Hull House (Addams, 1910). However, it is a continuing challenge to use
our imaginations and constantly make the connections within social work and
across disciplines such as education. Social workers and teachers have many
opportunities with the increased access to computer technology to study
neighborhoods that combat poverty through innovative projects such as the
school in Hyderabad (see textbox 7.4).

Social workers now apply systems theory to their understanding of toxic
environments on human development, but the instruments for making an
impact are in early stages. This chapter widens the lens to the full spectrum
of impact from basic needs to optimum conditions for families to thrive.
Maslow's hierarchy of needs is a classic approach of a pyramid of needs
from the basics of food, water, and shelter to education and self-actualization
(Maslow, 1968). In this book we expand the concept to a cycle of needs,
based on a constant flow of interaction within and between communities,
where we see people being creative and resilient despite contemporary barriers and lack of access to healthy environments.

As with earlier chapters, readers are encouraged to think from their own
experience at the micro level to the largest levels of macro interaction. For
example, the impact of the World Trade Organization and the World Bank on
southern nations is reviewed in the context of structural adjustment programs.
The Silent Valley Project was a structural program—financed internationally
in order to restructure the local economic community but without adequate

Textbox 7.4. Cyber Savvy in Slums

The Mustaidpura Government High School in Hyderabad demolishes the stereotype of a government-run school being a place where teachers play truant and students learn next to nothing.

The computer lab is full, with about 24 children busy at the 12 computers, two to each. They are engrossed and the visitor does not arouse much curiosity since their attention is focused on the assignment that they are doing on the computer. The school is fairly clean, classes are full with students dressed in neat uniforms, teachers are busy referring to books in the staff room. The school is functioning smoothly, as indeed it should. However, this comes as a surprise since it is a government school in Karwan area in the Old City of Hyderabad, in Mustaidpura, a locality dominated by poor rickshawpullers, vegetable vendors and labourers who push, pull, heave and carry huge sacks of vegetables to the nearby wholesale vegetable market.

The Mustaidpura Government High School which has about 400 students is one of the few government-run high schools in Hyderabad that demolishes the stereotype of a government-run school being a place where teachers play truant and students learn next to nothing. The other school is the Kulsumpura high school, barely a kilometre from Mustaidpura. No wonder then, two teachers of these schools, M Narayana of Kulsumpura High School and Sunita Yadav of Mustaidpura High School won the Innovative Teacher Awards of Microsoft in 2005. Their projects on using computers as part of classroom teaching were among the 10 winners from 1200 applicants across the country.

How it all began
Kulsumpura and Mustaidpura schools were fortunate to get 12 computers each under the MPLADS of former Hyderabad MP, Mr K M Khan, five years ago. While several schools that were similarly gifted computers did not even bother to unpack the computers, these two schools not only set up a computer lab but even appointed instructors to teach the students. The instructors were paid by pooling the contributions of teachers and some parents.

Last year Narayana and Sunita were nominated to a course run by Microsoft and the state government to train teachers in computers. Subsequently, they used the skills learnt at the two-week course and produced multimedia lessons. While Sunita's lesson was on the working of the heart, Narayana's was on how radio and TV work. These projects bagged them the awards.

An excited lot
The teachers are as excited with the accessibility to computers as the students. "The lessons literally take the students into the subject . . . they get to see the subject while in a classroom they have to only imagine," said the 35-year-old Sunita who teaches biological sciences. "For instance, the heart beat can be

(*continued*)

shown, so also the flow of blood. The process of photosynthesis is fascinating and when seen on the computer it is mind-boggling," she said. The students are allowed to work on the computers from fifth class. The lower classes, from first onwards are taught from animated lessons in primary subjects like language and arithmetic. The programmes, donated by Azim Premji Foundation, are screened on a 29-inch TV set donated by a private bank. "Even private schools that take Rs 50 as monthly fees do not provide the kind of access to computers like we do," said Sunita proudly.

The students have the computer lab twice a week and two students work on one computer. They are taught MS Word and later Excel. By the time they pass out from class 10, they are proficient in all applications and most can use English and Telugu while some become proficient additionally in Hindi too. The children have even entered competitions and bagged prizes at district and state levels. "Despite our inadequate facilities our kids have delivered wonder-fully," said Narayana.

The teachers believe the computer education that these two schools offer are attracting more students. According to Sunita, computers have helped generate interest for studies among the children. "Naturally, there's even personality growth; they have become more confident and their self-esteem has increased," she said. Other benefits of exposure to computers include strengthening of fundamentals, improved reading ability, improved grasp of English language and improved general knowledge. In fact, students hang on in the school and in the computer lab for at least an hour after school hours and need to be shooed out.

Tremendous impact

What about the impact of computers on the teachers? "Old and young, all teachers are now using CDs in the classroom," said Narayana as they have discovered that it is effective. The teachers' knowledge levels too have shot up and needless to say, they have lost the fear of technology. Sunita found she can complete a topic in one class with the help of a computer, while normally four classes are needed in the traditional classroom teaching. Interestingly, at times the teachers turn to students for help with the computers that not only makes teachers more humble but also empowers the students.

What next then, for these teachers? "We don't have Internet. Our task of preparing lessons will be more easy if we can access the Net," said Sunita. Even if they find a sponsor to fund the Net connection, the schools have a problem. There is no broadband/cable provider for several kilometres around them. But for these determined teachers who improved the school result from zero pass 15 years ago to 70–80 per cent now, that is hardly a difficult target to meet.

Source: By R. Akhileshwari, *Deccan Herald,* May 4, 2006.

Textbox 7.5.   Participatory Management of Water Resources

Dr. Leila Naryanan

INTRODUCTION

This case scenario presents two irrigation projects carved out to enable farmers to manage common water resources in two states in the Indian Union, i.e., Tamil Nadu and Kerala. This is based on the principle that water is not the property of an individual but common property. Hence, the community takes responsibility for rehabilitation of water tanks, utilization, and maintenance of these resources.

Abstract theories do not take us to a just world and participation has to be placed in a specific context. This case example presents a brief account of the experiences of the European Community in assisting the Tamil Nadu and Kerala minor irrigation projects.

PARAMETERS, INDICATORS, AND METHODS

Parameters that formed the basis for planning were those which characterized the traditional systems of Tamil Nadu, namely, "we feeling" leadership, which was called "Kavimanyam" in pre-British India.

TAMIL NADU SYSTEMS

Tamil Nadu had a long tradition of collective irrigations management, with villages having two sets of organizations, one to manage village affairs, and the other to manage common water resources. After independence government took over the irrigation tanks, which deteriorated as they became purely technical systems to be maintained by engineers, losing the social aspect.

In 1984 Phase I of a tank rehabilitation project with the European Community assistance was started; however, this fell far short of the objectives, as it was purely construction oriented and did not develop any social networks. Phase II went a little beyond; nevertheless, here again, formation of farmer associations was a mere formality —that is, merely served on paper associations. It was only in Phase III that the task of concretizing the participatory approach started, with the formation of the community organizer working group and recruitment of community organizers.

(*continued*)

SOCIAL INVESTIGATION OR SOCIAL SCREENING

The project started with social investigation to ascertain whether there was a positive social context for intervention. The variables to ascertain were divided into (a) necessary conditions and (b) facilitating conditions, and if (a) were not there the rehabilitations project would not be taken up. The necessary conditions were that (1) water had high value for the group, and (2) farmers felt that the proposed tank rehabilitation would improve the system. Even this appraisal was a participating appraisal and in some areas was entrusted to nongovernmental organizations (NGOs), which later also carried out the rehabilitation. A number of nongovernmental organizations (NGOs) were reviewed, and two, namely Speech and ASA, were selected. In the Tamil Nadu minor irrigation project, there were community organizers working directly under the rural sociologist and social worker of the government organization or under NGOs.

After the completion of projects an assessment was made. The indicators for participation were (1) individual empowerment, that is, knowledge of farmers or stakeholders; (2) group empowerment based on confidence of farmers in the leadership; and (3) "we" feeling.

Of all the rehabilitated systems the NGO-managed systems presented a very positive scene for participation and sustainability. Here we have to distinguish between transactional and transformational catalysts, the former focusing on the immediate task without trying to view the farmers' situation as a whole. Transformational catalysts engage with others in a way that raises the catalyst, leaders, and followers to high levels of motivation and morality. The majority of community organizers working with the government were transactional, while the employees of the NGOs were both technical and nontechnical. Thus, the community organizers functioned as transformational catalysts who attempted to combine tradition and modernity bringing together farmers, government officials, donors, and consultants.

KERALA

Kerala, situated on the western side of the subcontinent of India, differs from Tamil Nadu in being blessed with abundant water. However this is concentrated during the monsoon and there are four or five months when rivers and wells go dry. Farm size in Kerala is very small, with an average of only 0.3 hectares, and many participants were part-time farmers. With the implementation of land reforms, handing over land to the tillers, farms became fragmented. Since Kerala had no accepted leaders or tradition of collective effort, the community organizers formed ad hoc committees to organize farmers. The last phase of the new project focused on extension activities, and two strategies were adopted to strengthen the farmer associations.

Since the schemes were small, and farmers were part-time farmers they were grouped into clusters.

Community organizers were given a format to classify schemes into

1. Independent—when farmer associations were self-starters, these associations were likely to continue even after catalysts left
2. Dependent—no pressing issues, but would require external support for some more time
3. Problematic—there were specific constraints, technical or social, but they could be resolved by concerned technical and administrative personal.
4. Nonfunctional—the farmers consider the scheme to have failed and the community organizers hand over their reports to the government department

CONCLUSION

Forming farmer organizations is not easy; and as a capital-forming activity, it cannot be planned like construction works. The two case studies show how the community organizers achieved greater success in projects in Tamil Nadu, where the NGO functioned as transformational catalysts. In Kerala, it was difficult for community organizers to integrate farmers and develop "we feeling," due to small landholdings. Further, when farming was done on a part-time basis, catalysts have to be transformational, so as to develop the "we feeling"—the spirit of holism—in other words, they have to spread the message to farmers: "Develop in your own way. You have to take control of and be responsible for your own water resources."

local involvement or respect for local tradition. Professor Naryanan gives the encouraging example of engineers' coming to appreciate the critical role of local organizing and leadership (textbox 7.5).

The controversial question of transparency in communication concerning aid is also raised. Economically advanced nations both provide and disguise the disbursement of aid. For example in Iraq huge contracts have been awarded to U.S.-based organizations, including Subway, to feed and shelter the thousands of troops there. There is a disconnect with the well-being of the local communities. Similarly a number of international hotels establish water sources and purification systems adjacent to schools and villages where children are suffering from water shortages. This is a complex web of economic power structures colliding with natural resources and human need.

Social workers are key in this work to increase our stewardship of the earth in profound and practical ways. The IFSW Code of Ethics, the United Nations Declaration of Human Rights, and the Convention on the Rights of the

Child, all call for a valuing of human life and the right to survive. These are challenging goals, but social workers are at the forefront of generating and maintaining values in society. Social workers encourage the use of imagination in making connections between the child who falls asleep sewing baseballs and the students who play with them in a far off-field (UNICEF, 1999). Social workers design crisis interventions in times of disaster and implement them; they also work in multidisciplinary teams to build houses and waterways. The earth is precious and we know it and can share that knowledge and call to action.

STUDENT ASSIGNMENTS

1. Identify the sources of conflict in the case study below describing the Narmada Dam. Who are the "actors," what is the issue, who is affected by the decisions, and what could be positive and negative outcomes?

   Case Study:
   Deccan Herald » Front Page » Detailed Story
   Angry Modi threatens fast from today
   Narmada: ball in SC court
   DH News Service New Delhi:
   After failing to arrive at a consensus over the issue of suspending the construction of Narmada dam, the Review Committee meeting of Narmada Control Authority on Saturday asked the Supreme Court to determine the future course of action. Union Water Resources Minister Saifuddin Soz, who chaired the meeting, recommended to Prime Minister Dr Manmohan Singh the suspension of all construction work in the dam.

   Gujarat Chief Minister Narendra Modi, who was in the Capital to attend the meeting, reacted by saying he would undertake a 51-hour fast at Sabarmati Ashram in Ahmedabad from Sunday to protest against the decision.

   The meeting ended in a stalemate with the chief ministers of BJP-ruled states of Gujarat, Madhya Pradesh and Rajasthan toughening their stand over the issue.

   Mr Soz, Union Environment and Forest Minister A Raja and Maharashtra Chief Minister Vilasrao Deshmukh countered it by bringing in a resolution asking the prime minister to immediately suspend work till all affected persons were rehabilitated in accordance with the directives of the Supreme Court.

   Pointing out that they were not against the dam's construction, Mr Soz said in the statement: "We found that rehabilitation in Madhya Pradesh is not in accordance with the Supreme Court's directives. There is a tie over this issue. So we are recommending the suspension to the Prime Minister.

   "It is open to the Supreme Court to consider whether construction of the dam should be temporarily suspended till such time as rehabilitation and resettlement of the project's affected families is done in consonance with its directions. The ministry has not ordered suspension of the construction work on the dam," a statement from Mr Soz said.

Last week, the Union Cabinet had asked Mr Soz to chair the meeting after being pressurized by Narmada Bachao Andolan leader Medha Patkar who has been on hunger strike since March 29 demanding the immediate suspension of the construction of dam and the rehabilitation of 35,000 displaced families.

Mr Modi accused the Centre of succumbing to pressure from Patkar. "The issue is unresolved. There is a tie. Three-fourths of the states are in favour of increasing the height of the dam."

Stating that the dam would generate 1450 MW of power, Mr Modi said, "The Centre is pushing the country into darkness for political reasons. I appeal to people of Gujarat to exert pressure through democratic means." Later addressing a press conference here, Mr Modi questioned the authority of Mr Soz to recommend the suspension of the dam work.

2. What makes it important for social workers to focus on religious pluralism and understanding and counterreligious marginalization?
3. Would you say that the Hindu spiritualist Swami Vivekananda's saying on the record of religion, over 110 years ago, is relevant today? If yes, what is your rationale? If no, what is your rationale?
4. In your opinion, why is the concept of stewardship as part of collective well-being important?
5. Why is social investigation or social screening important?
6. What is your understanding of participatory management? Why is participatory management important?
7. What is green technology? What is your opinion about United States' commitment at the present time to green technology?

Chapter Eight

Global Visions in Action

You must *be* the change you wish to *see* in the world.

—Mahatma Gandhi

Reaching for common ground in social work across the globe is a task that involves recognizing paradox. The wealthiest nations have become used to resources in ways that make them vulnerable. Some of us panic when the lights go out or the elevator stops. In countries where the power grid is under pressure, people share computers and plan for the low amps at midday by taking the stairs. In countries where access to electricity is limited and expensive, alternative forms of cooking have provided effective heat sources and contributed to sustainable development (www.solarcookers.org).

The affluent societies, more often than not, during times of natural disasters, isolate themselves, and they also underestimate the potential for cooperation with countries perceived to be less capable. For example, India, a southern nation, was criticized by some global political leaders who cast doubts on its ability to cope in the aftermath of the tsunami disaster of 2004. This criticism was made after India decided not to take help from northern nations. Yet, within hours of the killer tsunami slamming into India's shores, India sent naval ships to its neighbor Sri Lanka to help in relief efforts. This was despite the fact that India lost more than 13,000 people as villages were wiped out along its southern coast, as well as on the islands of Andaman and Nicobar, where the economic damage estimated by the United Nations stood at \$2.5 billion (Ramanathan, 2009). Failing to include India in the initial response team countries could be due to prejudice and the inability to accept that a nation with many impoverished people is capable of helping others.

175

The tsunami of 2004 caused a devastating loss of human life (230,000 dead) and property damage in Indonesia (130,000 dead), Sri Lanka (31,000 dead), India (13,000 dead), Thailand (5,400 dead), and Maldives (81 dead). In addition to loss of human life there was major property damage as well (BBC Online, 2005; Government of India, 2005). One of the authors of this book (Ramanathan) conducted field research in Cuddalore district, Tamil Nadu (a southern state in India) in December 2008, which marked the fourth anniversary of the tsunami. In addition to the death toll in India, nearly 6,000 were missing, and 647,599 were displaced. Of the fatalities, 75 percent were women and children (Government of India, 2005). The tsunami's impact on the southern state of Tamil Nadu was on its beaches, shrines, and tourist areas along the coasts. The research findings support that the use of the private-public-NGO model in disaster relief produces desired outcomes. Findings also indicate that people who had lost material things depicted less severe post-traumatic stress symptoms, and were coping better with life challenges, compared to those whose loved ones had died (Ramanathan, 2009).

In reality, the communities that work best in the face of trauma are those where history is part of the narrated local story, where social capital, in the form of extended family networks and village forums, complement human capital in the form of relationships, compassion, reassurance, and understanding. Where people are willing to come together and share tents or pool resources they prove more resilient than people used to living in isolation from one another, where ownership, privacy, and preservation of material things are paramount. Certainly, the world over, people behave in more sociable ways when experiencing the first throes of disaster, but their responses are more chaotic when they are not used to sharing the bus.

Mathbor asserts that the opulent countries are not necessarily the best prepared in facing hurricanes, tsunamis, and tornadoes (Mathbor, 2006). When people are used to working as communities and village life includes natural organizing and inclusive communication, they are quick to mobilize help. Where people are affluent, however, they live behind walls or security fences, and they are isolated and vulnerable, especially in their lack of recognition of this reality of common vulnerability. Nevertheless, Kahn (2005), who used data set on annual deaths from disasters in 73 countries from 1990 to 2002, finds that though richer nations do not experience fewer natural disasters than poorer countries, richer nations do suffer less death as a result of such disasters. Kahn further concludes that economic development provides implicit insurance against nature's shocks (Kahn, 2005). This means that while the impact and hardship of disasters may be buffered by countries that are democracies with higher quality institutions, nonetheless village forums complement human capital in the form of relationships, compassion, reassurance, and understanding, thus helping in developing coping strategies after a disaster (Ramanathan, 2009).

Just as certain countries are claiming military power and superiority (even dominance) over others, social work is at the forefront of educating people for mutual respect, based on social knowledge rather than accumulation of wealth. This chapter reviews key aspects of large systems and assessment. The impact of globalization on social work is discussed, with attention to both the *positive* forces of cooperation and pooled knowledge, such as social work education that includes disaster relief, and antipoverty measures including micro credit projects, and the *negative forces* of camouflaged power and control. Finally, the chapter offers steps in reaching for common ground.

This closing summary weaves together key themes of the previous chapters. It also revisits the framework of six clusters of research and knowledge that present a synthesis for assessment and practice steps (see figures 1.2 and 8.1).

The Common Human Condition
Human Rights
Ethics
Cultural Diversity and the Toll of Terrorism
Migration and Free Movement of People
Earth as Precious Habitat and Sustainable Resource

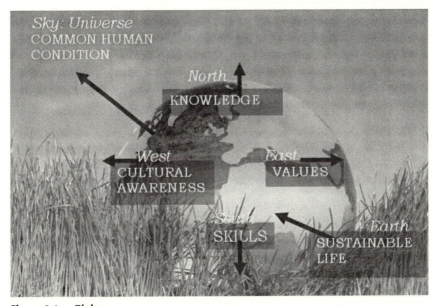

Figure 8.1. Globe

We have yet to thoroughly connect macro human behavior assessment and social development to practice with individuals and their families. It has been asserted that social work's research agenda in the 1980s was to blame the victim, and that inadequate attention was being paid to systemic issues and larger systems (Kagle and Cowger, 1984). Although we may ask why it has taken so long to appreciate our global interdependence, we set forth in this book the evidence and groundwork for accepting this reality by identifying the ways people are practicing across all system levels. The globalization of our communities is providing more opportunities for social work to respond to this need for broader perspectives on human well-being. Although, periodically, we have addressed linkages of poverty in the Global North to poverty in the Global South (limiting ourselves to national boundaries for comparisons), we have yet to address human condition adequately, in all its richness, urgency, and opportunity.

COMMON HUMAN CONDITION

In chapter 2, we discuss the idea that the concept of "human condition" is universal, but more often than not human condition is described within a particular context. Social work always discusses human behavior in relation to the environment, but it is easy for professionals who have access to power at a switch, cars that start, and food on the table, to forget what it means to be without access to basic resources to survive. Throughout this book we address the notion that all of us are subject to a "common human condition" and cannot live with dignity without our basic needs' being met. Earlier in chapter 2 we quoted our students' belief that the common human condition is part of everyone's life struggle. To grapple with and come to an understanding of the common human condition are a central part of the assessment process. We define the common human condition as

> The universal aspects of human existence such as the need for shelter, clean water, food, safety, identity, civil rights, intimacy, and song; that we step back from judging people without access to resources and recognize that all of us are vulnerable as individuals and stronger when we work in community.

Vandana Shiva refers to "cowboy" economics, whereby the corporation that finds "it" (be "it" gold, tin, diamonds, zinc, etc.) and has the money to extract it, keeps it. She suggests that we still find it hard to accept ourselves as citizens of an interdependent world (Shiva, 2002).

In 2005 we heard of a group of women in Ugborodo, Nigeria, who negotiated with an oil company to give them jobs and clean water. They peacefully filed into a refinery and took up residence until there were negotiations.

Unfortunately the complex relationships and systems of resources and boundaries that are a reality for planet Earth, more often lead to bloodshed and violence rather than the negotiated order in Ugborodo. *National Geographic* has documented the "curse of black gold," where villagers who used to be self-sufficient are overshadowed by vast oil wells and refineries whose spillages foul their water, kill their fish, and take food from their tables (Watts, 2007). Clearly too many people have yet to make the connection: peaceful negotiation is always preferable to violence. Peaceful interaction is the key, but when people have nothing to live for, it is also part of the common condition to become desperate. On a bus ride to meet a farmworkers' cooperative in Tolmin, Slovenia, Gabi Čačinovič Vogrinčič talked about her counseling with refugees from Sarajevo. She heard unbearable stories of escape and violence, experienced again and again as nightmares. She asked one of the authors of this book (Link): "What will you do to protect your child?"

Social work's role is to define and hold up the reality of human conditions and our common needs. Charlotte Towle wrote a classic volume in the 1945, discussing common human needs (Towle, 1945). Towle anticipated the need for dialogue and recognition that none of us can survive as an island, and all of us at some time in our lives are vulnerable. As we write and debate the common human condition in the twenty-first century, we are inspired by Towle's early expression of our need of each other.

HUMAN RIGHTS

Social workers are encouraged by the IFSW and the IASSW to utilize the Declaration on Human Rights in all their work. Often, country codes overlook the policies and convenants that have been painstakingly developed in international dialogue, and it is social work's role to ensure that these instruments are part of their practice. Malpractice occurs when instruments are ignored. Powerful case studies of the UNICEF *State of the World's Children* report remind us of the extent of human service taking place in global context (UNICEF, 2007).

As discussed in chapter 3, not all is well with the United Nations. The organization developed rapidly after World War II, but has been hampered in its global reach by the control of Western nations who currently dominate the Security Council. Also, as discussed in chapter 3, although the UN Declaration of Human Rights has helped advance individual rights, it continues to be a challenge to adequately address cultures with more collective orientation, for example the ancient cultures of China, India, Japan, Korea, and many other Asian countries, wherein the majority of the world's population resides. The interplay of individual and collective rights is the current reality and one in which social work leads the way in its attention to ecological systems, healthy communities, and cultural awareness.

As African and now Asian secretary-generals come to leadership, we all have the opportunity to support their call for more equitable sharing of decision-making power. To some, this sounds unrealistic, but with the increasing economic development and strength of countries such as Brazil, India, and China, the West cannot ignore this imbalance.

We have a perspective in social work, that human rights are rights inherent in nature. It follows that the sustainability of both humanity and our environment is important. Therefore, human rights and development are not two different entities but two sides of the same coin. It is imperative that we look at both individual and collective rights, self-determination and environmental rights, and in so doing reinvigorate the United Nations. Kofi Annan's parting speech as secretary-general (excerpt textbox 8.1), has reminded us of the original dreams for the United Nations that we could find peaceful ways to live together and recognize human rights. (This speech was one of the last public speeches in Annan's role as secretary-general of the UN.)

These five lessons from Secretary-General Annan are keynotes for social workers worldwide. They also speak to Annan's optimism, that we can learn from history and embrace a more just, cooperative, and humane future.

ETHICS

It is one of the strengths of the social work profession that practice is deliberately and carefully ethical. Just as we recognize that ethical behavior takes courage, we also see that it takes imagination. Now that we are faced with genome mapping, as social workers we are working to envisage the implications for gaining access to health insurance, interpreting reproductive health, planning family relationships—whom to marry, whom to adopt, what is the essence of being human. Currently national debates are taking place in the United States regarding President Obama's cancellation of the ban on federal funding for stem cell research (Stolberg, 2009). The twentieth century saw the horror of the concentration camps of the Hitler regime. It saw the failure of the idea of building a fatherland based on eugenics. Now the progress of science faces us all with questions of what it means to be sentient beings. The very essence may include our frailty.

In Selma Freiberg's early work on blind infants, she identified a critical role for social workers (Freiberg, 1974). When the family is responding with shock and quiet grief, the social worker is the advocate for the whole child—encouraging the parents to hold and celebrate this beautiful new life for all his/her potential—rather than having the "lost" attribute define their progress to secure attachment and joy.

Textbox 8.1. Kofi A. Annan Address

Secretary-General Kofi A. Annan,
Truman Library
December 11, 2006

As Secretary-General prepares to step down, five lessons learnt during difficult but exhilarating decade:

Thank you, Senator [Hagel], for that wonderful introduction. It is a great honor to be introduced by such a distinguished legislator. And thanks to you, Mr. Devine, and all your staff, and to the wonderful UNA chapter of Kansas City, for all you have done to make this occasion possible.

What a pleasure, and a privilege, to be here in Missouri. It's almost a home-coming for me. Nearly half a century ago I was a student about 400 miles north of here, in Minnesota. I arrived there straight from Africa—and I can tell you, Minnesota soon taught me the value of a thick overcoat, a warm scarf . . . and even earmuffs!

When you leave one home for another, there are always lessons to be learnt. And I had more to learn when I moved on from Minnesota to the United Nations—the indispensable common house of the entire human family, which has been my main home for the last 44 years. Today I want to talk particularly about five lessons I have learnt in the last ten years, during which I have had the difficult but exhilarating role of Secretary-General.

I think it's especially fitting that I do that here in the house that honors the legacy of Harry S Truman. If FDR was the architect of the United Nations, President Truman was the master-builder, and the faithful champion of the Organization in its first years, when it had to face quite different problems from the ones FDR had expected. Truman's name will forever be associated with the memory of farsighted American leadership in a great global endeavor. And you will see that every one of my five lessons brings me to the conclusion that such leadership is no less sorely needed now than it was 60 years ago.

My first lesson is that, in today's world, the security of every one of us is linked to that of everyone else.

- That was already true in Truman's time. The man who in 1945 gave the order for nuclear weapons to be used—for the first, and let us hope the only, time in history—understood that security for some could never again be achieved at the price of insecurity for others. He was determined, as he had told the founding conference of the United Nations in San Francisco, to "prevent, if human mind, heart, and hope can prevent it, the repetition of the disaster [meaning the world war] from which the entire world will suffer for years to come." He believed strongly that henceforth security must be collective

(continued)

and indivisible. That was why, for instance, he insisted, when faced with aggression by North Korea against the South in 1950, on bringing the issue to the United Nations and placing US troops under the UN flag, at the head of a multinational force.

- But how much more true it is in our open world today: a world where deadly weapons can be obtained not only by rogue states but by extremist groups; a world where SARS, or avian flu, can be carried across oceans, let alone national borders, in a matter of hours; a world where failed states in the heart of Asia or Africa can become havens for terrorists; a world where even the climate is changing in ways that will affect the lives of everyone on the planet.

- Against such threats as these, no nation can make itself secure by seeking supremacy over all others. We all share responsibility for each other's security, and only by working to make each other secure can we hope to achieve lasting security for ourselves.

- And I would add that this responsibility is not simply a matter of states being ready to come to each other's aid when attacked—important though that is. It also includes our shared **responsibility to protect** populations from genocide, war crimes, ethnic cleansing and crimes against humanity—a responsibility solemnly accepted by all nations at last year's UN summit. That means that respect for national sovereignty can no longer be used as a shield by governments intent on massacring their own people, or as an excuse for the rest of us to do nothing when such heinous crimes are committed.

- But, as Truman said, "If we should pay merely lip service to inspiring ideals, and later do violence to simple justice, we would draw down upon us the bitter wrath of generations yet unborn." And when I look at the murder, rape and starvation to which the people of Darfur are being subjected, I fear that we have not got far beyond "lip service." The lesson here is that high-sounding doctrines like the "responsibility to protect" will remain pure rhetoric unless and until those with the power to intervene effectively—by exerting political, economic or, in the last resort, military muscle—are prepared to take the lead.

- And I believe we have a responsibility not only to our contemporaries but also to future generations—a responsibility to preserve resources that belong to them as well as to us, and without which none of us can survive. That means we must do much more, and urgently, to prevent or slow down climate change. Every day that we do nothing, or too little, imposes higher costs on our children and our children's children.

My second lesson is that we are not only all responsible for each other's security. We are also, in some measure, responsible for each other's welfare. Global solidarity is both necessary and possible.

- It is necessary because without a measure of solidarity no society can be truly stable, and no one's prosperity truly secure. That applies to national societies—as all the great industrial democracies learned in the 20th century—but it also applies to the increasingly integrated global market economy we live in today. It is not realistic to think that some people can go on deriving great benefits from globalization while billions of their fellow human beings are left in abject poverty, or even thrown into it. We have to give our fellow citizens, not only within each nation but in the global community, at least a chance to share in our prosperity.

- That is why, five years ago, the UN Millennium Summit adopted a set of goals—the "Millennium Development Goals"—to be reached by 2015: goals such as halving the proportion of people in the world who don't have clean water to drink; making sure all girls, as well as boys, receive at least primary education; slashing infant and maternal mortality; and stopping the spread of HIV/AIDS.
- Much of that can only be done by governments and people in the poor countries themselves. But richer countries, too, have a vital role. Here too, Harry Truman proved himself a pioneer, proposing in his 1949 inaugural address a program of what came to be known as development assistance. And our success in mobilizing donor countries to support the Millennium Development Goals, through debt relief and increased foreign aid, convinces me that global solidarity is not only necessary but possible.
- Of course, foreign aid by itself is not enough. Today, we realize that market access, fair terms of trade, and a non-discriminatory financial system are equally vital to the chances of poor countries. Even in the next few weeks and months, you Americans can make a crucial difference to many millions of poor people, if you are prepared to save the Doha Round of trade negotiations. You can do that by putting your broader national interest above that of some powerful sectional lobbies, while challenging Europe and the large developing countries to do the same.

My third lesson is that both security and development ultimately depend on respect for human rights and the rule of law.

- Although increasingly interdependent, our world continues to be divided—not only by economic differences, but also by religion and culture. That is not in itself a problem. Throughout history human life has been enriched by diversity, and different communities have learnt from each other. But if our different communities are to live together in peace we must stress also what unites us: our common humanity, and our shared belief that human dignity and rights should be protected by law.
- That is vital for development, too. Both foreign investors and a country's own citizens are more likely to engage in productive activity when their basic rights are protected and they can be confident of fair treatment under the law. And policies that genuinely favor economic development are much more likely to be adopted if the people most in need of development can make their voice heard.

(continued)

- In short, human rights and the rule of law are vital to global security and prosperity. As Truman said, "We must, once and for all, prove by our acts conclusively that Right Has Might." That's why this country has historically been in the vanguard of the global human rights movement. But that lead can only be maintained if America remains true to its principles, including in the struggle against terrorism. When it appears to abandon its own ideals and objectives, its friends abroad are naturally troubled and confused.
- And states need to play by the rules towards each other, as well as towards their own citizens. That can sometimes be inconvenient, but ultimately what matters is not convenience. It is doing the right thing. No state can make its own actions legitimate in the eyes of others. When power, especially military force, is used, the world will consider it legitimate only when convinced that it is being used for the right purpose—for broadly shared aims—in accordance with broadly accepted norms.
- No community anywhere suffers from too much rule of law; many do suffer from too little—and the international community is among them. This we must change.
- The US has given the world an example of a democracy in which everyone, including the most powerful, is subject to legal restraint. Its current moment of world supremacy gives it a priceless opportunity to entrench the same principles at the global level. As Harry Truman said, "We all have to recognize, no matter how great our strength, that we must deny ourselves the license to do always as we please."

My fourth lesson—closely related to the last one—is that governments must be **accountable** for their actions in the international arena, as well as in the domestic one.

- Today the actions of one state can often have a decisive effect on the lives of people in other states. So does it not owe some account to those other states and their citizens, as well as to its own? I believe it does.
- As things stand, accountability between states is highly skewed. Poor and weak states are easily held to account, because they need foreign assistance. But large and powerful states, whose actions have the greatest impact on others, can be constrained only by their own people, working through their domestic institutions.
- That gives the people and institutions of such powerful states a special responsibility to take account of global views and interests, as well as national ones. And today they need to take into account also the views of what, in UN jargon, we call "non-state actors." I mean commercial corporations, charities and pressure groups, labor unions, philanthropic foundations, universities and think tanks—all the myriad forms in which people come together voluntarily to think about, or try to change, the world.
- None of these should be allowed to substitute itself for the state, or for the democratic process by which citizens choose their governments and decide

policy. But they all have the capacity to influence political processes, on the international as well as the national level. States that try to ignore this are hiding their heads in the sand.
- The fact is that states can no longer—if they ever could—confront global challenges alone. Increasingly, we need to enlist the help of these other actors, both in working out global strategies and in putting those strategies into action once agreed. It has been one of my guiding principles as Secretary-General to get them to help achieve UN aims—for instance through the Global Compact with international business, which I initiated in 1999, or in the worldwide fight against polio, which I hope is now in its final chapter, thanks to a wonderful partnership between the UN family, the US Centers for Disease Control and—crucially—Rotary International.

So that is four lessons. Let me briefly remind you of them:

First, we are all responsible for each other's security.

Second, we can and must give everyone the chance to benefit from global prosperity.

Third, both security and prosperity depend on human rights and the rule of law.

Fourth, states must be accountable to each other, and to a broad range of non-state actors, in their international conduct.

My fifth and final lesson derives inescapably from those other four. We can only do all these things by working together through a multilateral system, and by making the best possible use of the unique instrument bequeathed to us by Harry Truman and his contemporaries, namely the United Nations.

- In fact, it is only through multilateral institutions that states can hold each other to account. And that makes it very important to organize those institutions in a fair and democratic way, giving the poor and the weak some influence over the actions of the rich and the strong.
- That applies particularly to the international financial institutions, such as the World Bank and the International Monetary Fund. Developing countries should have a stronger voice in these bodies, whose decisions can have almost a life-or-death impact on their fate. And it also applies to the UN Security Council, whose membership still reflects the reality of 1945, not of today's world.
- That's why I have continued to press for Security Council reform. But reform involves two separate issues. One is that new members should be added, on a permanent or long-term basis, to give greater representation to parts of the world which have limited voice today. The other, perhaps even

(*continued*)

more important, is that all Council members, and especially the major powers who are permanent members, must accept the special responsibility that comes with their privilege. The Security Council is not just another stage on which to act out national interests. It is the management committee, if you will, of our fledgling collective security system.

- As President Truman said, "the responsibility of the great states is to serve and not dominate the peoples of the world." He showed what can be achieved when the US assumes that responsibility. And still today, none of our global institutions can accomplish much when the US remains aloof. But when it is fully engaged, the sky's the limit.

These five lessons can be summed up as five principles, which I believe are essential for the future conduct of international relations: collective responsibility, global solidarity, the rule of law, mutual accountability, and multilateralism. Let me leave them with you, in solemn trust, as I hand over to a new Secretary-General in three weeks' time.

My friends, we have achieved much since 1945, when the United Nations was established. But much remains to be done to put those five principles into practice.

Standing here, I am reminded of Winston Churchill's last visit to the White House, just before Truman left office in 1953. Churchill recalled their only previous meeting, at the Potsdam conference in 1945. "I must confess, sir," he said boldly, "I held you in very low regard then. I loathed your taking the place of Franklin Roosevelt." Then he paused for a moment, and continued: "I misjudged you badly. Since that time, you more than any other man, have saved Western civilization."

My friends, our challenge today is not to save Western civilization—or Eastern, for that matter. All civilization is at stake, and we can save it only if all peoples join together in the task.

You Americans did so much, in the last century, to build an effective multilateral system, with the United Nations at its heart. Do you need it less today, and does it need you less, than 60 years ago?

Surely not. More than ever today Americans, like the rest of humanity, need a functioning global system through which the world's peoples can face global challenges together. And in order to function, the system still cries out for far-sighted American leadership, in the Truman tradition.

I hope and pray that the American leaders of today, and tomorrow, will provide it.

Thank you very much.

Although a complex map of ethical decision making, the Seedhouse Grid (see figure 4.1) reminds us of the variety of components that need unraveling as we walk confidently into ethical discourse. Confidence may be challenged by the reaction of others. There is much debate about treatment of "whistle-blowers" and the repercussions plus isolation that ensues for those practicing moral courage (Strom-Gottfried, 2007). Holding corporations and nonprofits accountable will be a key aspect of social development in the coming century. Capitalism has failed to raise the well-being of those in poverty because the market has been manipulated. Competition does not flow freely because companies like Enron, Parmalat, and Chevron, as well as individuals such as Bernard Madoff, manipulate, pollute, and exploit. As these practices become more transparent, we have reason to be hopeful: the women of Ugborodo have taken an ethical stance and rely on wider support. In 2004, and 1999, one of the authors of this book, Ramanathan lamented about ethical issues and value dilemmas in the global economy, as they pertained to occupational social work. Ramanathan specifically talked about the unfortunate inverse relationship between increased economic activity in the Global South (economically developing nations) as it relates to health and safety of workers in these countires (Ramanathan and Link, 2004, 1999). It is encouraging to note that corporate social responsibility (CSR) has been gaining visibility in the corporate world in Western societies in this millennium. In some southern nations such as India, CSR has been more prevalent even in the previous millennium, as several large business enterprises were still family owned, and there was greater commitment to the community in which they did business, as opposed to larger corporations' allegiance to the shareholders. Increased visibility for CSR in Western societies in the current millennium is partly due to the economic crisis that was witnessed in the first decade of the millennium, and evolving business ethics as an important dimension of good corporate governance. Yet it is critical that the impact of increased economic activity on worker safety and health also be addressed through improved corporate governance of multinational companies. Social workers can and must play an important role in terms of advocacy on behalf of the individual workers, as well as collectively seek legislative protection of workers in the Global South, regarding health and safety. Social work values and human rights policy instruments, employed with insight, cultural awareness, and imagination, inform all our ethical decision making.

CULTURAL DIVERSITY AND THE TOLL OF TERRORISM

The social work educational community has a values-based and ethical responsibility to produce social work professionals who are actively inclusive and culturally aware in their myriad of professional encounters. An inclusive approach is critical both in terms of access to material resources and valuing of human dignity. This is critical to ensure human well-being that is focused on sustainable social development. In doing so, we need to urgently address the threats to civil liberties through religious and ethnic marginalization; promote, foster, and nurture economic democracy through initiatives of distributive justice; and be steadfast in our designing and implementations of peace acts in micro, mezzo, and macro aspects of social work practice. This means dissolution of the artificial demarcation of generalists versus specialists. When we deliberately aspire for an inclusive approach in our interventions, then we will be successful in our efforts for reaching common ground and move toward a just world. In this context, the following words from Martin Luther King Jr. see beyond 1963: "I can never be what I ought to be until you are what you ought to be. This is the way our world is made. No individual or nation can stand out boasting of being independent. We are interdependent" (King, 1963).

In the opening years of the twenty-first century, cultures seem more strained and separated in some parts of the world than ever before, particularly in the power play between those who would be the leaders of the "free world" and those who experience exclusion. The shadow of this first decade is the widespread use of terrorism to foment culture clash. The Latin word *terreo* means "to frighten." The *Oxford English Dictionary* defines terrorism as "government by intimidation, as directed and carried out by the party in power in France during the revolution in 1789–1794." Yet another definition of terrorism in the Oxford dictionary is "A policy intended to strike with terror those against whom it is adopted; the employment of methods of intimidation; the fact of terrorizing or the condition of being terrorized." On the other hand, *Webster's* definition of terrorism is "the systematic use of terror as a means of coercion." We define terrorism as "creation of an atmosphere of violence, destruction, and death." Thus, terrorism is a deliberate act that creates and exploits fear and creates an atmosphere of threat or violence, in the name of bringing about change. Generally, terrorist acts involve violence or the threat of violence. These violent acts are committed by individuals or nongovernmental groups—that is, by those who are neither part of nor officially serving in the military forces, law enforcement agencies, intelligence services, or other agencies of an established nation.

Terrorists attempt both to cause panic and to undermine confidence in the government and political leadership of their target country. Therefore, terrorism is designed to have psychological effects that reach far beyond its impact on the immediate victims or object of an attack. Terrorists mean to frighten and thereby intimidate a wider audience, such as a rival ethnic or religious group, an entire country and its political leadership, or the international community as a whole.

Terrorist groups generally have few members, limited firepower, and comparatively few organizational resources. For this reason they rely on dramatic, often spectacular, bloody and destructive acts, in order to attract attention to themselves and their cause. Through the publicity generated by their violence, terrorists seek to obtain the leverage, influence, and power they otherwise lack.

In broad terms the causes that have commonly compelled people to engage in terrorism are grievances borne of political oppression, cultural domination, economic exploitation, ethnic discrimination, and religious persecution. Perceived inequities in the distribution of wealth and political power have led some terrorists to attempt to overthrow democratically elected governments. As stated in chapter 7, at times, some national governments continue to engage in covert warfare, as they wage wars through terrorist surrogates. This is referred to as "state-sponsored terrorism."

The events of September 11, 2001, have no precedent in the history of terrorism in terms of planning and usurping technology. Similarly, Mumbai, the financial capital of India, has suffered several terrorist attacks. For example, in 2006, a series of bombs exploded on seven commuter trains, killing hundreds of people (Rai and Sengupta, 2006). Mumbai suffered further attacks in November of 2008, which left over a hundred dead.

As a response to the heinous attack on the World Trade Center of September 11, 2001, the United States, along with its allies, went to war to topple the Taliban regime in Afghanistan, and the war is still under way. While on the one hand we acknowledge that global terrorism has to be addressed, on the other hand, we agree with Jeffrey Sachs, a renowned economist, that the war against want is no less important than the war against terror. With the inauguration of President Obama and his administration in 2009, there is a renewal of commitment to the Global Fund, but the results have yet to be assessed.

It is no surprise that guns do not melt and that countries constantly trade in major conventional weapons, especially in war and periods immediately postconflict. While weapons of all varieties can kill millions and fall into the hands of terrorists, in contrast, weapons of mass salvation are lifesaving vaccines, medicines, food, and farm technologies. The constructive "weapons of salvation" avert millions of deaths each year in the wars against disease, drought, and famine. Although we have yet to find the mechanism to control the spread of conventional weapons across the globe that undo the work of organizations such as the World Health Organization and UNICEF, the Millennium Development Goals, with their intent to eradicate poverty, are a crucial commitment (www.un.org).

It is encouraging to note President Obama's emphasis on mutual respect in the world. An inclusive approach to dealing with nation-states is likely to reduce tensions and assist in the promotion of peace. In April 2009, while in Turkey, President Obama emphasized that the United States is not at war with Islam. He further stated, "In fact, our partnership with the Muslim world is critical in rolling back a fringe ideology that people of all faiths reject" (Tran, 2009). Later in April, while in Port of Spain, Trinidad, President Obama also pledged equal partnership in the Americas (Leighton and Feller, 2009).

Despite the encouraging words of President Obama, because of the current economic climate in the United States, and the visa-based employment restrictions placed on talented international workers, people of international, including Indian, origin continue to face biased and prejudiced treatment. For example, the Asian Indian population in the United States is becoming a target of epithets as demonstrated by the comments of radio talk show host Rush Limbaugh. On April 10, while discussing the outsourcing of jobs from America, Limbaugh viciously insulted India and her citizens, referencing the Danny Boyle 2009 film *Slumdog Millionaire* to make his point.

"There's a reason [these jobs] aren't coming back. They're outsourced for a reason, an economic reason, and they're not coming back," Limbaugh said, while speaking to a caller from Ohio. "If you're sitting out waiting for a job that's now being done by a slumdog in India, and you're waiting for that job to be cancelled, for the slumdog to be thrown out of work, and you to get the job, it ain't going to happen. It's not the way economics works" (*Rediff News*, 2009).

Around the globe, inequality is increasing, and as the world is globalizing economically it is leading to extreme gains in the wealth of a few. Half the world, that is, nearly three billion people, live on less than two dollars a day. The GDP (gross domestic product) of the poorest 48 nations (i.e., a quarter of the world's countries) is less than the wealth of the world's three richest people combined (UNICEF, 2007). Nearly a billion people entered the twenty-first century unable to read a book or sign their names. According to the International Labour Organization (ILO) report, the number of jobless worldwide in 2009, as compared to 2007, reached nearly 212 million in 2009 following an unprecedented increase of 34 million. During the same time frame, the number of unemployed youth worldwide increased by 10.2 million, the largest increase since 1991. Further, according to the ILO, the share of workers in vulnerable employment (wherein vulnerable employment is defined as the sum of workers accountable to themselves only and their contributing family workers) worldwide is estimated to reach over 1.5 billion, equivalent to over half (50.6 percent) of the world's labor force. In 2009, compared to 2008, the number of women and men in vulnerable employment is estimated to have increased by 110 million. The report also says that 633 million workers and their families were living on less than US$1.25 per day in 2008, with as many as 215 million additional workers living on the margin and at risk of falling into poverty in 2009 (ILO, 2010). According to UNICEF (2007), less than 1 percent of what the world spent every year on weapons was needed to put every child into school by the year 2000, and yet it did not happen. Therefore, as social workers, we see that there is a link between poverty, desperation, feelings of subjugation, and terrorism. Besides addressing precipitators and consequences of terrorism, we believe that we need to address poverty, a human-made disaster, along with effects of natural disasters on the human condition. Therefore, throughout this book we work to illustrate that sustainable social development must be rooted in economic democracy (Smith, 2006, 2009).

After the terrorist acts of September 11, 2001, racial and religious profiling and stereotyping of people became rampant, and still continue. In the words of President Barack Obama, "As for our common defense, we reject as false the choice between our safety and our ideals. Our Founding Fathers faced with perils that we can scarcely imagine, drafted a charter to assure the rule of law and the rights of man—a charter expanded by the blood of generations. Those ideals still light the world, and we will not give them up for expedience sake" (Obama, 2009).

When we continue to witness increased strife and communal violence due to religious differences, it is useful to remind ourselves of the saying of an enlightened Hindu spiritualist, Swami Vivekananda:

No other human interest has deluged the world in so much blood as religion: at the same time nothing has built so many hospitals and asylums for the poor . . . as religion. Nothing makes us so cruel as religion, nothing makes us so tender as religion. All religions seem to be susceptible to the disease of fanaticism. Each religion brings out its own doctrines, and insists upon them as being the only real ones. (Cited from the discourse on "The Ideal of a Universal Religion" by Swami Vivekananda, January 12, 1896, Hardman Hall, New York)

Given the current challenges and violence based on religious differences, the social work profession can no longer push religion under the rug, and needs to systematically focus on religious pluralism and understanding, and to counter religious marginalization, so as to support sustainable development. Therefore, it is imperative whether it is religious and/or racial marginalization of humanity, that as social work educators and practitioners we undertake multicultural interventions with understanding of our own roots and culture, which gives us a sense of grounded identity from which we to need to transcend so as to learn and value others. Additionally, we need to have a grounded understanding of our common humanity, and convey respect for local uniqueness and indigenous traditions. One of the greatest threats facing

Earth is the readiness to stereotype and dehumanize people who are different and hence seem threatening, given to desperate acts, or different in their approach to life than the state we happen to live in.

For effective promotion of sustainable development, peace, and security, the social work profession needs to be effective in cross-cultural communication. This requires that we be reflective practitioners, and transcend awareness of our own culture and the impact of our behaviors, especially in relation to stereotyping, to be culturally competent professionals.

Even though in the United States soon after September 11, 2001, initial policy reactions threatened well-established rights under habeas corpus, in a welcome turn in June of 2008 the Supreme Court ruled 5–4 in favor of habeas corpus rights for those being held in Guantanamo Bay (*Boumediene et al. v. Bush*, 2008). This was a momentous turnaround, holding unconstitutional the provision of the 2006 Military Commissions Act (MCA) and paving the way for prisoners to seek freedom through federal habeas corpus claims (www .nytimes.com/2008/11/07/washington/07gitmo.html).

Even though they may become targets of profiling, people of color are loyal to their countries of citizenry, as seen in Britain, where Asians and blacks feel more British than whites, who fragment into English, Scottish, Welsh, and Irish identities (Stone and Muir, 2007). So one has to ask if legal and political identity structures are superseding cultural identities, and if this is by design by the dominant culture or minority culture, and, if so, we need to look at the related ramifications for social policies.

MIGRATION AND FREE MOVEMENT OF PEOPLE

Even though the United Nations guarantees free movement of people as a universal right, insular immigration policies are resulting in unfair worker-immigration laws in Europe including the UK, France, and the Netherlands. Basically, all nations are a nation of immigrants. If we go back far enough, we will find that all of us can be linked to a common DNA. The immigrant experience, however, in the United States is justly celebrated, as no aspect of that experience is more American than the long heritage of early immigrants who settled illegally. Yet we wouldn't know it from the immigration debate that went on in the United States in 2005. It is ironic that America's pioneer values developed in a distinctly illegal context. In 1763, George III drew a line on a map from modern-day Maine to Georgia, along the Appalachians, and declared it illegal to claim or settle west of the line (which he reserved for Native Americans). Nevertheless, George Washington, and Ethan Allen, either grabbed land and/or engaged in selling land to other illegals.

Both historically, as well as now, it is quite deadly to bring a family across the line. Nevertheless, during the early settler times, illegals avoided arrest and settled down. Border patrols (both the British army and provincial militias) were not able to prevent such undocumented migration. George Washington continued to amass a lot of land without valid titles. After the revolution, when the British law was no longer valid, Washington's titles to the amassed land became legal. To celebrate their arrival and inform ourselves of their historical arrival on American soil, descendants of these immigration experiences (especially of those from Europe during the nineteenth and twentieth centuries) visit the Ellis Island Immigration Museum. Further, we celebrate the trials and tribulations of these ancestors who risked much to become Americans, and helped found a nation (Hogeland, 2006).

Today, representing the interests of the bulk of humanity that reside in southern nations, India is asking the United Nations to focus on issues of global migration. Specifically, India wants the United Nations to focus on promoting teamwork among nations to maximize the benefits of international migration while reducing its negative effects. "In the context of globalization, there is a need to recognize the inevitability of international migration." These salient issues were debated in the UN General Assembly committee debate on "Globalization and Interdependence." Besides the increased demand for specialists in developed countries, which can be matched by their availability in developing countries, economically advanced northern nations also expect southern nations to be more receptive to enhanced market access. It is interesting to note that even the World Bank's *Global Economic Prospects 2006* report documents that a rise in migration from developing countries raises incomes of natives in high-income countries. While the revolution in information and communication technologies provides the needed tools to tackle the challenges of globalization, Basu asserts that, even though the world is shrinking due to technology and communications, it is ironic this is accompanied by restricting of movement of people from the developing world (Basu, 2006).

In chapter 5, cultural competence is discussed, and in chapter 6 migration issues are discussed. Now when immigration is viewed in the context of cultural competence, it is germane to note that people of Asian Indian origin have become targets of racist behaviors including acts of violence perpetrated against both Asian Indian immigrants, as well as students who have come to Australia to pursue higher education. In fact, Australia's former defense force chief, General Peter Cosgrove, is asking his country to confront racism, and has stated that the attacks against Indians are a "major problem," and due to the nature of these attacks, in Melbourne, Australia, concluded that they were racially motivated (Cosgrove, 2010). Nevertheless, more recently, Australia's police chief, Simon Overland, has advised Indian students to keep a low profile and "try to look as poor as you can," to avoid attacks (*Deccan Herald*, 2010b). These kinds of comments clearly demonstrate the various ways in which insidious racism can raise its ugly head. Therefore, it is incumbent upon social workers to address these racist behavior patterns at the micro, mezzo, and macro levels of interventions.

EARTH AS PRECIOUS HABITAT AND SUSTAINABLE RESOURCE

In his research into differential giving following "disasters," Sundby discussed the different perception and definitions of what constitutes a disaster—10 people dead, or 100, man-made or natural (Sundby, 2006). The perception of how the disaster occurs, completely naturally as in the tsunami in 2004 or as a result of some political involvement, meaning that people hold some responsibility, influences giving and relief projects. In the film *Earth on Edge* (2006), Bill Moyers contrasts disasters such as polluted groundwater or mudslides with natural events and suggests that human beings have been slow to realize their interaction with the earth as a precious habitat. The Mississippi River is the arterial river of the United States, but often it has been used as the dumping ground of chemicals, household waste, old cars, debris of all sorts. Although it is a disaster that a dead zone is developing at the mouth of the Mississippi in the Gulf of Mexico, very little attention has been directed toward the deeper causes and collective responsibility.

Golam Mathbor (2006) contrasts the approaches of more and less developed countries toward habitat awareness and disaster relief. As we track the experience of disasters such as the 2004 tsunami or the 2005 hurricanes or 2010 earthquake in Haiti, we can identify the key elements of relief. These elements include preparation, response, relief, and reconstruction. Where natural disasters are a common occurrence we can learn the most about environmental factors. Most recently, on January 5, 2010, Haiti was the struck with the worst earthquake in the region in more than 200 years, which left the country in the American hemisphere in shambles (Romero, and Lacey, 2010). According to Carroll and Batty (2010), it was predicted that the death toll in Haiti would reach 200,000.

With regard to the areas where hurricanes are prevalent, Shiva (2000) as well as Mathbor refers to the realization that coastal deforestation is a problem. The band of mangrove or coconut trees in Sri Lanka served to protect and offer people shelter. Similarly, deep-rooted trees prevent soil erosion and flooding. Shiva, in her work on the "water wars," laments the trade-driven changes from natural, deep-rooted oaks in the foothills of the Himalayas to the water-absorbing and lighter root systems of the more marketable eucalyptus. Additionally, the health impact of climate change is a critical issue that policymakers should be aware of while setting priorities for action and investment to mitigate the impact of global climate change. This is the key message that WHO experts delivered at the "Climate Change Global Risks, Challenges, and Decisions" conference in Copenhagen. Building on research, WHO has identified three key health arguments for stronger climate change measures:

1. Climate change has adverse consequences for health: as carbon goes up, health goes down
2. Reducing greenhouse gases emissions can be beneficial to health: as carbon goes down, health goes up
3. The health impacts of climate change are felt unequally: effective response requires global action. (WHO, 2009)

Former president of the United States Bill Clinton acknowledges that the United States is the largest emitter of greenhouse gases. He points out the fact that the United States, with 5 percent of world's population and 21 percent of economic output, accounts for 25 percent of the emissions (Clinton, 2007). Two years after the U.S. Supreme Court finding (2007) on carbon emission in one of the most important environmental decisions in years, the Supreme Court ruled that the Environmental Protection Agency has the authority to regulate heat-trapping gases in automobile emissions. The court further ruled that the agency could not sidestep its authority to regulate the greenhouse gases that contribute to global climate change unless it could provide a scientific basis for its refusal (Greenhouse, 2007). Consequently, President Obama's administration has declared greenhouse gases a threat to public health, marking a major step—both practically and symbolically—toward federal limits on the carbon dioxide emissions scientists blame for global warming. This confirms that greenhouse gas pollution is a serious problem now and for future generations. With President Obama's call for a low-carbon economy, the pollution problem has a solution—one that will create millions of green jobs. This action opens the door to broad emissions limits in all other parts of the economy, including power plants and construction sites, which critics say could further chill an already recessionary economy. Administration officials insist they would prefer to let the United States Congress set those limits and that they will help spur millions of clean-energy jobs in the years to come (Tankersley, 2009).

If environmental issues are not systematically attended to, they are likely to threaten the sustainability of inhabitants of planet Earth. For example, decreased access to a safe, stable water supply in Asia "will have a profound impact on security throughout the region" (Asia Society, 2009). The cascading set of consequences that reduced access to freshwater will trigger include impaired food production, the loss of livelihood security, large-scale migration within and across borders, and increased economic and geopolitical tensions and instabilities. Although Asia is home to more than half of the world's population, the region has less freshwater per capita than any continent except Antarctica. While solutions are within reach, they require high-level political will and significant investments. Governments need to develop policies that can address multiple problems simultaneously, with the aim of reducing security risks and vulnerabilities and providing economic benefits such as investments in infrastructure for water conservation and management. Asian countries forging a regional approach in which governments and other key stakeholders, including nongovernmental organizations, civil society groups, and businesses work together to clarify responsibilities and coordination mechanisms to address water security concerns, will be beneficial (Asia Society, 2009). The Asia Society is an international organization dedicated to strengthening relationships and deepening understanding among the peoples of Asia and the United States. If a regional approach is wanting, then, the transboundary river systems that cut across countries will drive hydropolitics in the region. Therefore, we need to address the "universal environmental concerns," even though the solutions could vary due to regional uniqueness. Therefore, global environmental problems cannot be solved by perpetuating poverty in the southern nations. Additionally, with regard to energy usage, and types of energy consumption, there is a definite need for greater energy efficiency and the development of new technologies.

Central to this is the viewpoint that social work advocates: we are an interdependent planet and share responsibility for sustainable growth and the availability of resources for future generations.

Thus, human future on the earth means valuing our connection to our habitat. As presented in chapter 7, Chief Seattle speaks of the shining streams while alerting us to the possibility of defiling our bed. We have seen the consequences of pollution through the industrial revolutions in the United States and Europe and now in Asia. Sustainable projects, such as that of the irrigation projects of Professor Naryanan (see textbox 7.5) and the projects of Nobel Prize winner Wangari Maathai, need wider visibility. The *New Internationalist* consistently reports on the destruction of habitat by transnational corporations; occasionally they report better news (www.newint.org). As social workers we too can give visibility to the successes, as we have in the case studies offered in this text.

SOCIAL WORK EDUCATION IN GLOBAL CONTEXT

At the Annual Program Meeting of the Council on Social Work Education in the United States in 2006, an international group of educators came together to discuss the issues facing less developed countries as they build their social work programs. Peta Anne Baker, from Jamaica, recognized the universals in social work, such as concern about the spread of HIV/AIDS, human trafficking, disaster relief, and human rights, but stated that this is not enough. Baker and her colleagues in the Caribbean sought to go beyond global awareness to seek a parallel process of social work that is context-specific, that reflects the local culture and traditions, rather than a model imposed from outside. The outside models in this instance were cited as the United States and European forms of social work curriculum and their emphasis on individual problems rather than societal and community work.

The preface to the Indian Declaration of Social Work Ethics similarly calls for less developed countries to generate their own models of work that better reflect their social networks, social justice, and community group focus (Desai, 1998). In his call for something with the "smell of Africa" Abbye Tasse (2006), president, International Association of Schools of Social Work, based in Ethiopia, speaks of the need for analytical tools that reflect the reality of absolute poverty. He asked for respect for a variety of approaches to democracy (in jest he listed several definitions of democracy, including "one man, one vote, once") and greater insight as to the impact of uneven access to resources. There is an arrogance on display when educated social workers from more developed countries automatically assume that they can help less-well-resourced countries. They may go in a spirit of goodwill, but also with the camouflaged belief in their superior lexicon of knowledge. Giving up the superiority means claiming the human connection.

Tasse (2006) refers to the "paradox of poverty," where some people in the Global North underestimate the skills and resilience of people and countries experiencing poverty. As social workers this is familiar: we know the dynamic of underestimating capacities from attitudes toward people experiencing financial and employment crises in the United States or United Kingdom. Welfare reform has been embraced in punitive and demeaning ways, and social workers are part of the implementation—for example, of sanctions that reduce monthly income, regardless of the age and nutritional needs of children in the family. The International Labour Organization identifies work as including the work of child raising and child minding and challenges the West's current focus on structural adjustments forced on people experiencing poverty, also known as welfare reform (ILO, 2010). Gradually the informal work sector is being given recognition and the "right to sit" and sell their homemade wares.

Tasse, from the school of social work in Ethiopia, asks, "Are you qualified to help me?" The response from a Western-trained educator or social worker needs to be, "Perhaps, but tell me what your reality is and let me pay attention to your capacities, to what you have here, and to how you cope before I assume I have something to offer."

Our challenge in reaching common ground is for people in the West to move away from the arrogance of measuring our status by our degrees and the pile of things we own. Instead we can reach for the recognition that many of us have been pampered and are vulnerable because of the way we take for granted the resources at our fingertips. The impulse to work together is to be trusted in the context of a complex interplay of understanding. A process is becoming apparent at the Center for Global Education in Minneapolis. It has been part of the preparation of students traveling to fieldwork and homestays in Mexico and Namibia, where the travelers are asked to keep a reflective journal, to educate themselves about the culture they are visiting, and to step back from their daily expectations and be respectful, curious, and open to new learning.

In a recent visit to Mexico, a North American student locked herself in her dorm room after a visit to the city center and refused to answer the door. She literally closed down, overwhelmed by the poverty she had been unable to imagine. From the perspective of the educator who coaxed her out (Link), the student had joined people lined up to buy tortillas. A small boy with a toddler on his shoulders came begging and in her hesitant Spanish she explained that she would buy them tortillas. When at the front of the line, she looked around for the child, only to see him rush round the corner with a whole clan of siblings. The student had insufficient money to buy for all of them and fled. Suddenly she realized that she cannot only respond on the micro level, one by one, but can find her role as she seeks to understand the structural reasons for the children's abject poverty. Then she can act on that understanding.

For experienced educators, closing down and being exhausted are typical responses to heat, population pressure, dehydration, and lack of food, but millions of people experience this every day. In their local and other worlds dialogue, the Center for Global Education encourages us to make a ritual of leaving our habitual existence when traveling to another country, especially one that is less materially resourced. Stepping out deliberately and identifying what we are leaving behind invokes an open approach to learning from others. Stepping consciously into a new world of encounters, friendships, sights, scents, food, traditions, and greetings, enhances learning. Cali Breese describes her encounters in China in textbox 8.2 and illustrates this "stepping out." The process involved in appreciating context includes at least the following phases:

- *Preparation* through personal experience, contacts through technology, media (such as Allafrica.com, the Hindu, and so forth), advance planning, reading, finding mentors.

Textbox 8.2. Description of Event: Peace Corps Volunteer in China

Cali Breese

Date: 6/30/02 to 4/12/2003

Summary: After a competitive application process stressing my skills, adaptability, and cross-cultural understanding, I was invited into Peace Corps service following my graduating from college. I was assigned to teach English as a Foreign Language at Qingyang Teacher's College in Gansu Province, People's Republic of China.

I entered training on June 30, 2002, participating in an intensive 10-week program in the cities of Chengdu and Yibin, China. Area studies included 45.5 hours in history, economics, political development, and cultural norms of China. Technical training included 93 hours in the methodology of teaching English as a Foreign Language and curriculum design. As part of the technical training, I completed three weeks of practice teaching in a model school at Yibin University. I thought I was ready.

My host city of Yibin was located three hours north of Chengdu by bus. Each day, I felt challenged to understand the dialects of the lecturers who originated from different parts of the country, to intensely focus on the history of China and culture of China, and to move in with a Chinese host family with whom I would be living for two months. I remember how difficult it was to acclimate to a new city, filled with strange city smells and unique sounds to which I was not accustomed. Walking down the street, I found myself surrounded by others who resembled my short stature and midnight black hair color, and this was reassuring. I did not understand the social rules however, for example to the nationally acclaimed game of Mahjong, or when it was appropriate to spit bones from meals on the floor, and how to communicate with my family that could not speak English but spoke many dialects.

My time in Yibin challenged me to think of my experience as a "sink or swim" time in my life. I struggled each week to learn how to do the grocery shopping, how to balance at 6:00 AM during our Tai-Chi morning exercises, and to find the words from my limited Chinese vocabulary to tell them how much I appreciated their patience and genuine interest in me. They made a huge display of my birthday by taking me to a breakfast of hot noodles and throwing an evening party with my friends and their extended family. I always felt that they welcomed my friends into their home as they did with their daughter. My host parents even gave up their bedroom so that I could have privacy within the home for two months. Their thoughtfulness and sincerity helped me to feel comfortable in slowly releasing my grasp of my American cultural tendencies, including being individualistic rather than communal, in the hopes of learning and experiencing what it is to be included and welcomed as a member in a Chinese family.

- *Self-review* of ability to be flexible, respectful, patient, willing to try new food, welcoming, calm in a variety of settings.
- *Exposure* to new culture—this can be successful learning but it can also be too much too quickly in ways that cause a shutting down or backing off the original good intent.
- *Graduated contribution*—the best way to settle into a new place is to patiently observe and be ready to be useful in small ways.
- *Acceptance of others' preconceptions.*
- *Readiness for exchange of skills.*
- *Receptive attitude toward the hard conversations.*
- *Engaging in ongoing reciprocal learning.*

During the nineteenth and twentieth centuries, many countries were colonized and occupied by European and North American countries for trade and extraction of resources, especially minerals and oil. The story unfolding in the twenty-first century is the effort by many people to reach for greater understanding, for more respectful and peaceful interaction. Common ground is sought that does not minimize the local context and allows for appreciation of identity, history, and culture. Although the media manipulate and make money from the jolts per second of war and terror, we are entering a period of fewer wars and increased innovation, for example, in the ways professionals are cooperating across borders—in Doctors without Borders, Farmers without Borders, and the more recently proposed Social Workers without Borders (Boston College International Social Work Conference, March 2007). The Peace Force that entered Sri Lanka in 2004 was one of the first to use the strength of their peaceful human strength to be present and deescalate aggression. In the spring of 2007, Irish newspapers were full of the headlines "Peace Is Breaking Out." Bitter foes were coming together in words of reconciliation. The leaders of Sinn Fein Republicans and the Northern Ireland Protestant Unionists sat together in Stormont and acknowledged the suffering and pain experienced on both sides during the decades of struggle, known as the "troubles."

Similarly, even though we hear about the heavily armed young men protesting the exploitation of their local communities by oil companies, there are quieter and more constructive approaches. In 2005 the women of Ugborodo filed quietly in the early morning into the Chevron plant and took the security guards by surprise. They thought they had arrived in heaven: "we did not know what lay across the river from our village, the shine, the floors, the clean water." Although there is much negotiating to do, such community organizing and taking of power are frequently found (see discussion of Luz y Libertad, in chapter 2 of this book).

Apparently it is not the most commercial news when communities make peace—social workers every day are waging peace. The Dalai Lama is heard in his call for compassion. The possibilities of the profession are inspiring as we seek common ground while respecting our local context and traditions. The Christian Peacemaker Teams (CPT) in Colombia has posted its mission statement and many social workers are taking part in peacemaking missions in Colombia:

> CPT Colombia is a community made up of trained volunteers from different cultures that forms part of the international, ecumenical organization, CPT. Our work is based in, though not limited to, the Middle Magdalena region of Colombia. We work together on grassroots initiatives to expose and transform structures of domination and oppression through active nonviolence in order to make possible a world grounded in respect, justice and love, even of enemies. (Read more at www.cpt.org)

It is one of the most encouraging aspects of contemporary social work, that we begin to see the connections between structural issues of poverty lived out in the actions of workers who travel across borders to offer their service to whole communities, believing in their common humanity.

CONCLUSION

There is a wealth of knowledge awaiting social workers when we venture to listen to global voices. All our communities are now drawn closer, or in Friedman's terms, on a more level playing field, with access to Internet cafes and cell phones in the remote places and highest mountain villages (Friedman, 2004). As this book demonstrates, this increased ability to communicate is developing in tandem with the migration of labor and the globalization of the marketplace. Such rapid change brings both opportunities and challenges to the social work profession. It may be easier for a practitioner to focus on a client and his or her family in the home or immediate community with goals that relate to the daily needs of surviving—whether it be food, shelter, education, health, or work. It is no longer ethical, however, to focus only at the personal or "micro" level of interaction; the social work profession is by nature systemic. Also, our human relationships whether social, economic, political, or cultural are inextricably global and interdependent (Lyons, Manion, and Carlsen, 2006). A case example of this interdependence is the transfer of sanitation technology from a global southern nation that is economically challenged (India) to a global northern nation that is economically advanced (Japan). Specifically, we are referring to Sulabh International's (a leading sanitation NGO in India) decision to start its operation soon in Japan by constructing low-cost toilets popularly known as "Sulabh Sauchalaya." The decision was made in the light of the initiatives by the Japan International Cooperation Agency, on whose invitation Sulabh founder Bindeshwar Pathak—winner of the coveted Stockholm Water Prize in 2009, for his efforts in the field of sanitation to improve public health—visited Tokyo to throw light on effective methods for easy disposal of human waste (*Deccan Herald*, 2010a).

Social work practice role-models to other disciplines, such as education or law, that no one exists in a vacuum and when we work in one system it has ripple effects across many. The metaphor of chaos theory works for human service: that a butterfly flapping its wings in Hong Kong becomes a tornado in Florida (Wheatley, 2000). Similarly, when a farmer in Kansas puts too much pesticide on his fields it drains off with rainwater and contributes to the dead zone developing at the base of the Mississippi, in the Gulf of Mexico. This in turn affects the Mexican fisherman's family livelihood so that he thinks of becoming a migrant worker to the United States (Moyers, 2006). The family who hopes to adopt a child from another country is encouraged to think through their cultural roots and the "language of blood" (Trenka, 2003). Parents must be able to rely on professionals who practice ethically and are fully aware of global policy instruments, such as the Convention on the Rights of the Child, that affect their work. The migrant laborer or refugee expects to meet a worker who can find the resources necessary to help with integration into the new community. Social workers must interpret, listen to cultural traditions, and walk beside children recovering from the trauma of losing their roots or taking part in long journeys searching for safety. At borders, social workers are people who can prevent human trafficking and exploitation. The list of connections to social work and globalization is a long one that is just begun.

As we close this book we encourage readers to take the broadest global view of their work and their future. We see many opportunities for peaceful community building despite the daily imagery of our television screens. Commercially, headlines like "Peace Is Breaking Out All Over" do not hold the public's attention as well as violence, but in some countries, reporting of violent acts is left to the last pages; we can relearn being peaceful (Arun Gandhi, 2007). Many countries are focusing on their positive steps: In this context the politicians, families, and children of Northern Ireland are putting peace first. In Ugborodo, the women are taking charge. In the organization Luz y Libertad, people are working with confidence for a better world. We offer in closing a poem from Lavanya Krishnan that echoes this belief, that we can build well together and treasure this planet:

> "The Earth Breathes Again"
> The colors are golden . . . rich;
> They stand a while
> Then burst into flame . . .

But the land is bare . . . brown;
Smoky gray earth
And sighs of pain . . .

Sometimes, in the darkness
I hear voices coarse and screeching
Like ravens fighting in the dust
Like angry people weeping . . .
But, sometimes when
These voices pause
As if listening to another,
The strangest music
Slowly floats . . .
And the voices melt together.

Note by note they weave a song . . .
Golden, jeweled, breathing!
Like a seamless layered tapestry
Boundlessly flowing . . .
One breathing golden drop
(Before the burst of flame)
Falls and frozen dreams
They thaw, and the earth,
She breathes again!

References

CHAPTER 1. SOCIAL WORK PRACTICE IN A GLOBAL SOCIETY

Aaronson, S. & Zimmerman, J. (2006). "Fair Trade? How Oxfam Presented a Systematic Approach to Poverty, Development, Human Rights, and Trade." *Human Rights Quarterly, 28*(4).

Addams, J. (1930). Address to the Women's International League for Peace and Freedom at The Hague.

Aslam, A. (2002). *Land Rights for Women*. Washington, DC: International Food Policy Research Institute. www.ifpri.org/resources

Augsburg College. (2003, summer). *Human Services in Mexico: Semester Debriefing with Faculty and Students*. Minneapolis: Augsburg College, Center for Global Education.

Barash, D. (2000). *Approaches to Peace*. New York: Oxford University Press.

Burningham, K. & Thrush, D. (2001). *Rainforests Are a Long Way from Here*. York, UK: Joseph Rowntree Foundation.

Council on Social Work Education. (2004). *Education Policy Standards*. Alexandria, VA: CSWE.

Council on Social Work Education. (2008). *Educational Policy Statement*. Alexandria, VA: CSWE.

Dominelli, L. (2009). "Repositioning Social Work." In *Social Work: Themes, Issues and Critical Debates*, ed. R. Adams, L. Dominelli, & M. Payne Basingstoke, UK: Palgrave Macmillan.

Feller, E. (2001). *Introduction to the UN High Commissioner for Refugees Report*. Geneva: UNHCR, p1.

Friedman, T. (2004). "It's a Flat Earth after All." *New York Times*.

Gangrade, K. D. (1987). "Development of Voluntary Action." In *Encyclopaedia of Social Work in India*. 2nd ed. New Delhi: Government of India, Ministry of Welfare.

Garcia, T. (2002, November 20). "Geography Survey Report." Public Broadcasting Service.

Germain, C. (1991). *Human Behavior in the Social Environment*. New York: Columbia University Press, 1991.

Gould, K. (1995). "The Misconstruing of Multiculturalism: The Stanford Debate and Social Work." *Social Work, 40*(2), 198–205.

Havel, V. (2000). "The Politics of Responsibility." In *Approaches to Peace*, ed. David Barash, pp. 257–261. New York: Oxford University Press. Reprinted from the *World Policy Journal* 12, no. 3 (1995): 81–87.

Hell to Pay. (1991). Video. New York: Women Make Movies.

Kielburger, C. & Kielburger, M. (2004). *Me to We: Turning Self-Help on Its Head.* Mississauga, ON: Wiley.

Link, R. (1995, spring). "British Family Centres and Parent Participation: Child Protection through Empowerment." *Community Alternatives International Journal of Family Care, 7*(1) 81–106.

Link, R. & Bibus, A. (2000). *When Children Pay*. London: Child Poverty Action Group.

Link, R. & Čačinovič, G. (2004). "US–Slovenia Exchange Program." In *Models of International Collaboration*. Washington, DC: CSWE.

Link, R. & Healy, L. (2005). *Teaching International Content*. Washington, DC: CSWE.

Martin, Chris. (1999, October). "Banana Split." *New Internationalist*, 317.

Mayadas, N., Ramanathan, C. S. & Suarez, Z. (1999). "Mental Health, Social Context, Refugees and Immigrants: A Cultural Interface." *Journal of Intergroup Relations, 25*(4), 3–14.

Moyers, B. (2000). *Earth on Edge*. PBS video.

Obama, B. (2010). "Remarks by the President in the State of the Union Address. January 27, 2010." Washington, DC: Office of the Press Secretary, The White House. www.whitehouse .gov/d-press-office/remarks-president-state-union-address

O'Connell, P. (2007). "Globalization and Human Rights." *Human Rights Law Review, 17*(3).

Oneindia (2007, September 8). "Pharma Company to Provide Free Insulin to the Poor." news .oneindia.in/2007/09/08/pharma-company-to-provide-free-insulin-to-poor-1189254852 .html

Potocky, M. (1996). "Toward a New Definition of Refugee." *International Social Work, 39*(3), 245–256.

Prothrow-Stith, D., with Weissman, M. (1991). *Deadly Consequences*. New York: Harper Collins, 8.

Ramanathan, C. S. (2002). "Diversity and Inclusiveness: A Hindu American View." Paper presented at the Religious Pluralism and Democratic Societies Conference, Kuala Lumpur, Malaysia.

Ramanathan, C. & Link, R. (Eds.) (1999, 2004). *All Our Futures*. Pacific Grove, CA: Thomson/ Brooks/Cole.

Ramanathan, R. & Beverly, C. (1999). "International Travel Experiences: African-American High School Students and Urban School Communities." *Journal of Intergroup Relations, 25*(4), 15–29.

Roy, A. (2004). *An Ordinary Person's Guide to Empire*. Cambridge, MA: South End Press.

Ryan. (1976). *Blaming the Victim*. New York: Vintage.

Sachs, J. (2005, March 14). "Sustainable Development." *Time*, p. 48.

Saleeby, D. (2002). *Strengths Perspective in Social Work Practice*. 3rd ed. Boston: Allyn and Bacon.

Sen, A. (2004). *Development's Unfreedoms*. New York: Anchor.

Singer, P. (2004). *One World*. New Haven, CT: Yale University Press.

Skarnulis, E. (2004). "Quality of Life Assessment." In *All Our Futures*, eds. C. Ramanathan & R. Link. Pacific Grove, CA: Thomson/Brooks/Cole.

Sullivan, M. (1993). "Social Work's Legacy of Peace Echoes from the Early 20th Century." *Journal of Social Work, 38*(5), 513–520.

Tan, Ngoh-Tiong. (2004, June). "Crisis Theory and SARS: Singapore's Management of the Epidemic." *Asia Pacific Journal of Social Work and Development, 14*(1), 7–17.

Titmus, R. (1968). *Commitment to Welfare*. New York: Pantheon.

UN. (2000). *Development Report*.

UNICEF, (1997) *State of the World's Children*. New York: UNICEF.

———. (2000). *Progress of Nations*. New York: UNICEF.

———. (2010). *State of the World's Children*. New York: UNICEF.

UNHCR. (2007). *Statistical Yearbook*. www.unhcr.org/statistics.html

Watkins, K. (1995). *The Oxfam Poverty Report*. www.oxfam.org

CHAPTER 2. COMMON HUMAN CONDITION

Amnesty International. (2005). *Nigeria Report, Ten Years On: Injustice and Violence Haunt Oil Delta*. www.amnestyusa.org/business/nigeriareport/report.pdf

Ashford, J., LeCroy, C. & Lortie, K. (2006). *Human Behavior in the Social Environment*. Belmont, CA: Thomson.

Bibus, A., Link, R. & O'Neal, M. (2005). "The Impact of US Welfare Reform on Children's Well Being: Minnesota Focus." In *Safeguarding and Promoting the Well Being of Children, Families and Their Communities*, eds. J. Scott & H. Ward. London: Jessica Kingsley.

Burningham, K. & Thrush, D. (2001). *The Rainforests Are a Long Way from Here*. York, UK: Joseph Rowntree Foundation.

Clinton, H. R. (2009, February 12). "The 50th Anniversary of Martin Luther King, Jr.'s Trip to India and Black History Month." Treaty Room, Washington, DC, U.S. Department of State. www.state.gov/secretary/rm/2009a/02/117269.htm

Cooley, C. (1908). "A Study of the Early Use of Self Words by a Child." *Psychological Review, 15,* 339–357.

Cronin, A. (1937). *The Citadel*. Canada: Little, Brown and Company.

Fulford Family Centre. (2002). *Parent Handbook*. Bristol: Barnadoes.

Gaudier, M. (1993). "Poverty, Inequality, Exclusion: New Approaches to Theory and Practice." In *Social Exclusion: Rhetoric, Reality, Responses*, eds. G. Rodgers, C. Gore & J. B. Figueiredo. Geneva: International Institute for Labour Studies, International Labour Organization (ILO) Publications.

Healy, L. (2001, 2008). *International Social Work: Professional Action in an Interdependent World*. New York: Oxford University Press.

International Labour Organization. www.ilo.org

Korten, D. C. (1995). *When Corporations Rule the World*. West Hartford, CT: Kumarian Press and Berrett-Koehler.

Link, R. & Healy, L. (2005). *Teaching International Content*. Alexandria, VA: CSWE.

Maslow, A. H. (1968). *Toward a Psychology of Being*. Princeton, NJ: Van Nostrand.

Midgley, J. (2003). "Assets in the Context of Welfare Theory: A Developmentalist Interpretation." *Social Development Issues, 25*(1–2).

Norton, D., Brown, E. F., Brown, E. G., Francis, E. A, Murase, K. & Valle, R. (1978). *The Dual Perspective: Inclusion of Ethnic Minority Content in the Social Work Curriculum*. Alexandria, VA: CSWE.

Patel, A. (1998, February 22). "Operation Flood." Keynote Address to the Second Pan Commonwealth Veterinary Conference. Bangalore.

Ramanathan, C. & Link, R. (Eds.) (1999, 2004). *All Our Futures*. Pacific Grove, CA: Thomson/Brooks/Cole.

Ryan, W. (1976). *Blaming the Victim*. New York: Vintage.

Sartre, J.-P. (1960). *Roads to Freedom*. Paris.

Scottish Education Authority Report. (2004). *The Rainforests Are Far from Here*.

Sherraden, M. (Ed.). (2003). "Asset Building and Social Development." Special issue, *Social Development Issues, 25*(1–2).

Shiva, V. (2002). *The Water Wars*. Cambridge, MA: South End Press.

Specht, H. & Courtney, M. E. (1994). *Fallen Angels: How Social Work Has Abandoned Its Mission*. New York: Free Press.

UNICEF. (1997). *The State of the World's Children*. New York: UNICEF.

———. (2000). *The Progress of Nations*. New York: UNICEF.

———. (2002). *The State of the World's Children*. New York: UNICEF.

———. (2006). *The State of the World's Children*. New York: UNICEF

Wheatley, M. (2000). *Leadership and the New Science: Discovering Order in a Chaotic World*. San Francisco: Berrett-Koehler.

World Bank (1982). *World Development Report: Environment, Economics, and Policies*. Volume 1.

CHAPTER 3. HUMAN RIGHTS AND SOCIAL AND ECONOMIC JUSTICE

Adams, P. & Nelson, K. (1992). *Reinventing Human Services: Community and Family-Centered Practice*. Hawthorne, NY: Aldine de Gruyter-Bloom.

Annan, K. (2003). Foreword to *The State of the World's Children*. Geneva: UNICEF.

Anti-Discrimination for the Judiciary. (2006). www.europa.eu,int/comm/employment_social/fundamental_rights/index_en.htm

Ball, O. & Gready, P. (2006). *The No-Nonsense Guide to Human Rights*. Oxford: New Internationalist.

Bellamy, C. (1998). Quoted by J. Csete in "Challenges to Children's Well-Being in a Globalizing World." Fedele & Fauri Memorial Lecture. University of Michigan School of Social Work.

Bibus, A., Link, R. & O'Neal, M. (2005). "The Impact of Welfare Reform on Children's Well-Being." In *Safeguarding and Promoting the Well-Being of Children, Families, and Communities*, eds. J. Scott & H. Ward. London: Jessica Kingsley Publishing.

ENOC. (2005, 5 July). *European Network of Ombudsmen for Children—Submission to the Europe and Central Asia Regional Consultation Conference*. Ljubljana, Slovenia.

"Face-to-Face." (1999). Case Study 6.2 in *All Our Futures*, eds. C. Ramanathan & R. Link. Pacific Grove, CA: Thomson/Brooks/Cole.

Figueiredo, J. & de Haan, A. (1998). *Social Exclusion: An ILO Perspective*. Geneva: International Institute for Labour Studies.

Financial Times. (2005, March 2). Editorial, p. 2.

———. (2005, May 10). "Supreme Court Rejects Death Penalty for Juveniles." Editorial, p. 17.

Free the Children. (2004). *An International Network of Children Helping Children*. www.freethechildren.com

Garbarino, J. (1999). *Lost Boys: Why Our Sons Turn Violent and How We Can Save Them*. New York: The Free Press.

Germain, J. (1995, April 1). "To Reduce US Domestic Abuse, Outlaw Spanking, as in Sweden." *Minneapolis Star Tribune*.

GNP Media. (2002). *Children of the World: Society and the Children of Italy*. Program No. 1. Lincoln, NE: GNP Media.

Goodwin, J. (2005, July). "Too Young to Kill." *Oprah Magazine*, pp. 188–208.

Human Rights Ombudsman of the Republic of Slovenia: Who Is the Ombudsman? www.varuh-rs.si

IFSW. International Federation of Social Workers. (2002). *Social Work and the Rights of the Child.* Berne, Switzerland: IFSW.

Kielburger, C. & Kielburger, M. (2004). *Me to We: Turning Self-Help on Its Head.* Mississauga, ON: John Wiley.

KLJUC [Center for Fight against Trafficking in Human Beings]. (2005). Ljubljana, Slovenia: KLJUC.

Link, R. & Bibus, A. (2000). *When Children Pay.* London: Child Poverty Action Group.

Link, R. & Čačinovič Vogrinčič, G. (2000). *Models of International Collaboration.* Alexandria, VA: CSWE. See chapter 4.

Link, R. & Healy, L. (2005). *Teaching International Content.* Alexandria, VA: CSWE.

Mandela, N. (2000, May 6). "Building a Global Partnership for Children." Johannesburg Conference on the Convention on the Rights of the Child.

Obama, B. (2010). "Remarks by the President in the State of the Union Address. January 27, 2010." Washington, DC: Office of the Press Secretary, The White House. www.whitehouse.gov/d-press-office/remarks-president-state-union-address

Oxfam. (1996). *Answering Back: Testimonies from People Living in Poverty around the World.* Oxford. See pp. 12–13.

PBS. (1998). *Childhood* [television series]. Part 1 of 7.

Reichert, E. (2007). *Challenges in Human Rights.* New York: Columbia.

Samar, S. (2005). *The History of the Commission for Human Rights in Afghanistan.* New York: UNHCR.

Scott, J. & Ward, H. (Eds.). (2005). *Safeguarding and Promoting the Well-Being of Children, Families, and Communities.* London: Jessica Kingsley.

Shukovsky, P. (2003, December 17). "Feds Claim Adopted Orphans Had Parents, U.S. Agents Break Up Local Agency Dealing in Cambodia." *Seattle Post-Intelligencer,* p. A1.

Slovenian Association of Friends of Youth. (2002). *Human Rights Ombudsman of the Republic of Slovenia: Who Is the Ombudsman.* Retrieved January 13, 2007, en.zpms.si/home

Slovenian Committee for UNICEF. (1995). *Situation Analysis of the Position of Children and Families in Slovenia.* Ljubljana, Slovenia: UNICEF.

"State of the Union Address." (2003). Complete transcript of President's Bush's speech to Congress and the Nation, Office of the Press Secretary, January 28, 2003, the White House.

Stones, C. (1994). *Focus on Families: Family Centres in Action.* Basingstoke, UK: Macmillan.

Strong, R. (1998). *The Story of Britain: A People's History.* London: Pimlico Random House.

Traylor, G. (2002, February 16). "Closed Records Leave Those Who Were Adopted at Risk." *Star Tribune.*

Trenka, J. J. (2003). *The Language of Blood.* St. Paul: Minnesota Historical Society.

United Nations. (1948). *Universal Declaration of Human Rights.* General Assembly resolution 217A.

——. (1987). *Human Rights: Questions and Answers.* New York: Reichert.

——. (1989). *The UN Convention on the Rights of the Child.* www.un.org.

UN Convention on the Rights of the Child. (1989). Human Rights Resource Center, University of Minnesota. www.umn.edu.humanrts

UNHCR Representation in Slovenia, Asylum Section of the Ministry of Interior of the Republic of Slovenia Association Kljuc. (2004). *Dictionary.* Ljubljana, Slovenia: UNHCR.

UNICEF. (1997). *The State of the World's Children.* New York: UNICEF. See cover image.

——. (2003). *The State of the World's Children.* New York: UNICEF. See p. 1.

——. (2004). *The State of the World's Children.* New York: UNICEF.

Waldmeir, P. (2005, March 2). "Top Court Abolishes U.S. Death Penalty for Juveniles." *Financial Times,* p. 10.

CHAPTER 4. VALUES, INTERNATIONAL ETHICS, AND THEIR ROLE IN SOCIAL WORK PRACTICE

Accident Facts. (1996, 2006). Itasca, IL: National Safety Council.

Barash, D. (2000). *Approaches to Peace: A Reader in Peace Studies.* New York: Oxford University Press.

Bibus, A. (1995). "Reflections on Social Work from Cuernavaca, Mexico." *International Social Work, 38*(3), 243–252.

Bibus, A. & Link, R. (1997, November). "In Partnership with Families: A Global View." *National Family Based Services Conference Proceedings.* Minneapolis.

British Association of Social Workers. (1996). *The Code of Ethics for Social Work.* Birmingham, UK: BASW.

Čačinovič Vogrinčič, G. (1997). *Constructionist Concepts in Social Work Education: A Framework for Professional Ethics.* Ljubljana, Slovenia: University of Ljubljana Plaidoyer.

Collopy, M. (2000). *Architects of Peace.* Hong Kong: Publishers Group West.

Council on Social Work Education. (2008). *Educational Policy and Accreditation Standards.* Retrieved February 11, 2010, www.cswe.org

Cross, T. (1986). *Cultural Competence Continuum.* Seattle.

Desai, M. (1998). "Indian Declaration of Ethics." Presentation at the International Consortium for Social Development Conference, Jerusalem.

Elliott, D. & Mayadas, N. (2004). "Infusing Global Perspectives into Social Work Practice." In *All Our Futures*, eds. C. Ramanathan & R. Link, pp. 59–60. Pacific Grove, CA: Thomson/ Brooks/Cole.

Envall, E. (1997). *President's Message: International Federation of Social Workers.* Oslo, Norway: IFSW.

Freire, P. (1989). *Pedagogy of the Oppressed.* New York: Continuum.

French, H. (1997, October 8). "AIDS Research in Africa: Juggling Risks and Hopes." *New York Times*, pp. A1, A8.

Gray, M., Coates, J. & Yellow Bird, M. (2008). *Indigenous Social Work around the World: Towards Culturally Relevant Education and Practice.* Burlington, VT: Ashgate.

Healy, L. (2008). *International Social Work Professional Action in an Interdependent World.* 2nd ed. New York: Oxford University Press.

Hill Gross, S. (1992). *Wasted Resources Diminished Lives.* St. Paul: Upper Midwest Womens' History Center.

Hirshberg, C. & Barasch, M. (1995). *Remarkable Recovery.* New York: Riverhead.

IASSW/IFSW. (2004). International Association of Schools of Social Work/International Federation of Social Workers. *Ethics in Social Work: Statement of Principles.* Retrieved March 7, 2010, www.ifsw.org/en/p38000324.html.

Lewis, M. B. (1986). "Duty to Warn versus Duty to Maintain Confidentiality: Conflicting Demands on Mental Health Professionals." *Suffolk Law Review, 20*(3).

Loewenberg, F. M. & Dolgoff, R. (1992). *Ethical Decisions for Social Work Practice.* Itasca, IL: Peacock.

Media Network. (1991). *In Her Own Image: Empowering Women for the Future* [film and guide]. New York.

Midgley, J. (2000). *Social Welfare in Global Context.* New Delhi and Thousand Oaks, CA: Sage.

Mwansa, L. (forthcoming). "Social Work in Africa." In *Handbook of International Social Work*, ed. L. Healy & R. Link. New York: Oxford University Press.

National Association of Social Workers [US]. (1996). *Code of Ethics.* Washington, DC: NASW Press.

National Association of Social Workers [US]. (1997, February 2). "Privacy of Ethics Procedures Upheld." *NASW News, 42*.

National Association of Social Workers. (1999). *Code of Ethics*. Washington, DC: NASW.

Orwell, G. (1953). *Such, Such Were the Joys*. New York: Harcourt, Brace.

———. (1963). *1984*. London: Penguin.

Parry, J. K. & Shen Ryan, A. (1995). *A Cross-Cultural Look at Death, Dying, and Religion*. Chicago: Nelson Hall.

Postman, N. (1992). *Technopoly*. New York: Vintage.

Powell, J. (2006). *Social Theory and Aging*. New York: Rowman and Littlefield.

Ramanathan, C. S. (1992). "EAP's Response to Personal Stress and Productivity: Challenges for Occupational Social Work." *Social Work, 37*(3), 234–239.

———. (1994). "Health and Wellness at the Workplace in Developing Nations: Issues Confronting Occupational Social Work." *Employee Assistance Quarterly, 10*(1), 79–90.

Ramanathan, C. S. & Link, R. (Eds.) (2004). *All Our Futures: Principles and Resources for Social Work Practice in a Global Era*. Pacific Grove, CA: Brooks/Cole/Wadsworth.

Reamer, F. G. (1995). *Social Work Values and Ethics*. New York: Columbia University Press.

Seedhouse, D. (Ed.). (1989). *Ethics: The Heart of Health Care*. Oxford: Alden; New York: Liss.

Shukovsky, P. (2003, December 17). "Feds Claim Adopted Orphans Had Parents: U.S. Agents Break Up Local Agency Dealing in Cambodia." *Seattle Post-Intelligencer*, p. A1.

Sisneros, J., Stakeman, C., Joyner, M. C., & Schmitz, C. (2008). *Critical Multicultural Social Work*. Chicago: Lyceum Books.

Skarnulis, E. (2004). "Quality of Life Assessment." In *All Our Futures*, ed. C. Ramanathan and R. Link. Pacific Grove, CA: Thomson/Brooks/Cole.

Srivastava, K. D. (1967). *Commentaries on the Factories Act, 1948*. Delhi: Eastern Book Company.

———. (1988). *Commentaries on the Factories Act, 1948*. Delhi: Eastern Book Company.

Trainer, T. (1994). *Developed to Death*. London: Green.

Walljasper, J., Spayde, J. & the editors of the *Utne Reader*. (2001). *Visionaries: People and Ideas to Change Your Life*. Minneapolis: Utne Reader Books.

Whitaker, W. H. & Federico, R. C. (1997). *Social Welfare in Today's World*. New York: McGraw-Hill.

Zavirsek, D. (1997). *Empowerment in Mental Health Networking*. Slovenia, Ljubljana: University of Ljubljana.

CHAPTER 5. CULTURAL COMPETENCE IN LOCAL AND GLOBAL RELATIONSHIPS

ACLU. (2003, November 14). *News Letter*. www.aclu.org/safefree/resources/17343res20031114.html.

Aguillar Lutterman, A. (2005). "Low and High Context Culture." Presentation to the Social Work Peace class, Center for Global Education, Augsburg College, Minneapolis.

Aylwin-Foster, N. (2006, January 12). "Conventional Warfare." *The Guardian, UK*, p. 1.

Barash, D. (Ed.). (2000). *Approaches to Peace*. New York: Oxford University Press.

Belgum, M. (2000, October). "Multicultural Humor." Augsburg College Homecoming Presentation, Minneapolis.

Bhalla, S. (1997). *Quotes of Gandhi*. New Delhi: U.B.S. Publishers.

Carter, R. T. & Qureshi, A. (1995). "A Typology of Philosophical Assumptions in Multicultural Counseling and Training." In *Handbook of Multicultural Counseling*, eds. J. Pontevotta, L. A. Suzuki & C. Alexander. Thousand Oaks, CA: Sage.

Cross, T. (1986). *Cultural Competence Continuum*. Seattle: University of Washington Press.

Department of Justice. (n.d.). "The USA PATRIOT Act: Preserving Life and Liberty." http://www.justice.gov/archive/ll/highlights.htm.

Finn, J. & Jacobsen, M. (2002). *Just Practice*. Peosta, IA: Eddie Bowers.

Green, J. (1999). *Cultural Awareness in the Human Services*. Boston: Allyn and Bacon.

Hall, E. (1976). *Beyond Culture*. New York: Doubleday.

Herman, S. (2003). "The USA Patriot Act and the US Department of Justice: Losing Our Balances?" *Jurist Legal Intelligence* forum. jurist.law.pitt.edu/forum/forumnew40.htm.

Leigh, J. (1998). *Communicating for Cultural Competence*. Boston: Allyn and Bacon.

Link, R. & Bill, R. (2005). "Lessons without Leaving: A Report on the Department of State Educational Ambassador Grant. Presented to the Annual Conference of the Council on Social Work Education." New York.

Mayadas, N., Elliott, D. & Ramanathan, C. (1999, 2004). "Infusing Global Perspectives into Social Work Practice." In *All Our Futures*, eds. C. Ramanathan & R. Link. Pacific Grove, CA: Thomson/Brooks/Cole.

Mayadas, N., Ramanathan, C. S. & Suarez, Z. (1999). "Mental Health, Social Context, Refugees & Immigrants: A Cultural Interface." *Journal of Intergroup Relations, 25*(4), 3–14.

McIntosh, P. (1988). "White Privilege and Male Privilege: A Personal Account of Coming to See Correspondences through Work in Women's Studies." Wellesley, MA: Wellesley College, Center for Research on Women.

Norton, D. (1997). "Dual Perspective." In *Human Behavior in the Social Environment*, eds. Lortie et al., pp. 4–6. Pacific Grove, CA: Brooks/Cole/Thomson.

Obama, B. H. (2009a). Interview with *Al Arabiya*. www.alarabiya.net/articles/2009/01/27/65096.html

———. (2009b, February 5). "Remarks of President Barack Obama National Prayer Breakfast." Washington, DC. blog.beliefnet.com/stevenwaldman/2009/02/obamas-remarks-at-the-national.html

Orwell, G. (1953). *Such, Such Were the Joys*. New York: Harcourt Brace.

Oxfam. (2000). "An Agenda for Change." In *Approaches to Peace*, ed. D. Barash. New York: Oxford University Press.

Pinderhughes, E. (1989). *Understanding Race, Ethnicity and Power*. New York: The Free Press.

Ramanathan, C. S. & Link, R. J. (1999, 2004). *All Our Futures: Principles and Resources for Social Work Practice in a Global Era*. Pacific Grove, CA: Thomson/Brooks/Cole.

Sen, A. (1999). *Development as Freedom*. New York: Anchor.

———. (2002). "Civilizational Imprisonments." *The New Republic, 226*(22), 28–33.

Tan, Ngoh-Tiong, & Rowlands, A. (2004). *Social Work around the World III*. Berne, Switzerland: International Federation of Social Workers.

Tan, T., Rowlands, A. & Yuen, F. (2007). *Asian Tsunami and Social Work Practice*. New York: Haworth Press.

Webster, Michael. (2008, February 15). "The Patriot Act: How It Affects You." American Chronicle, http://www.americanchronicle.com/articles/view/52560.

Wheatley, M. (2000). *Leadership and the New Science: Discovering Order in a Chaotic World*. San Francisco: Berrett-Koehler.

CHAPTER 6. MIGRATION AND
THE BORDERS THAT DIVIDE US

Ahluwalia, M. S. (2009, February 17). "H1B Visa Bar Bad Economic Decision." *NDTV Correspondent*.

Associated Press. (2001, May 28). "20 Injured in Rekindled Racial Strife in Northern Britain." *New York Times*. www.nytimes.com/2001/05/28/world/28BRIT.html?ex=1175227200&en =8248ae60a43a0936&ei=5070

Balgopal, P. R. (1997). "Asian Indians." *Encyclopedia of Social Work*, pp. 256–260. Washington, DC: National Association of Social Workers.

Basu, A. (2006). *Globalization and Interdependence: International Migration and Development*. Second Committee of the 61st session of the U.N. General Assembly, October 19, 2006. www.un.int/india/2006/ind1271.pdf.

Bernstein, N. (2009, November 2). "U.S. to Pay $ 1.2 million to 5 detainees over abuse law suit." *New York Times*. http://www.nytimes.com/2009/11/03/nyregion/03jail.html.

Byrne, J. (2009, April 9). "Asians Should Simplify Their Names, GOP Lawmaker Says." *The Raw Story*.

Census of India. (2001). Office of the Registrar General of India. www.censusindia.net

Center for Global Education. (2006, June). Human Services in Mexico Semester. Re-entry Debriefing, at Augsburg College, Minneapolis.

Chandrasekhar, S. (1982). "History of the United States Legalization with Respect to Immigration from India." In *From India to America*, ed. S. Chandrasekhar, pp. 11–28. La Jolla, CA: Population Review Publications.

Cosgrove, P. (2010, January 20). "Attacks on Indians Racially Motivated: General Cosgrove." *Deccan Herald*. www.deccanherald.com/content/47778/attacks-indians-racially-motivated -gen.html

Deccan Herald. (2006a, October 17). "UK Varsities to Spy on 'Asian-Looking' Students."

———. (2006b, December 11). "Immigrants Better Educated than Britons: Reports."

———. (2007, January 30). "India Warns UK of Unfair Worker-Immigration Laws."

Erlanger, S. (2002, January 30). "A Jumpy Anti-Immigrant Europe Is Creeping Rightward." *New York Times*. www.nytimes.com/2002/01/30/world/a-jumpy-anti-immigrant-europe-is -creeping-rightward.html?pagewanted=1

Express India. (2009, February 14). www.expressindia.com/latest-news/US-stimulus-bill-to -hit-Indians-H1B-visa-holders/423542/

Golden, D. (2006). *Price of Admission*. New York: Crown.

Gupta, S. (2006, December 31). In "300 Million Melting Pot or Meltdown," by Anderson Cooper, CNN.

Hart, J. M. (1988). *Roots in the Sand* [Video]. San Francisco: National Asian American Telecommunications Association.

Hess, G. R. (1976). "The Forgotten Asian Americans: The East Indian Community in the United States." In *The Asian American*, ed. N. Hundley, pp. 157–158. Santa Barbara, CA: Clio.

Kelkar, R. (2006, November 27). "Au Revoir Freedom in America." *Rediff*. www.rediff.com/ news/2006/nov/27guest.htm

Krishnan, I. (1990). *Knowing Her Place* [film]. New York: Women Make Movies.

Mayadas, S. M., Ramanathan, C. S. & Suarez, Z. (1999). "Mental Health, Social Context, Refugees, and Immigrants: A Cultural Interface." *The Journal of Intergroup Relations*, 25(4), 3–14.

Morland, Maria Roots. (2003, June). Master of Arts in Leadership Final Project Presentations. Augsburg College. Minneapolis.

Phan, P. T. (1994, September–October). "Haunted by a Circle." *Colors, 3*(5).

Ramanathan, C. S. (2007, May). Interview of Mr. Parasuram Ramalingam, Board Member, ECOMWELL.

———. (2007, June). Interview of Mr. Parasuram Ramalingam, Board Member, ECOMWELL.

Ramaswami, V. K. (1968). "International Factor Movement and the National Advantage." *Economica*, pp. 309–310.

Rao, V. K. (1982). *Indian Socialism, Retrospect, and Prospect*. New Delhi: Concept.

Rappaport, J., Davidson, W., Wilson, M. & Mitchell., A. (1975). "Alternatives to Blaming the Victim or the Environment: Our Places to Stand Have Not Moved the Earth." *American Psychologist*, 30, 525–528.

Rediff India Abroad. (2005, December 15). "How BPO staff can fight racial abuse, India Abroad as it happens." http://www.rediff.com/money/2005/dec/15guest.htm

Rivera-Batiz, R. (1982). "International Migration Non-Traded Goods and Economic Welfare in the Source Country." *Journal of Development Economics, 11*, 81–90.

Ross-Sheriff, F. (2004). "Muslim Refugees in the United States." Presentation to the Annual Program Meeting of the Council of Social Work Education. Anaheim, CA.

Sen, A. (2007). Keynote Address at the NASSCOM 2007 India Leadership Forum in Mumbai on 7 February 2007. http://www.hindu.com/nic/itindia.htm.

Sharma, Meena. (2006, April 18). "Canadian Akhil Sachdeva wants apology from US Govt. for unlawfully detained in Jail." http://www.nriinternet.com/NRI_Discrimination/USA/After%20Sep%2011/CasesUpdated/Akhil_Sachdeva/index.htm.

Sharma, P. (2006, September 14). "Sikh Youths Allege Hair Cut in Algeria." *Times News Network.*

Silicon India. (2005, December 5). "Indian Techie Files Suit against US Firm." www.siliconindia.com/shownewsdata.asp?newsno=30117

———. (2006a, April 18). "Indian Threatened by US Agents." www.siliconindia.com/shownewsdata.asp?newsno=31620

———. (2006b, October 20). "India Seeks UN Focus on Global Migration." www.siliconindia.com/shownews/33589

Stark, O. & Bloom, D. (1985). "The New Economics of Labor Migration." *American Economic Review, 75*, 173–178.

UNHCR. (1991). *Refugees Dossier: United States of America: A Marvelous Mosaic*. UNHCR, Geneva, #82, p. 15.

U.S. Bureau of the Census. (2003). *American Community Survey*. Washington, DC. www.census.gov/acs/

Wadhwa, V. (2009, March 2). "Why Skilled Immigrants Are Leaving the US." *Business Week.*

Wayne, L. (2001, April 29). "Workers and Bosses in a Visa Maze." *New York Times.*

Yardley, J. (2002, July 29). "Immigrants Found Dead in Truck; Two Drivers Are Charged." *New York Times*. www.nytimes.com/2002/07/29/national/29TRUC.html?ex=1028977083&ei=1&en=273492fc16a3a498

CHAPTER 7. PLANET EARTH AND SUSTAINABLE LIFE

Addams, J. (1910). *Twenty Years at Hull House*. New York: MacMillan.

Agarwal, A. & Narain, S. (Eds.). (1985). *State of India's Environment, 1984–1985: The Second Citizen's Report*. New Delhi: Center for Science and Environment.

Apuzzo, M. (2007, March 14). *Chiquita to Pay 25 Million in Terror Case: Bananas and Business*. www.mindfully.org/industry/2007/chiquita-colombian-terrorist14mar07.htm

Balakrishnan, M. (1984). "The Larger Mammals under Endangered Habitats in the Silent Valley Forests of South India." *Biological Conversation, 29*, 277–286.

Basha, S. (1987). "Studies on the Ecology of Evergreen Forests of Kerala with Special Reference to Silent Valley, and Attapady (South India)." PhD thesis, University of Kerala, Trivandrum.

Berk, L. E. (2004). *Development through the Lifespan*. Boston: Allyn and Bacon.

Bradsher, K. (2009, April 27). "Assessing the Danger of New Flu." *New York Times*. www.nytimes.com/2009/04/28/health/28hong.html?scp=3&sq=h1n1%20swine%20flu%20pandemic&st=cse

Burningham, K. & Thrush, D. (2001). *The Rainforests Are a Long Way from Here.* York, UK: Joseph Rowntree Trust.

Cooney, R. & Michalowski, H. (Eds.). (1987). *The Power of the People: Active Nonviolence in the United States.* Philadelphia: New Society.

Deccan Herald. (2010, January 23). "India and China Almost Certain to Sign Copenhagen Accord." www.deccanherald.com/content/48396/india-china-almost-certain-sign.html

Gandhi, A. (2007). "Principles of Non-violence." Presentation to the Convocation Series, Augsburg College, Minneapolis.

Glendinning, Lee. (2007). "Anita Roddick, Pioneer Whose Dreams Turned the High Street Green, Dies at 64.". The Guardian. http://www.guardian.co.uk/business/2007/sep/11/ethical living.lifeandhealth.

Harnden, T. (2009, April 7). "Barack Obama in Turkey: US Will Never Be at War with Islam." *Daily Telegraph.* www.telegraph.co.uk/news/worldnews/northamerica/usa/barack obama/5115044/Barack-Obama-in-Turkey-US-will-never-be-at-war-with-Islam.html

Jayson, E. (1990). "Community Ecology of Birds in Silent Valley." *Ecological Studies and Long Term Monitoring of Biological Processes in Silent Valley National Park,* pp. 13–53. Kerala, India: Kerala Forest Research Institute.

Kelkar, R. (2006, November 27). "Au Revoir Freedom in America." *Rediff.* www.rediff.com/ news/2006/nov/27guest.htm

Kerala Forest Research Institute. (1990). *Ecological Studies and Longterm Monitoring of Biological Processes in Silent Valley National Park.* Kerala, India: Kerala Forest Research Institute. Research report.

Maathai, W. (2006, March). "Peacemaking with the Environment." Presentation to the Peace Prize Forum, Luther College.

Manilal, K. (1988). *Flora of Silent Valley Tropical Forests in India.* Calicut, India: The Manthrubhumi Press.

Martin, Chris. (1999, October). "Banana Split." *New Internationalist* 317.

Maslow, A. H. (1968). *Toward a Psychology of Being.* Princeton, NJ: Van Nostrand.

Mathbor, G. (2006). "Disaster Response and Social Work's Role." Presentation to the Annual Program Meeting of the Council on Social Work Education, Chicago.

Mathew, G. (1990). "Studies on the Lepidopteran Fauna of Silent Valley." In *Ecological Studies and Longterm Monitoring of Biological Processes in Silent Valley Park,* pp. 55–107. Kerala, India: Kerala Forest Research Institute.

Moyers, B. *Earth on Edge.* PBS video.

Nair, P. V. & Balasubramanyan, K. (1984). *Long-Term Environmental and Ecological Impacts of Multipurpose River Valley Projects: Wildlife Studies in Idukki, Periyan, and Silent Valley.* Kerala, India: Kerala Forest Research Institute Report.

Nelson-Pallmeyer, J. (2004, October 12). "Making Sense of US Foreign Policy: The Costs and Consequences of Empire." Kessel Memorial Lecture. Minnesota State University.

Ransom. D. (2002). *Fair Trade: Small Change, Big Difference.* London: New Internationalist.

Obama, B. H. (2009, April 3). "Transcript: Obama's Strasbourg Remarks." CBS News. www .cbsnews.com/stories/2009/04/03/politics/100days/worldaffairs/main4918137.shtml?source =RSSattr=Politics_4918137

Onishi, N. (2002, December 29). "Nigeria's Oil Wealth Flows Out, Not Down." *New York Times.*

Postman, N. (1992). *Technopoly.* New York: Vintage Books.

Powell, W. E. (1988). "The Ties That Bind: Relationships and Traditions." *Social Casework, 11,* 556–562.

Prigoff, A. (2000). *Economics for Social Workers: Social Outcomes of Economic Globalization with Strategies for Community Action.* Belmont, CA; Wadsworth.

Rahmani, A. R. (1980). "Silent Valley: India's Last Tropical Forest." *Tiger Paper Number 7,* (1), 17–19.

Rai, S. & Sengupta, S. (2006, July 12). "Series of Bombs Explode on 7 Trains in India, Killing Scores." *New York Times.*

Ramanathan, C. S. (2009). "Public-Private-NGO Partnership in Providing Relief to Victims of Tsunami of 2004: A Reality Check in Cuddalore, India." Unpublished manuscript.

Ramanathan, C. & Link, R. (Eds.). (2004). *All Our Futures.* Pacific Grove, CA: Thomson/ Brooks/Cole. See chapter 4.

Reed, B. (2009, February 17). "Analysis: President Obama's New Green Stimulus Law." Green.TMCnet.com. green.tmcnet.com/topics/green/articles/50701-analysis-president -obamas-new-green-stimulus-law.htm

Rogge, M. (2004). "Social Work and Toxic Environments: The Impact of Lead Paint in Schools." Presentation to the Annual Program Meeting of the Council on Social Work Education, Atlanta.

Shiva, V. (2002). *Water Wars: Privatization, Pollution, and Profit.* Cambridge, MA: South End Press.

Singer, P. (2004). *One World.* New Haven, CT: Yale University Press.

Smith, J. W. (2006, 2009). *Economic Democracy: A Grand Strategy for World Peace and Prosperity.* Sun City, AZ: The Institute for Economic Democracy Press.

Stone, L. & Muir, R. (2007). *Who Are We? Identities in Britain, 2007.* London: Institute for Public Policy Research.

Tan, R. (2004, June). "Crisis Theory and SARS: Singapore's Management of the Epidemic." *Asia Pacific Journal of social Work and Development, 14*(1), 7–17.

UN. (1989). *Convention on the Rights of the Child.*

UNEP (UN Environment Programme). (2003). *Global Environment Outlook Year Book.* Geneva: United Nations. www.unep.org/yearbook/2003/.

UNICEF. (1999). *Progress of Nations.* Geneva: UNICEF

———. (2006). *State of the World's Children.* New York: UNICEF.

———. (2007). *State of the World's Children.* New York: UNICEF.

Unnikrishnan, N. (1989). *Silent Valley National Park Management Plan: 1990, 91–99, 2000.* Mannarghat: Silent Valley Park Division.

Vijayan, V. S. & Balakrishnan, M. (1977). "Impact of Hydro-electric Project on Wildlife. Report of First Phase of Study." Peechi, India: Kerala Forest Research Institute.

Vivekananda, S. (1896, January 12). "The Ideal of a Universal Religion." Address delivered at Hardman Hall, New York.

Wolters, L. (2007, April 13). "Invista to Correct EPA Violations." http://wichita.bizjournals. com/wichita/stories/2009/04/13/daily13.html.

World Health Organization (2010). *Pandemic H1N1 2009: Update 84, Global Alert and Response (GAR).* www.who.int/csr/don/2010_01_22/en/index.html

Worldwatch Institute. (2006). *State of the World 2006 Special Focus: China and India.* Washington, DC: Worldwatch Institute.

Zoological Survey of India, (1986). *Records of the Zoological Survey of India, 84*(1–4).

CHAPTER 8. GLOBAL VISIONS IN ACTION

Annan, K. (2006, December 11). "Farewell Speech." Truman Library, Kansas City, MO.

Asia Society. (2009, March 14). "Asia's Next Challenge: Securing the Region's Water Future." http://www.asiasociety.org/policy-politics/environment/asias-next-challenge-securing-regions-water-future.

Basu, A. (2006). *Globalization and Interdependence: International Migration and Development.* Second Committee of the 61st session of the U.N. General Assembly, October 19, 2006. www.un.int/india/2006/ind1271.pdf

BBC Online. (2005). "Tsunami." www. news.bbc.co.uk/2/hi/south_asia/7887670.stm

Boumediene et al. v. Bush. (2008, June 12). www.supremecourtus.gov/opinions/07pdf/06-1195 .pdf

Carroll, R. & Batty, D. (2010, January 16). "Haiti Earthquake: Aid Effort Ramps Up As 200,000 Dead Predicted." *The Guardian.* www.guardian.co.uk/world/2010/jan/16/haiti-earthquake -update-toll-aftershock

Clinton, B. (2007). *Giving: How Each of Us Can Change the World.* New York: Alfred A. Knopf .

Cosgrove, P. (2010, January 20). "Attacks on Indians Racially Motivated: General Cosgrove." *Deccan Herald.* www.deccanherald.com/content/47778/attacks-indians-racially-motivated -gen.html

Deccan Herald. (2010a, February 1). "Sulabh to Construct Low-Cost Toilets in Japan." www .deccanherald.com/content/49954/sulabh-construct-low-cost-toilets.html

———. (2010b, February 7). "Victorian Top Cop Asks Indians to 'Look Poor' to Avoid Attacks in OZ." www.deccanherald.com/content/51341/victorian-top-cop-asks-indians.html

Desai, M. (1998). "Indian Declaration of Ethics." Presentation at the International Consortium for Social Development Conference, Jerusalem.

Freiberg, S. (1974). "Blind Infants and Their Mothers: An Examination of the Sign System." In *The Effects of the Infant on Its Caregiver,* eds. M. Lewis & L. A. Rosenblum. New York: John Wiley.

Friedman, T. (2004). "It's a Flat Earth after All." *New York Times.*

Gandhi, A. (2007). "Principles of Non-violence." Presentation to the Convocation Series, Augsburg College, Minneapolis.

Government of India. (2005, January 5). *India Tsunami Situation Report.* www.searo.who.int/ linkfile/countries_sit_rep_ind_5jan.pdf

Greenhouse, L. (2007, April 3). "Justices Say EPA Has Power to Act on Harmful Gases." *New York Times.* www.nytimes.com/2007/04/03/washington/03scotus.html

Hogeland, W. (2006, December 27). "Our Founding Illegals." *New York Times.* www.nytimes .com/2006/12/27/opinion/27hogeland.html?ex=1324875600&en=ecb31dfb21ba7c20&ei= 5088&partner=rssnyt&emc=rss

International Labor Organization. (2010, January). *Global Employment Trends.* Geneva: ILO. www.ilo.org/global/About_the_ILO/Media_and_public_information/Press_releases/lang --en/WCMS_120465/index.htm

Kagle, J. D. & Cowger, C. D. (1984). "Blaming the Client: Implicit Agenda in Practice Research?" *Social Work,* 29(4), 347–351.

Kahn, M. E. (2005). "The Death Toll from Natural Disasters: The Role of Income, Geography, and Institutions." *The Review of Economics and Statistics,* 87(2), 271–284.

Kelkar, R. (2006, November 27). "Au Revoir Freedom in America." *Rediff.* www.rediff.com/ news/2006/nov/27guest.htm

King, M. L. (1963). "The World House Essay." In *Why We Can't Wait.* New York: Harper & Row.

Leighton, A. & Feller, B. (2009, April 17). "Obama to Trinidad for Summit of the Americas." *The Huffington Post.*

Lyons, K., Manion, K. & Carlsen, M. (2006). *International Perspectives on Social Work Global Conditions and Local Practice.* Basingstoke, UK: Palgrave/Macmillan.

Mathbor, G. (2006). "Disaster Response, Relief, and Recovery." Presentation to Council on Social Work Education Annual Program Meeting, Chicago.

Moyers, B. (2006). *Earth on Edge.* PBS video.

Obama, B. (2009, January 21). "Inaugural Address." www.whitehouse.gov/the_press_office/President_Barack_Obamas_Inaugural_Address/

Onishi, N. (2002, December 29). "Nigeria's Oil Wealth Flows Out, Not Down." *New York Times.*

Rai, S. & Sengupta, S. (2006, July 12). "Series of Bombs Explode on 7 Trains in India, Killing Scores." *New York Times.*

Ramanathan, C. S. (1999, 2004). "Ethical Issues and Value Dilemmas in Global Economy: An Example of Occupational Social Work." In *All Our Futures*, eds. C. Ramanathan & R. Link. Pacific Grove, CA: Thomson/Brooks/Cole.

Ramanathan, C. S. (2009). "Disaster Management and Tsunami of 2005: India a Case in Point." Unpublished manuscript.

Ramanathan, C. & Link, R. (Eds.). (1999, 2004). *All Our Futures*. Pacific Grove, CA: Thomson/Brooks/Cole.

Rediff News. (2009, April 17). "Limbaugh Denigrated Indian Citizens by Calling Them Slumdogs." Washington, DC. news.rediff.com/report/2009/apr/17/limbaugh-denigrated-indian-citizens.htm

Romero, S. & Lacey, M. (2010, January 12). "Fierce Quake Devastates Haitian Capital." *New York Times.* www.nytimes.com/2010/01/13/world/americas/13haiti.html?th&emc=

Shiva, V. (2000). *The Water Wars: Privatization, Pollution, and Profits.* Cambridge, MA: South End Press.

Silicon India. (2006, October 20). "India Seeks UN focus on Global Migration." www.siliconindia.com/shownews/33589

Smith, J. W. (2006, 2009). *Economic Democracy: A Grand Strategy for World Peace and Prosperity.* Sun City, AZ: The Institute for Economic Democracy Press.

Stolberg, Sheryl Gay. (2009, March 9). "Obama Lifts Bush's Strict Limits on Stem Cell Research." *New York Times.* www.nytimes.com/2009/03/10/us/politics/10stem.html?_r=2&scp=2&sq=stemcell%20research&st=cse

Stone, L. & Muir, R. (2007). *Who Are We? Identities in Britain, 2007.* London: Institute for Public Policy Research.

Strom-Gottfried, K. (2007). *Ethics and Moral Courage.* Manuscript submitted for publication.

Sundby, N. (2006). "The Nature of Disasters." Presentation to the International Consortium for Social Development, Warsaw, Poland.

Tankersley, J. (2009, March 29). "Surge of College Students Pursuing 'Clean Energy' Careers." *Los Angeles Times.* articles.latimes.com/2009/mar/29/nation/na-energy-students29

Tasse, A. (2006). "Report from the President of the International Association of Schools of Social Work." Panel presentation to the International Consortium for Social Development, Warsaw, Poland.

Towle, C. (1945). *Common Human Needs.* Washington, DC: National Association of Social Workers.

Tran, M. (2009, April 6). "US Is Not at War with Islam Says Barack Obama." *Guardian.* www.guardian.co.uk/world/2009/apr/06/barack-obama-turkey-armenia.

Trenka, J. (2003). *The Language of Blood.* St. Paul: Minnesota Historical Society.

UNICEF. (2007). *State of the World's Children.* New York: UNICEF.

Watts, M. (2007). "Curse of the Black Gold: 50 Years of Oil in the Niger Delta." *New York Times.*

Wheatley, M. (2000). *Leadership and the New Science: Discovering Order in a Chaotic World.* San Francisco: Berrett-Koehler.

WHO. (2009). *Health Impact of Climate Change Needs Attention.* Geneva. www.who.int/mediacentre/news/notes/2009/climate_change_20090311/en/

Index

Note: Page numbers followed by *f, tb,* or *t* indicate figures, tables, or textboxes, respectively.

About the Authors

Rosemary J. Link, PhD, LISW, was born in St. Albans, England, and gained her undergraduate honors degree in modern history and politics with sociology from the University of Southampton and her postgraduate diploma in Applied Social Studies from the University of London. After ten years as a school social worker, team leader, then educational administrator in England, Dr. Link came to the University of Minnesota for her PhD in social work with a special interest in children's rights and social policy. Dr. Link served as a professor of social work and dean of graduate studies at Augsburg College, Minneapolis, and is currently associate vice president for academic affairs at Simpson College, Iowa, where she is primarily responsible for building undergraduate and graduate programs for adult learners.

In addition to administration, Dr. Link chaired the board of Southside Family Nurturing Center (www.ssfnc.org) for six years (2003–2009) through their capital campaign and renovation. The agency is featured as a star program by the Children's Defense Fund. Dr. Link has ongoing research interest in children's well-being and human rights. Dr. Link has served as external examiner to the University of the West Indies at Mona, Jamaica, and the University of Bharathair, Coimbatore. Dr. Link has published numerous articles relating to child poverty, human rights, and social development, as well as four books, including *When Children Pay*, a study of child poverty together with Dr. Anthony Bibus; *All Our Futures*, a textbook in human behavior together with coauthor Dr. Chathapuram Ramanathan; *Models of International Curriculum in Social Work*, a curriculum design text together with Dr. Lynne Healy; and a forthcoming *Handbook for International Social Work*.

In 2005–2006, Dr. Link received a State Department grant to serve as an educational ambassador in Slovenia, India, and Singapore. The project included working with a technology specialist, Robert Bill, and international colleagues, Dr. Tiong Tan, Dr. Gabi Čačinovič Vogrinčič, and Dr. Lea Bohinc setting up exchanges for students of social work and human service, plus generating interactive video classrooms. Dr. Link describes herself as an educational administrator, writer, social worker, and human rights advocate.

Chathapuram S. Ramanathan, PhD, ACSW, LMSW, CAC, was born in Nagpur, India, and earned his undergraduate degree in Natural Sciences, and after receiving a master's degree in social work from the Madras School of Social Work, came to the United States, and received an MSW specializing in community mental health. After working as a clinical social worker in a mental health center, he earned an interdisciplinary PhD in social work and human resource management. Dr. Ramanathan has worked in the human service area over three decades. Dr. Ramanathan holds a master's and a doctoral degree from the University of Illinois at Urbana-Champaign. His practice and scholarship focus is on addiction recovery, cross-cultural issues, social development, and clinical social work. Dr. Ramanathan has been providing psychotherapy services for over 30 years, and is a licensed marriage and family therapist.

Dr. Ramanathan has taught full-time in graduate schools of social work for over 10 years. He has published 20 refereed articles and coauthored the book *All Our Futures* in 1999. Dr. Ramanathan has received many awards and honors, including a tribute from the Michigan legislature and Michigan governor in October 2008 for helping people pursue their freedom of religion and engaging Asian American businesses in job development. He recently coauthored an article that was recognized as the best article by the National Human Rights Workers Association. This article, "Mental Health, Social Context, Refugees and Immigrants," appeared in the *Journal of Intergroup Relations*. In 2004, he was awarded a Fulbright scholarship to lecture on social work as a full professor, to students and professionals, at the Tata Institute of Social Sciences, a deemed university (first social work program in Asia—established 1936), and at the National Institute of Mental Health and Neuro Sciences. In 2002, Dr. Ramanathan, as a speaker through the U.S. Speaker and Specialist Program, presented "Diversity and Inclusiveness: A Hindu American View," at the conference "Religious Pluralism and Democratic Societies: United States and South East Asia," Kuala Lumpur, Malaysia.

In the late 1980s and early 1990s, Dr. Ramanathan served on the Michigan Governor's Multicultural Mental Health Education Task Force. Dr. Ramanathan served on the Council on Social Work Education's (CSWE) International Commission from 1992 to 2004. He has been serving CSWE as a trained site visitor for over 15 years, reviewing graduate and undergraduate programs for accreditation. He has served on several agencies' boards of directors. Dr. Ramanathan has been serving NASW's National Ethics Committee as an alternate member since 2007. He serves on the editorial boards of two major journals: *Drugs and Society* and *Social Development Issues*. In 2007 and 2008, Dr. Ramanathan provided pro bono advice to the Michigan Economic Development Corporation. Dr. Ramanathan has presented over 50 papers and workshops in the United States, Canada, South Africa, Portugal, Malaysia, Netherlands, the UK, Turkey, India, Sri Lanka, Thailand, Ireland, Germany, Poland, Brazil, and Hong Kong. Dr. Ramanathan has trained participants in addiction recovery and clinical social work, as well as on social development issues. Additionally, Dr. Ramanathan has also trained participants in the area of diversity issues through many organizations, such as the University of East London; National Human Rights Workers Association; Larsen & Toubro, LTD; Phillips Software, LTD; National Association of Social Workers, Michigan Chapter; Southfield School District, Michigan; and Plymouth-Canton Community Schools.

Dr. Ramanathan is the founding chair of the Michigan Indo-American Democratic Caucus, the first statewide caucus formed on behalf of Indo-Americans in the history of United States of America.

Breinigsville, PA USA
05 August 2010
243046BV00004B/2/P

Merton, Thomas, *The Ascent to Truth*, London: Burns and Oates, 1976.

Morel, Georges, SJ, *Le sens de l'existence selon Jean de la Croix*, 3 vols, Paris, 1960-61.

O'Donoghue, OCD, *The Holy Mountain*, Wilmington, Delaware: M. Glazier, 1983.

_____, *Lovelier than the Dawn*, Dublin: Carmelite Centre of Spirituality, 1984.

Peers, E. Allison, *Spirit of Flame. A Study of St. John of the Cross*, London: SCM Press, 1943.

Ruiz Salvador, Federico OCD, *Introducciòn a San Juan de la Cruz*, Madrid, 1968.

Stein, Edith, *The Science of the Cross. A Study of St. John of the Cross*, London, 1960.

Surgy, P. de 'La source de l'échelle d'amour de Saint Jean de la Croix', *RAM*, 27, 1951, pp 18-40.

_____, 'Les degrès de l'échelle d'amour de Saint Jean de la Croix', *RAM*, 27, 1951, pp 237-259, 327-346.

Sutter, Amatus de, 'La fe ilustradísima, Apropos d'un livre recent', *Eph C*, 9, 1958, pp 412-422.

_____, 'Foi et contemplation chez Saint Jean de la Croix', *Eph C*, 13, 1962, pp 224-256.

_____, 'La méditation chez Saint Jean de la Croix', *Eph C*, 11, 1960, pp 176-196.

Tillyer, Desmond, *Union with God. The Teaching of St. John of the Cross*, London & Oxford: Mowbray, 1984.

Trueman Dicken, E.W., *The Crucible of Love. A Study of the Mysticism of St. Teresa of Jesus and St. John of the Cross*, London: Darton, Longman & Todd, 1963.

Vilnet, Jean, *Bible et mystique chez Saint Jean de la Croix*, Paris, 1949.